"*Capable is the book I wo...*
of every couple who has..."

—GARY CHAPMAN, PhD, Author of *The 5 Love Languages*

CAPABLE

A STORY OF TRIUMPH FOR CHILDREN THE WORLD HAS JUDGED AS "DIFFERENT"

DEBORAH WINKING PhD

Foreword by Temple Grandin

Capable: A Story Of Triumph For Children the World Has Judged As "Different"
Published by High Expectations Press
Ft Collins, Colorado

ISBN: 978-0-578-84162-5

FAMILY & RELATIONSHIPS / Parenting / General
FAMILY & RELATIONSHIPS / Autism Spectrum Disorders

Cover and Interior design by Victoria Wolf,
www.wolfdesignandmarketing.com

Names: Winking, Deborah, author.
Title: Capable : a story of triumph for children the world has judged as "different." / by Deborah Winking, PhD.
Description: First trade paperback original edition. | Fort Collins [Colorado] : High Expectations Press, 2021. | Index included. | Also published as an ebook.
Identifiers: ISBN 978-0-578-84162-5
Subjects: LCSH: Parents of autistic children. | Autism in children.
BISAC: FAMILY & RELATIONSHIPS / Autism Spectrum Disorders. | FAMILY & RELATIONSHIPS / Parenting / General.
Classification: LCC RJ506.A9 2021 | DDC 616.8588 WINKING–dc22

**HIGH
EXPECTATIONS
PRESS**

One imperfect person intentionally parenting with high expectations to help her child see himself as able to take on whatever the world throws his way.

DEAR READER

THIS BOOK REPRESENTS my best recollection over 20 years. Many experiences are imprinted on my heart with a white-hot intensity that is reserved entirely for mothers. All the events herein are true, but I have changed names; and have merged some personal characteristics, identities, and locations to maintain anonymity. I retell my story for the sole purpose of helping others on their way to raising "capable" sons and daughters. I will be entirely satisfied if my journey provides some small spark of inspiration for those in the thick of the humbling odyssey that is parenting.

CONTENTS

ACKNOWLEDGMENTS

MY UNENDING THANKS TO:

…all the caring teachers, therapists, nurses, doctors, and specialists who have come through the revolving door of our lives; many of you we see no more, but you have left your mark on our hearts.

…Lori, my precious sister for pressing me hard on every dream I have ever had; first for burning the midnight oil critiquing and spurring me on as I added one last stroke to an overworked canvas, and now for doing the same for the contours of this manuscript.

…Veronica, Cara, Carol, Beth, Angie, Shannon, Rosanne, Joanne, Bridget, Dana, Steve, Megan, Cheree, and all the early readers whose honest critiques and first-hand insights kept me grounded and brought incomplete ideas into focus.

…Jack's sisters and brother Livie, Rosie, and Will, who cinched the deal during a ski trip, saying "Mom, you know you ought to finish that book." How could I not?

…My amazing husband for forcing me to be organized, for editing and re-editing; for clearing a path for this writing by cooking countless dinners and folding numerous loads of laundry, and perhaps most of all, for always believing in me, even when I did not.

... The team at My Word Publishing, you lifted me up and carried me throughout this process.

...God, who gives me strength at all times. He alone gets the credit for all decisions (parenting and otherwise) that defy my selfish nature.

And finally, to:

...Jack, now no longer a little boy, but a man of strength, perseverance, faith and humor: Thank you for loving me through, and in spite of, all my mistakes and maternal overreach. You, along with your sisters and brother, are my pride and joy!

FOREWORD

I REALLY LIKE STEPHEN HAWKING'S statement about disability. Shortly before he died, he offered this in a New York Times interview, "concentrate on what your disability does not prevent you from doing well." There were countless things that were difficult and painstakingly slow for him. Imagine having to train your cheek muscle to make the small movements that type letters. But one thing he could do quite well was mental mathematics. By focusing on math instead of his disability, Hawking supplied the world with enduring explanations of black holes.

In *Capable*, Dr. Winking chose to see not "what was" but "what was possible" for her son, Jack. She consistently stretched him just beyond his comfort zone. On the surface, *Capable* is the story of how one mom motivated her son to beat the odds given the rare genetic syndrome which dealt a hand that included physical and cognitive challenges. He would never be a star basketball player, but he was selected for an environmental science fellowship and is graduating

1

from college. If *Capable* were simply an uplifting tale of triumph for a single boy that would be enough, but it is so much more than that. Throughout the book, Dr. Winking speaks directly to all parents who find themselves raising a child who has been judged as "not quite measuring up" by the world's standards. She provides critical insights about the messages parents send every day that impact their child's success over time. She also offers them the tools to avoid passing their fears on to their child.

Similarly, I have found that far too many parents overprotect their children and as a result they are not acquiring basic skills such as learning to shop or how to open a bank account. Parents have difficulty letting go when I suggest that their child should be challenged with new experiences and in many cases, these children have a much milder disability than Jack faced.

I was the product of high expectations parenting. My mother had natural instincts about how much to stretch me as well. She would also give me choices. When I was fifteen and afraid to go to my aunt's ranch, she gave me a choice. I could go all summer or go for only a week, but not going was not an option. When I got out to the ranch, I loved it. Going to the ranch led me to a career in the cattle industry. I became interested in ranching because I was exposed to it.

Kids have got to get out and do things and *Capable* provides parents with a prescription for ensuring that their child is able to pursue his or her best life despite the challenges they face.

Temple Grandin, Author
Thinking in Pictures
The Autistic Brain

Introduction

THE POWER
OF ONE

*Narrative is radical, creating us at the very
moment it is being created.*

-Toni Morrison

NOBODY EVER SAID BEING A PARENT WAS EASY. It is alternatingly joyous, angst-provoking, exhausting, crazy-making and exhilarating—and that is on a good day. The job becomes exponentially more difficult when, based on some measure, your child has been labeled "different," "special," or "disabled." It is my greatest desire that you will come away from this book thinking, *this woman parented with high expectations and it changed her kid's life, and just maybe it could help me and my kid too.* Instead of offering prescriptions based solely on numbers and descriptive vignettes, I put skin and bones on the research which proclaims that parental beliefs and behaviors actually *do* impact a child's success over the long haul. It is my goal to offer useful insights by untangling the messy complexity of parenting because that is where we parents live: smack-dab in the middle of the mess. Of course, we too are part of the mess, as we bring our own strengths, vulnerabilities, and demons to the party.

I set out to shed light on the mess through the use of "story" combined with the tempering lens of research. I believe this is the best and perhaps only way to inspire you to parent intentionally, fearlessly, and with high expectations to help your child live their best life no matter what circumstance or label the world has pronounced.

I get vulnerable and lay bare my parenting odyssey, warts and all, while weaving in current science and the experiences of others along the way. I encourage you to consider and "try on" for yourself the lessons that lie within each chapter. While the story speaks for itself and provides a powerful prescription for any parent of a child with special needs, I also offer a companion guide that provides a go-to summary of key learnings to help you on your own unique journey toward parenting with high expectations.

Why tell a story when you can make a list or show the numbers?

A good portion of my career has been devoted to using educational research to make sense of changes in student performance and behavior. However, long before I got distracted with tallying numbers and aggregating large data sets, I believed in the power of one. I was schooled in the case study method by the granddaddy of case study research, Dr. Bob Stake. This bespectacled, pipe-smoking academician, who sported a full beard long before they were millennial chic, transfixed wide-eyed undergrads with the virtues of using "the single case" to illuminate human experience. As opposed to statistics, which are stripped raw of context and are therefore too blunt to detect uniqueness, the case study uncovers nuance, subtlety, emotion, and idiosyncrasy—all the complexities that go into understanding deeper truths. Using the case study method in my own work taught me firsthand that when we immerse ourselves in a single contextualized case, we get a far richer and more instructive understanding of that which matters most.

I concede that statistics make for succinct sound bites, breaking news clips and tidy tweets. For example, I could tell you that 7 million or 14% of all US public school children are "labeled." That 34% of these children have a specific learning disability, 19% have a speech/language impairment, 14% have an "other health impairment," 10% have autism, 7% have a developmental delay, 6% have an intellectual disability, and 5% have emotional disturbance.[1] I could further tell you that my son Jack was one of 14,000 babies born every year with a rare genetic syndrome called Sotos. I could end by reporting that in the 6th grade he was one of only .4 % of all school age children nationwide (who are labeled with more than just a speech disorder) to exit special education for general education. This all fits within the 140 character tweet limit and we could be done with it right there.

Statistics etch bold black lines on the canvas, but they do nothing to fill the space between with the brilliant colors that create depth and dimension. I made the conscious choice to use memoir, the less academic cousin of case study, to provide the vivid color, texture, and subtle shading that illuminate the research and bring the complete picture into focus. Having read scores of self-help and parenting resources over the years, I knew that my experience would make for a better story than handbook. First, because it exists not in disconnected, bite-sized examples but as one continuous "becoming" that has unfolded over the course of a childhood and, secondly, because I wanted to humanize the research rather than catalog it. In short, I believe that the context-rich "case" embedded in this account will provide parents with a more "meaty" and actionable understanding of high expectations parenting.

So, on these pages it is with undying gratitude for and permission from my son that I undertake the telling of one story: the account of being "mom," teacher, helper, and witness during the 21 years I have existed on the planet with my amazing son, Jack. To be sure, this is not his story, because I could never presume to tell his story. That is his and his alone to tell. And just like any two people witnessing the same event, accident, or miracle, each has their version of what happened. This is mine. It offers more than a single data point on the expectations and mindset research landscape. It provides a compelling illustration of what can happen when we unleash the power of "yet" in the realm of parenting. It proves that, with sustained effort, things we never imagined are possible for our children.

Also, to be sure, this is not Jack's dad's story. He too has his own to tell. Even though Pete was with me and loved us unconditionally through it all, we were not always walking side by side, in lock step on each fateful parenting choice. Like many fathers of fragile infants, he initially had a hard time bonding with Jack for fear of crushing loss. In the early years, he did not always share in my high expectations vision turned holy war. There were many times when I had to drag him along kicking and screaming, as evidenced by my campaign to get a regulation-size basketball hoop in the driveway back when Jack could only turn away from a ball being tossed in his direction.

However, over time, Pete has witnessed the fruits of sending "capable" messages and he is now Jack's biggest cheerleader. I deduced that to support readers on their parenting journey, it was most helpful to focus on the path I forged rather than complicate matters by weaving in Pete's circuitous route toward high expectations. Fascinating in itself, but another book indeed.

That being said, *Capable* IS for you if someone or some circumstance has put a limitation on your child. Perhaps a professional has handed down a diagnosis, or a loved one has offered their projection. Or maybe an accident or traumatic event has altered life for your child. This book is for you if your child has Down syndrome, attention deficit/hyperactivity disorder (ADHD), autism, obsessive compulsive disorder (OCD), is deaf or blind, has cerebral palsy, or uses a wheelchair.

This book is for you if experts have told you that your child has a developmental delay, has severe emotional disturbance, is on the "spectrum," has a visual impairment, multiple disabilities, or has been judged "health impaired." Because it deals with the ways in which our beliefs, behaviors, and fears affect our children, this book is for you if your child has chronic anxiety or an eating disorder that makes you likely to transfer your fears on to your child. Some have argued that this book is for you even if your child is "typical" and going through oppositional teen years, certainly a fear-inducing time for us all.

Being entrusted with raising a child with special needs is among the most humbling experiences that life has to offer. I draw from my expertise, but I write with an equal measure of humility, as one among the great unwashed masses of moms and dads who have regrets about entire chunks of their parenting. To be sure, I am not suggesting, as some parent advocates have, that I have cured my child. I don't pretend to have all the answers. This book does not promise an easy time or one devoid of regrets. Rather, I offer one story and will be supremely gratified if it causes you to parent more intentionally and courageously in ways that send your child the message that he or she is capable!

Chapter 1

ADAM'S BELLY BUTTON

There are no ordinary people. You have never met a mere mortal.

—CS Lewis

THE ANCIENT-LOOKING SHOE BOX sat perched atop the cluttered card table that served as a permanent piece of furniture in the extra bedroom of my parents' modest Indianapolis home. These days, consistent with the frenetic pace of life, I was accustomed to breezing in and out, staying only a night or two. My regular visits to Mom and Dad's had been reduced to stopovers. I would check in for barely 48 hours on the way to or from work in some distant locale and then, just as quickly as I arrived, I would rush home to the people, pets, and responsibilities that awaited there. But for some reason, on this evening, a pause in the action caused me to not just eye the box, but to actually crack open its lid. I took out first one envelope and then the next, until I was devouring the contents of the tissue-paper-grade translucent pages. The letters fanned out around me on the floor like a yellowing peacock tail, each neatly headed with an assortment of dates all ending in the year "1964."

These pages, when assembled chronologically, tracked the ongoing dialog between Mom, who was staying in a borrowed room in St. Louis' Cardinal Glennon Children's Hospital, and Dad, who was back home in Quincy, a historic Illinois river town situated proudly on the bluffs overlooking the Mississippi. Carefully, in uniformly scrolling cursive, my mom had laid out the details of each surgery, usually closing with a lighthearted anecdote. Like how surprised the nurses were that I didn't flinch as the long needle pierced my thigh and was held there for what seemed like forever until its syrupy solution filled my veins. And how I stubbornly refused to drink the Dixie cup of Coca-Cola that was intended as a "chaser" to the syringe. The Coke was necessary, they said, to mix with the concoction in the syringe to light up my organs like a pinball machine so the doctors could get a better look. (Funny thing, to this day you still can't pay me to drink a soda.)

Other times, the stories were not so funny, like when Mom wrote to Dad about how I came into possession of a new batch of my beloved 2-by-4-inch miniature Golden Books because the little boy a couple of rooms down from me had just died. His mother, with vacant eyes, held them out to Mom with lifeless arms murmuring that she no longer had any need for them. Or how I would call out to the inconsolable little guy in the bed next to mine, "Don't cry Gordy, Debbie's here." Advice offered with all the worldliness of a precocious 19-month-old who knew her way around the children's ward. Throughout this long-distance, handwritten dialog, I am struck by

Mom's quiet courage and how, even fifty years later, it still brings a tear to my eye. Dad had to stay back and work at the post office in order to pay the hospital bills and care for my older brother. So, it was Mom on her own with me in Children's Hospital those endless weeks. Today, as I go about my "grown-up" days of Zoom conferences, teaching, and racking up frequent flyer miles, a persistent thought lives somewhere on the edge of my consciousness that I am here today because of the faith and resolve laced through those brittle pages, and because of the fateful decisions my parents made that led up to their writing.

You see, on the 29th day of April, 1963, seven months before JFK was shot, a second child was born to Jeanette and Marvin Winking. A little girl with a pelvis not curved, but as flat as a pancake, and a bladder and reproductive organs on the outside instead of on the inside where they belong. The Catholic priest on hand baptized me unceremoniously, should I not make it. To my parents' joy, I came through that first night. In the morning, at one day old, I was flown to the Mayo Clinic in Rochester, Minnesota. Although my survival was no longer at issue, the doctors at that esteemed institution threw up their hands, not seeing any way to fully put me back together. Another more optimistic surgeon, in another hospital, said that he could not remake my bladder, but he would set it up so that I could pee into a bag that would be externally attached to my body.

Mom and Dad toted me and my broken body from doctor to doctor and did not give up until they found a St. Louis urologist who was willing to try an experimental technique. It would involve closing my organs inside my body and breaking my pelvic bones, molding them into the normal concave shape so that I would not forever walk like a duck. All this could be possible, he said, but I would never be able to have children. Of this he was certain.

By the time I was a year and a half, I was big enough to begin this untested process. There were multiple surgeries, months in a hard cast that went from my toes to my chest, and countless four-hour round-trip drives to the hospital, where they manipulated my hips and legs and tested my bladder to ensure that I could urinate. My parents' overriding worry was that I would not be able to walk when the doctors finally cut off the plaster cast, but learn I did... first to walk, and then to run. Next came years of teaching my new bladder to work, and trips back and forth to the St. Louis hospital for painful catheterizations, but, for all intents and purposes, I was fixed.

In this real-life Humpty Dumpty tale, in order to put me back together again, they folded my organs into my lower abdominal cavity and held them in place with a wire, taking with them my navel, evidence of the umbilical cord that had connected me to my mother and to life itself.

Unbeknownst to me, as I wriggled in my crib, my parents quietly endured this protracted medical odyssey. It challenged their faith, as well as the prevailing medical science of the day. As it always is with kids who are insulated from their grown ups' struggles to care for them, I knew nothing of the emotional pain and financial burden that my parents shouldered to bring me home in one piece.

Incongruous as it was, compared to the gravity of their concerns, as I grew, the overriding concern that tormented this consummate child of the seventies was my non-existent belly button. After all, this was the decade that gave the Western world hip huggers, halter tops, and bikinis. My lingering medical problems included a weak pelvic floor, reoccurring infections, scoliosis, incontinence, and remaining amenorrheic well into my twenties. All of these I took in stride. What scarred me more than my considerable physical scars, though, was the absence of that universal mark that has united all of mankind (with the exception of the Biblical first man who ironically had no need for one.) In high school, as other girls, in classic Sneetch-like fashion, lamented being cursed with an "outie" when they wanted an "innie," I longed just to have either. Even as my little sister sported sassy two-piece swimsuits, Mom strategically outfitted me in tank suits to avoid the questions and presumably inevitable taunts. All this angst over a belly button. What are they good for anyway? I am sure herein lies one more lesson about the inexhaustible human pursuit to avoid being different.

What is it about even the slightest perceived oddity that is so fascinating to kids? It inevitably got around the neighborhood that I did not "have one." Even now I have not forgotten the trauma I experienced at the hands of David Sayer, an older kid who chased me down our back alley wielding a big stick, shouting over and over, "She doesn't have a belly button!" as if the absence of this abdominal indent was as contagious as a nasty case of herpes. It happened more than a few times that my brother and his friends took me behind the old oak tree in our back yard and made me show them my scar.

As I shed my self-conscious teen years, preoccupation about the physicality of my story gave way to a kind of awe and reverence. I learned what could have been and was captivated by my parents' courage in the face of something they could not have fully understood at the time. I was humbled by their dogged persistence in searching for what they thought I needed to be whole. What was the quality that prevented them from caving to the bleak prognosis offered by the Mayo Clinic elites? What allowed them to dismiss the surgeon who wanted to fit me with an ileostomy bag and send me on my way? My parents did not possess any of the requisite college degrees that would have put them on even footing with the countless medical professionals they encountered. Even so, I was struck that the absence of these credentials did not demur them in the least or cause them to settle for anything less than *everything* they imagined for their little girl.

I can't say for sure how my story of early adversity, as unique and quirky as it was, shaped how I view the world today. But I passionately believe that each one of us has a place deep inside from which we draw inexhaustible strength, our own personal tangle with adversity. This was mine.

Now on to another dance with adversity that began in 1998.

Chapter 2

DREAMS OF GIVING BIRTH

*There are two things in life for which we
are never truly prepared: twins.*

—Josh Billings

TWINS, BEAUTIFUL TWINS. Many envy the blessing of twins, two
beings the same, yet unique…double-the-fun. Parents dress them
in identical outfits for as long as they can get away with it. Amateur
photographers set up their own fantastical Anne Geddes-esque
photo-ops of their multiples peeking out of matching flowerpots.
Since these two would be our first, my husband Pete and I had no
idea what we were in for. Having never been entrusted with one
child, let alone two, we were blissfully ignorant. We had no concept
of parenting, and particularly not parenting on steroids: double the
feedings, double the baths, and double the diaper changes. We had
just bought our first home in the San Francisco East Bay. Six and a

half months pregnant, I occupied myself by painting the baby room turquoise with fuchsia accents. Noah's Ark was our nursery theme and I thought myself clever for choosing it. It was appropriately androgynous since we were expecting a boy and a girl, cute but not too cute, and the religious overtones couldn't hurt, since we would need all the help we could get—divine or otherwise.

I had talked my sweet father, a woodworking genius who never wanted to disappoint his little girl, into building a shelf of biblical proportions for the baby room. He constructed a nearly six-foot-long ark, complete with cut-outs of giraffes, hippos, and lions, overlooking a mantel made to resemble the whimsical galley of Noah's mythical vessel. As I finished edging paint into the corners of the room, I imagined the army of stuffed animals that would someday call this shelf home. Noah's Ark was a tribute to all God's creatures entering a new world two-by-two. Now sharing precious real estate in my belly, these two were due to make their entrance in mid-April.

But that was not meant to be. Ours came early, as twins often do. There's nothing particularly noteworthy about that fact except that they were really early. It was Super Bowl weekend, and my girlfriend Keri was visiting from Minneapolis. On Saturday we shopped for the crib that the babies would one day share.

Then came Sunday and the Denver Broncos were facing the Green Bay Packers. I didn't really know much about the teams on the field or the game itself. We would not live in Colorado, the state where I developed a modest interest in football, for four more years. This ambivalence did not deter me from exploiting the occasion as an excuse for a party. So, there we were, my friend and I, chopping veggies and concocting dips for the festivities when I registered a barely perceptible sensation of cramping in the vicinity we jokingly called "the area." The feeling would have passed unnoticed in the flurry of pregame activity. I was thirty-three years old and had never been pregnant before. Furthermore, I had not expected to ever be, given the dire projection the doctors had given my parents all those years ago regarding their daughter's child-bearing potential. Keri was as inexperienced as I was—early 30s and no kids.

But then I felt it again.

Instead of immediately calling my obstetrician or speeding to the nearest emergency room, we followed our natural female impulse—we phoned a friend. She was a work colleague back home in the Midwest who had given birth to a little girl only a couple of years prior.

Mary, our resident expert in Minnesota, confirmed our suspicions. The "cramps" occurring at that moment in California were, in fact, bona fide labor pains. An unorthodox route to a diagnosis, perhaps, but with her corroboration, Pete sped me to the hospital. I was in shock as I was barely 27 weeks pregnant. However, there was no time to ponder the unlikelihood of it all.

A quick cervical check by the inexplicably cheery, but matter-of-fact emergency room attendant made it official: I was having these babies soon. As my mind raced imagining all the meanings that the word "soon" could take in this context, efficient medical personnel in green scrubs were busy instructing me to remove all jewelry and were inserting IV tubes into my forearm. It did turn out that soon really did mean *soon*, but not immediately. These were not to be Super Bowl babies.

The truly life-saving medical virtuosos on the obstetrics floor did everything they could to delay my labor and succeeded in doing so for the better part of the next week. During those endless days,

I lay in my hospital bed, a human incubator. Flat on my back with nothing to contemplate but my feet, I remember being grateful more than a few times that Keri and I had treated each other to pedicures during our crib-shopping excursion. As shifts changed and nurses came and went, more than a few made small talk about my "nice toes" in an unconvincing effort to distract me.

Great, I may be giving birth to seriously premature babies, but at least I had that going for me, I mused with grim irony. But always the pleaser, I laughed along, not wanting to spoil this compassionate attempt at humor. Their joking bolstered me. I reasoned that if my condition were dire, these highly qualified nurses would be solemn-faced, or at least stoic, right?

By Thursday I had reached the magical number "28." In the neonatal world, 28 is the number of weeks when labor and delivery nurses breathe a guarded sigh of relief and doctors consider the odds in favor of the child if labor can no longer be stopped and the baby (or this case, babies) must be delivered.

So it was, on that afternoon in late January, that they made their entrance—almost three months early. Through the joint miracles of C-section and corticosteroids designed to accelerate fetal lung development, my beautiful babies arrived. Jack, the "big brother," weighed in at a whopping 2 pounds 7 ounces, and Olivia, the younger and more petite, just skimmed 2 pounds 4 ounces. I liked the idea that Jack would always be thought of as "big brother" by virtue of arriving two minutes before his sister. While it should not have mattered either way, and was admittedly a tad sexist, I secretly liked the idea of the boy coming first. Bigger and stronger, he would be the protector who would watch over his little sister. I imagined him sticking up for her against bullies in elementary school and sizing up boyfriends in high school.

At just over 2 pounds each, I was resigned to the fact that the babies would be in the hospital for a while. However, as the one-day-olds matured into one-week-olds, it became apparent that Jack was the "big brother" by birth and weight only. He was weaker and was not responding like his sister to the careful ministrations of the neonatal intensive care staff.

"Wait," I comforted myself…anyone who knows preemies or who has hung around a Neonatal Intensive Care Unit (NICU) for any amount of time will tell you that premature girls are noted for being more robust than premature boys. As a matter of fact, during the week that I lay in waiting to give birth, one of my favorite NICU nurses educated me regarding the apparently legendary preemie hierarchy. According to her, barring other illness, black girls were the alphas, the strongest and most resilient among premature babies. Then came Hispanic girls, and finally white and Asian girls. (That tracked with my experience of the world; my black women friends were some of the strongest and most perseverant people I knew.) The nurses' pecking order followed the same for boys: black, then Hispanic, with the lowest rung on the preemie food chain reserved for white and Asian boys. These lesser specimens even had a nickname among the nurses. They were dubbed the "wimpy white boys." That was the reason, I told myself, that our beautiful boy was listless, flaccid in tone, barely reacting to touch, and would not open his eyes. That explained why his grip was weak and why his arm would drop flat when we let go instead of curling up in an infantile show of muscle like his twin sister's.

At the same time, Livie, as she was known by everyone on the floor, was the debutante of what appeared to be a party in the NICU. Dropping weight as all babies do in the hours and days after exiting the birth canal, Livie fell to just slightly below two pounds. Seeing the impossibly low number 1.92 lb. register on the scale built into her incubator should have terrified us. But it did not. Even though her brother dwarfed her in length and weight, she was kicking and cooing in her plastic pod-like enclosure and was breathing on her own after only one day on this earth.

We marveled at Livie's tiny arms and legs, barely formed and so devoid of fatty tissue that Pete could slide his wedding band all the way up her arm. I recently learned the history of how well-meaning parents in the early 1900's were advised to surrender their hopelessly premature babies to a man who had set up shop on New York's Coney Island boardwalk. This man, Martin Couney, had no medical credentials, but would eventually go on to invent the incubator. He was the same man who sold tickets to the public to gaze upon these miniature curiosities, these fragile, bird-like beings, in order to raise the money needed for their care. His unorthodox ways saved countless babies, some whose adult children and grandchildren tell the story today.[2]

The account of Livie, sporting her daddy's wedding band, a little show of bling on her tiny bicep, may sound like the stuff circus sideshows are made of, but it was all true and we have the photos to prove it. The skilled NICU nurses, accustomed to frail, complicated cases, were delighted to be charged with a hearty baby who came without breathing machines and feeding tubes, a baby with whom they could just play. They brought in frilly doll dresses, adorned Livie in them and made jokes about her being the "girlfriend" to another tiny boy in the incubator next door.

Still, as my conscious mind clung to the comforting theory of the "wimpy white boys," somewhere deeper inside I registered a lingering sense of unease. I could not shake the feeling that something was wrong as I gazed at my babies—Livie, effortlessly breathing on her own, and her big brother Jack, who was bound to a ventilator—a metal monstrosity that looked like a throwback to a circa-1959 B-rated sci-fi movie. It extruded tubes and cables, with blinking lights, and emitted a constant low-pitched whirring sound. Most vital was the transparent plastic coil that went all the way down my son's esophagus and was doing the lion share of his breathing for him. Without this marvel of medical automation with its cords, hoses, and gauges, our boy would not be with us.

The signs that all was not well mounted as we whiled away the days in the NICU. Because the twins were delivered via caesarian section, I had to stay in the hospital for a few days. During those first days, I would shuffle out of the maternity ward clad in my standard issue hospital gown and down the elevator to the NICU to hold, cuddle, and just generally stare amazed at these new creations. As any new mom will attest, these moments constituted the best part of every day. I would sit in the NICU as long as they would let me, rocking one baby and then the other "kangaroo style."

Kangaroo Care was the term given to the literally life-giving practice by which a parent rearranges whatever clothing is covering his or her chest so that it is out of the way in order to hold their newborn against them, skin to skin, beating heart to beating heart. In fact, less than five years after the twins were born, a woman in Australia brought her pre-term boy back to life using Kangaroo Care after he had been officially pronounced dead by doctors. Wanting nothing more than to say good-bye, this mom begged to hold the lifeless boy she had given birth to three hours earlier. Medical personnel had long since turned off the machines and gone back to the business of caring for the living, when, after holding her son skin-to-skin for more than two hours, this mom felt a faint flutter. That flutter accelerated into a full-blown heartbeat, defying the proclamations and expertise of all in attendance that day.[3] Even the most jaded doctors on the scene, when interviewed, could not explain the phenomena without resorting to the word "miracle."

At this point, with two-pound twins, I could use all the supernatural energy I could muster. So, I rocked like a determined (read demented) modern-day, Grandma Moses under the glare of the florescent lights that flooded the ward. Just holding, cooing, watching, and hoping. Although my flimsy hospital gown welcomed an immodest draft and the hum of the ventilators was torturously dull and unforgiving, I could have been rocking my babies in front of a roaring fire amid the wafting aroma of fresh baked cookies for all the warmth and contentment I felt. After work, Pete would drive over to the hospital and join me in this vigil of perpetual rhythmic movement, cradling one baby while I cradled the other.

But even the mystical juju of Kangaroo Care did not jumpstart Jack's frail countenance. Still, I maintained, "It is only a matter of time." After all, the lore of the wimpy white boys as foretold by the NICU nurses loomed large. It held that although these boys started out as weaklings, biology evened out over weeks and months and, in time, they fared as well as any other baby, boy or girl, dark or light. Jack would grow out of this and be my big, strong boy. I waited and prayed, and prayed and waited, but circumstances did not change. He did not ween off the ventilator as did the other babies around him.

As sad and envious as I was, I was not a monster. I could not help but join in the accolades for other babies born after Jack, as one by one their ventilators were turned down little by little each day, some babies getting stronger even in a matter of hours until they were liberated from their machines. I regaled with ecstatic parents as they saw for the first time their child's lips curl up, no longer obscured by the ventilator tube, in what was perhaps a lopsided smile. Even so, my own baby remained listless, not breathing on his own, without muscle tone, and eyes unopened.

Chapter 3

FACING GOLIATH

Small stars still light up big skies.

—Matshona Dhliwayo

THE DOCTORS WERE STUMPED. They could find no ready answer for Jack's delays. True, a number among the medical staff wrote off Jack's troubles to the wages of premature birth. This was plausible. I knew that prematurity did not simply mean "miniature" baby, as if humans were Snickers bars and could be "fun-sized" while keeping everything else constant. Prematurity is known to cause any number of serious health issues, including impaired vision, a fragile immune system, sensory problems, and even cerebral palsy. None of these were a picnic, even so, a part of me wanted to chalk up Jack's difficulties to prematurity because somehow the word "prematurity" had a seductive temporary ring to it—as if the difficulties stemmed solely from that pesky little prefix. As if once we crossed the threshold from "pre" to "maturity" all would be well. Like with pro sports, you had your "pre-season" and then your "season." One did not hurt the other, in fact the "pre" was intentionally designed to make the "season" stronger. I challenged a silent God to reveal His intentional design as we watched our baby struggle.

Days turned into weeks and Jack remained a puzzle. He remained frail, slack, and unresponsive as his twin, Livie, by now mini-diva of the NICU, continued to hold court among the nurses in her little cluster of incubators. As happy as I was to watch the nurses gush over Livie, my joy was stunted and hollowed out. It turned out my friends with older kids were right—we are only as happy as our saddest child and, forget sadness, at times Jack seemed to be barely there. Eventually he had to be transferred from the Walnut Creek Hospital level-three NICU to Oakland Children's Hospital, which specialized in more complicated infants. He did two stints at Children's, a level-four facility where smaller, more fragile, sicker, and drug-addicted babies precariously hung onto life.

Despite such complications, babies are joy personified. Perhaps all the more so because of our gnawing uncertainty, we actively sought out reasons to smile. Even if slightly forced, we found them— moments of levity that buoyed our spirits as we puzzled through. The first time Jack was transferred to Oakland Children's was for a somewhat routine operation to close a valve in his heart. This, we were told, was a relatively common surgery among the preemie set. As they suited up, the jovial docs mused that it was fortunate that it was our boy twin who required the Patent Ductis Arteriosis operation, because the procedure came complete with a long scar that sliced all the way down between the shoulder blades. When we looked confused, not quite comprehending how they could joke about maiming our child, the doctors pointed out that Jack would later have bragging rights to say he had earned the scar in a sword fight, a story they assumed a boy would have way more fun telling than a girl would.

I seized upon these lighthearted exchanges like a drowning woman grasping for a life preserver. The surgeons' banter alluded to a future, a typical childhood where kids battled with brightly colored Styrofoam swords and exchanged tall tales, a future where breathing machines, IV's, feeding tubes and the insistent glare of fluorescent light on white linoleum were a distant memory.

Unfortunately, Jack's second transfer to Children's was not so routine. It was on the orders of one Dr. William T. Friedrich. Dr. Friedrich was a stern clinician whose countenance was made all the more severe by his thick German accent. Unlike most of the deliberately soft-spoken NICU docs, he had neither the time nor inclination for treading lightly on the tender feelings of desperate, sleep-deprived moms and dads. If Dr. Friedrich was aware that he was the puppet master pulling the very strings that animated the fragile mix of fear, expectation, and hope churning in the guts of hapless parents, nothing in his demeanor betrayed it. Pete and I were no exception to this rule. Instead of allowing us to take shelter in the comforting explanation that Jack's delays were merely the result of a premature multiple birth, Dr. Friedrich exhorted that there was "more going on with 'Baby Boy Winking'" as he liked to call him. He maintained his brooding stare whenever he surveyed Jack. His expression seemed to grow more ominous with each update on Jack's condition. He did what parents fear most, he didn't keep his suspicions to himself, but gave full-throated voice to his concerns. His guttural cadence made each theory sound more menacing than the last.

"There is something we are missing," he mused out loud as his ever-knitted brows joined in pronouncing sentence over Jack. Two among the possible diagnoses he unceremoniously threw out were cerebral palsy and cystic fibrosis.

I avoided him like the plague and rejoiced on the days he was off duty. I sought out the company of other doctors who, with a ready smile, threw out comforting platitudes like, "Jack's coming along," and "getting bigger every day," which stood in stark contrast to Dr. Friedrich's prognostications, ever ringing in my ears like a death sentence. When I ventured to ask one of the safe, amiable docs why his colleague was so adamant that something was wrong with my child, he said Friedrich was a thorough clinician who was inclined to look for "zebras," when it was likely he had just a plain old horse before him. I took his meaning. Friedrich was drawn to searching out the unusual and unlikely, instead of accepting the obvious.

Still, I was frustrated that Friedrich would not leave our baby be. Zebras be damned, Jack was just taking his time catching up. This indomitable man left no stone unturned, ordering test after test to rule out his hunches.

As if Dr. Doom was not enough, Children's Hospital NICU itself was an unnerving place. Who could say what it felt like to be an infant resident there? This hard-edged, antiseptic world was the sum total of their life experience. Helpless as we were to remedy the situation, we parents knew where babies really belonged—HOME, in rooms fancifully themed with airplanes, choo-choo trains, giraffes, princesses, and teddy bears, swaddled in plush cribs and bathed in natural light. Although nurses and volunteers tried their best to create a cheery veneer, the NICU was a cold place stripped bare by an unforgiving glare 24 hours a day, seven days a week. We knew that these scrubbed, sterile wards masked hidden dangers. Not the least of which was the ever-present threat of infection traveling through intravenous tubes that pierced impossibly tiny veins, obscenely visible through tissue-paper-thin skin. These infections could run roughshod through tiny systems in a matter of hours and cause problems that would make mere prematurity seem like a walk in the park. Faced with these threats, we parents lived in an impossible paradox…both despising the place that was our lifeline and being anxious to get our babies home even though home was a place where they could not yet survive.

Because of the extra fragile state of Children's lilliputian inhabitants, moms and dads could not venture into the nursery to view their babies without donning hospital scrubs. The antiseptic-chic ensembles included scrubs, a shower cap-like bonnet, and booties constructed with a green synthetic blend—an inexplicable cross between paper and fabric. Once suited up, parents were required to suds up to their elbows in a pungent yellow-green iodine solution. In a macabre way, it reminded me of those sci-fi movies where scientists climb into complex hazmat suits before daring to make contact with the beings they had created. But this was standard practice for sustaining life in the NICU. Even though the entire ritual screamed, "Your baby is not okay," I could not wait to begin it, because at its conclusion I could see my child.

Jack's second stint in this place was to investigate one of Dr. Friedrich's most pernicious hunches: cystic fibrosis. Ruling out this grim prediction involved exploratory surgery slicing open Jack's tiny stomach in search of a particular enzyme that would confirm the condition. We scrubbed-up, suited-up, and bootied-up. We cooed our good-byes to Jack as his incubator was wheeled down the hall and into the elevator bound for surgery. Then began the waiting game. We sat among other parents, superficially polite to one another, but each of us isolated, existing within our own personal pain. After what felt like an eternity, Jack was wheeled back into the nursery. As it turned out, Dr. Friedrich was foiled again. The procedure did not yield the sinister enzyme. It seemed that, at least for the moment, Jack had escaped the deadly diagnosis, but even so his condition continued to confound. He hung on, fragile, but alive. Even here in this excruciating limbo there was hope. He wasn't getting worse, he wasn't getting better, but he existed. Through it all I just wanted him home.

Feeding my babies also fed my fears. While tiny Livie ate like a champ, Jack would not breastfeed. His suck was so weak he could not eek out even a drop of milk. Since putting on weight was a major prerequisite to getting discharged from the NICU, it was imperative that Jack eat. So as much as I willed him to master breastfeeding, I had to cry 'Uncle.' Every two hours after putting him to my breast, I reluctantly gave in and relinquished him to the adept nurses who solved the problem in short order by suspending a tube, little thicker than a piece of dental floss, down his throat to deliver precious drops of pumped breast milk. I wanted so badly to feed my sweet boy that I would end up just nuzzling him—not unlike the crazy, homeless woman I had seen in an alleyway in San Francisco desperately cradling a doll she believed was her real-life child. I was stubbornly pretending that breastfeeding was working, but the act did more for me than Jack. I was fooling myself; he wasn't catching on.

At about this time, Livie was discharged. Now we experienced another impossible tug. The tug between celebrating the homecoming of a healthy child and agonizing over the sick one who lay attached to tubes in the hospital, suspended in an endless state of limbo between beginning life and what?

Like any parent with a compromised child, I continued to scan the landscape for even the slightest sign that Jack was with us and that he was fighting. Mercifully, one came during another of Dr. Friedrich's "hunting expeditions." The doctor had insisted upon what the nurses explained in hushed tones was a painful test whereby a needle is inserted into the lower abdomen and directly into the infant's bladder to obtain urine. This test was yet another in search of that ever-elusive enzyme that Friedrich was convinced was the source of all Jack's troubles. I dreaded the idea of seeing my baby subjected to any type of pain. "If it is uncomfortable for you, you may choose to not be present for the procedure," dripped Friedrich's accent. The good doctor clearly did not know who he was dealing with. You bet your goose step I was going to be there. No way was I going to let my baby go through this ordeal alone.

So, there I stood, pressed against the cold steel of the examining table, stroking Jack's flaccid forearm. Dr. Friedrich, whose character, at this point, I have completely villainized (unfairly maybe, but never underestimate the power of post-natal hormones to elevate the crazy) was poised with a needle that looked like a deadly weapon in comparison to Jack's spare frame, his chest imperceptibly rising and falling with the hum of the ventilator. Friedrich lowered the needle toward Jack's exposed abdomen and was just about to puncture the tissue-thin skin, when my son fought back the only way a three and a half pounder can. He shot a stream of pee directly into the air. The urine was a heat seeking projectile that found its target as surely as if there was a bull's eye painted squarely on the good doctor's face. A slow smile spread on mine. The nurse in attendance and I side-eyed each other and suppressed a shared giggle. Friedrich motioned to the same nurse, who resumed a straight face as she dutifully handed him a surgical towel. He stoically mopped his brow, abandoning his mission, grumbling as he walked away something about how "now there was no point to the test as there was nothing left to collect." Excusing the bad pun, I admit that Jack was not the only one who was "relieved." I quietly reveled in the fact that my son had escaped the giant needle. I looked for the procedure to be rescheduled, but it was not. To this day I cannot explain why.

Was what I witnessed that day the involuntary biological function expected of any organism or a sign of personal agency? Irrational: maybe, but I grabbed hold of this incident as a sure sign that Jack was gaining ground. At the same time, I too was gaining ground. I clung to the thought that Jack showed what in today's parlance might be termed "grit." And so it was that "peepee-gate" became the symbol for an expression of will, of presence, a life force that was emerging within my son.

Time in the NICU was not marked by the clock or the calendar, but rather from feeding to feeding, from vitals check to vitals check, from one medication administration to the next. As I existed in this alternate time-space continuum, I whiled away the hours by spinning peepee-gate into a superhero tale of sorts. My personal David and Goliath story featured Jack as the underdog protagonist who uses his only superpower to deliver a knockout blow to "Doctor Doom." The story itself was sophomoric and a bit absurd, but the subtext was a world in which sick babies get strong, where purity and innocence win over suspicion and cynicism and, more specifically, a world in which my son prevails. I dreamed of a future NICU reunion where the nurses and doctors retold the story to a strapping, sandy haired boy of 9 or 10. In my mind, Jack and everyone within earshot had a good laugh at Friedrich's expense. My son was a fighter, with a sense of humor to boot. That was how I always ended the story that I told myself and anyone else who would listen. As I look back now, this was not only a tantalizing fantasy for a frazzled mom with a sick child—it was the moment when I first dared to hope for a future for Jack.

Chapter 4

JAILBREAK

Preparation can only take you so far. After that,
you have to take a few leaps of faith.

—Michael Scofield

ALL TOLD DURING HIS TIME IN THE NICU, Jack toughed out numerous procedures, two full-blown surgeries, two blood transfusions, powerful courses of antibiotics, and an infection brought on (inevitably, I thought) by an intravenous tube lodged in his arm. True to form, Dr. Friedrich wanted to conduct "just one more test," as he was still dogged by the confounding case of Jack. But we would have none of it. By now, Jack had some heft to him. He had unceremoniously weaned off the ventilator. There was no longer a thick tube thrust down his throat obscuring his face. It was replaced with a relatively benign breathing device, just a small clear cannula at his nostrils delivering a constant stream of oxygen.

My parents had ventured out to California from Illinois and were stationed at our house at the ready for double baby detail. Livie, long since discharged, was the epicenter of joy and activity at home. Even so, I could not help but feel sad that she was the lonely inhabitant of a nursery outfitted for two. It was time to get our boy home.

The first week of April, 17 days before the twins would have been born save prematurity, my mom and I staged an infantile jailbreak at the hospital. An unlikely mother-daughter Bonnie and Clyde, we delighted in our crime, giggling as we lifted Jack from his incubator after convincing a sympathetic nurse to remove his IV, his final tie to the NICU. We gathered the few belongings he had accumulated during his 2½-month stay, swaddled him in donated hospital blankets, and hustled him off the ward like illegal contraband. We did not stop until we reached our getaway car, an unassuming mini-van outfitted with two infant seats. Now laughing out loud, I pulled away with Gabe strapped in the back and Mom riding shot gun, peering behind us to make sure Dr. Friedrich was not in hot pursuit with a dripping syringe, determined to order "just one more test."

Laughter triggered a sense of relief that was nothing short of intoxicating. It was good fun to pretend we were making a covert escape. But truth be told, we got little pushback as we exited with our pastel baby bundle. The amiable NICU docs (aka the non-Friedrich types) had run out of theories and did not know what to do with Jack. His nurses were willing accomplices to our benign crime. We had come to know them well over languid weeks on the ward and they too felt Jack should be home. It was just that no one in authority would say with confidence that he was fit to be discharged. In the absence of anyone taking the initiative, we had taken matters into our own hands. Jack was not necessarily progressing, but he was a whopping five pounds, 15 ounces, well beyond the weight threshold for sending a preemie packing. Still slack and lifeless in my arms, my boy was coming home!

We were off, happy to put as much distance as we could between Jack and the hospital where he had spent the entirety of his short life. I was certain that all he needed to catch up to his sister was the love and nurturing that could only be provided in the comfort of home. He needed a chance to sleep in the crib alongside his sister, feeling her next to him just like before he was pulled abruptly from me and into this confusing world. He needed to rest in natural light away from the fluorescent beams, humming ventilators and medication-dispensing IV's. He needed unhurried time to gently coax breastfeeding, away from the prying eyes of medical personnel who were scrutinizing our performance at this most fundamental skill in service of "keeping feedings on schedule." I was sure that together these "home remedies" would do the trick.

But they did not. I bristled as Pete became increasingly irritated with Jack's slow eating and listless behavior. For the first full week home, almost three months after he was born, he still was not alert. His limbs were slack and eyes only partially opened—sometimes one and then the other. My husband adopted an air of impatience with Jack. I could tell, like many parents who were terrified to lose a child, Pete was wary about bonding with him. I confess we did not talk about his fears. I was overwhelmed, just absorbing the rhythm of caring for two infants— feeding, changing, rocking, feeding, changing, rocking—times two. Somewhere I knew that Pete's hesitancy and shortness with Jack was his way of protecting himself should the unthinkable happen. It may have been a logical defense mechanism for my husband, who was just trying on this new "daddy" thing, but it did not prevent me from becoming equally impatient with him. How could he not love this sweet boy, how could he not see that Jack needed his daddy to cuddle him just as much as he needed his mom? Impatience turned to anger.

The incongruent, yet equally powerful forces of exhaustion and hope conspired to suppress reason so that it lurked just below the surface. The concerns that were driving Pete's behavior were undiscussable and I didn't allow myself to go there on a conscious level for fear I would have to confront reality.

In late April our friends and neighbors threw us the baby shower that never happened in mid-February because, at the time, when I should have been enjoying the last months of my pregnancy, we had already been thrust in parent mode occupied with the task of keeping our babies alive. Now with both kids home from the NICU, it felt safe to celebrate. One neighbor, a baker, came over with two identical fondant cakes, one salmon color and one teal. This neighbor was followed by many other friends whose well wishes were delayed by our long hospital stint. Many who worried and prayed alongside us were now relieved and ready to party. They came bearing gifts. There were boy-girl twin outfits, onesies out the wazoo, oodles of primary-colored plastic toys, and, consistent with our theme, every Noah's Ark nursery accoutrement imaginable. The well-wishers cooed at the babies, dangled things in front of them, trying to coax a smile, and a few hearty moms jockeyed to hold first one and then the other. Most who detected a difference between the babies were polite enough to say nothing. Among those who did venture a comment, it was always something upbeat like, "he'll catch up" or "just give him time." These throw-away sentiments were meant to sooth, but for me they had the opposite effect. They shouted, "These people notice that something is amiss." Paranoid, I wondered if they were already creating a pecking order among my twins. I wondered if they pitied Jack, I wondered if they were thinking, "What is wrong with that baby?" I tried hard to allow the frivolity of the moment drown out those thoughts.

Chapter 5

2 X WOKE

*Anything can make me stop and look and
wonder, and sometimes learn.*

—Kurt Vonnegut

THE EVENING UNFOLDED with the predictable rhythm of every other since the grandparents cleared out and we were left to our own devices. Pete and I juggled two nearly identically sized baby bundles, bottled breast milk, burp cloths, binkies, forks, and inevitably cold food, as we attempted to resume "normal" dinners. Just as we finished what could not quite be called a meal, Pete cradled Jack while I breastfed Livie. Holding her calmed me. Her face flushed pink after eating. Although I had to pinch myself, it was unmistakable... she was filling out. Still beyond petite, at just under five pounds, Livie had transformed from the bird-like being who resembled a 3D version of a grainy ultrasound image into my sweet round baby, all soft edges, alert, and uncomplicated. With her, I did not have to deal with sideways glances or quizzical looks.

One down, one to go, I thought as I slid her back into the navy polka-dot Pack 'n Play that she now shared with her brother. Having prepared a tiny vial of breast milk so small it resembled an oversized test tube more than a baby bottle, I leaned back in a dining room chair to feed Jack. This was our ritual because his suck reflex was too weak to take the breast. Just like every other evening, soft light from the chandelier above the table danced on surfaces and played with the pink twilight outside. I relaxed, settling in, pillow on my lap, for a painfully slow feeding session.

I was slumped over, close to dosing off, when seemingly out of nowhere, Jack's eyes flickered open. These were not the lazy, half-open lids we had become accustomed to: sometimes one then the other lifting, each one betraying its partner by moving out of sync. No, this was a big-eyed stare, both eyes working in coordination, glistening and awake. He rolled them around displaying unmistakable cognition. The overhead light was the subject of his wonder as if he were just seeing it for the first time. Jack's gaze followed the light and then landed on me. There was sweet recognition in those eyes. They seemed to say, "You are my Mommy." My own eyes, glassy with tears, replied, "Yes, you are right, I am your Mommy, and you are perfect." One might think I would not dare move lest I break the spell that conjured this fairy tale moment, but I could not contain myself, I was already up, Jack in my arms, calling for Pete who had moved into the living room to kick back in front of the TV with Livie.

"Honey, he is awake!" I yelled. Both of us, now energized by our boy's bright eyes, began cooing in encouraging tones and suspending objects in front of him to see what else might capture his attention. For me, it was as if the heavens had opened, and for a few precious moments all was right with the world. Jack was going to be okay.

Before bed that night, I gazed down at my precious twins lying together in their shared crib, reassuring myself: they were perfect. Of course, Jack had been suffering from a particularly pernicious case of "wimpy white boy lag," just as predicted by the omniscient NICU nurses. Dr. Friedrich be damned! Tonight's performance vindicated Jack against all the doctor's dire prognostications. Being of German ancestry myself gave me license to be particularly critical, I felt. The whole race was too stern, too unfeeling, and certainly on the wrong side of history in not one, but two world wars. The doomsday proclamations fell away. That night, I consigned Dr. Friedrich, the German, to the wrong side of what was now Jack's history in the Children's Hospital Oakland California Neonatal Intensive Care Unit. I slept well as visions of my twins chasing each other in the yard danced in my head.

I had an unbeatable sense of optimism borne out of those bright eyes following the twinkling light. What I had seen that evening was nothing short of a miracle: life demanding to be noticed. Convinced this was the first sign of Jack emerging from temporary malaise, we set up preemie boot camp in our combined kitchen-family room. The get-fit regime came to include lots of tummy time for Jack with eye-catching objects suspended just above his head to flex those slack neck muscles and coax his head up and off the floor. At first, he could not lift his head, but if you put your nose to the floor and caught his attention, you could see his eyes lifting, interested in doing the work that his cranium could not yet manage. Stamina was low, but we pressed on.

Once we settled into a routine, visits began from the early interventionist. Giving birth prematurely puts you in a club that nobody wants to be in, and at the same time entitles you to lots of "free" stuff.

There were all kinds of complimentary developmental toys distributed by charitable organizations, as well as eligibility for modest Social Security Disability Insurance payments for your child. But most significantly, prematurity entitles your child to developmental intervention services from the state. In California, all premature babies receive visits from an early intervention specialist to help them catch up on critical developmental milestones. Since the only criteria for services was being born earlier than 32 weeks gestation, our assigned interventionist began working with both Jack and Livie.

It is surely true that time is a friend to the prematurely born. Most preterm babies quickly outpace the work of the interventionist, making strides in weightbearing, sitting, grasping, and pulling up between visits. These strides move them rapidly into the category of "typically developing," dropping them off the interventionist's caseload. Like a miniature Olympic gymnast, Livie quickly nailed all her compulsory developmental milestones and graduated. Unfortunately for Jack, our DIY baby boot camp and regular visits from the interventionist did not make up the ground he needed in order to move on.

But life with the twins was not all work and no play. Before long we planned our first family vacation for early June when the twins had been home from the hospital for about two months. This was to be our annual pilgrimage to the New Jersey shore to soak up the sun with Pete's parents at their shore house, except this time we were four. Excited to show off our double blessings, I stuffed the suitcase to the gills with ridiculously cute twin outfits, matching floppy sun hats, and little pink and blue sunglasses (of course). Each day we would suit up Jack in tiny American flag trunks and Livie in an even tinier American flag bikini and tote them down to the beach. Livie was feisty, bubbly, and nearly sitting up on her own. She smiled and babbled as the sea breeze tickled her face. But the New Jersey humidity did not agree with Jack. He remained frail and limp and was able to assume only two positions on our umbrella-shielded beach blanket. He either lay flat on his back, arms splayed out to his sides or lounged supported in Pete's or my arms, not able to hold himself up.

Pete's friend Jack was the best man at our wedding. He was also our Jack's godfather and namesake. He and his wife joined us at the shore with their new baby, a boy born three months before the twins. The identical American flag swimsuits were a gift from them, and they matched the suit they had gotten for their own boy. Three babies on a beach blanket all sporting American flags. As you might expect, our adorable patriotic threesome caught the attention of more than a few beachcombers strolling the shoreline. Although overwhelmingly cute, a double take of the lineup drew a sharp contrast. Jack's son was a sturdy little guy with all his developmental building blocks firmly in place. As if the differences between Jack and his sister were not enough, this other boy only brought into stark relief the fragility of our own son. Jack would often cry or sleep through our stints at the beach as if the wind and exertion of the brief trip were too much for him. He simply did not have the stamina.

Perhaps frustrated or embarrassed by the harsh developmental lines drawn between Jack and his friend's fine specimen of a boy, one day Pete suggested we "change it up." We juggled applying sunscreen with the task of loading up our kiddie convoy of strollers, diaper bags, coolers, towels, beach umbrellas and three babies. Just as we were about to set off on our daily two-block sojourn to the beach, he offered, "Why don't we just head down without Jack this time, he is just a flesh blob. Let's let him sleep here. My mom will take care of him."

Just an off-hand comment: How should I take it? Not purposefully cruel; after all, Pete had been handed his "Dad Card" abruptly by the twins' premature births. He was uncomfortable with all of the objectively ugly, plastic baby paraphernalia and lost freedom that comes with the job. He, like a lot of guys in his position, still wanted to travel light. The comment was offered casually, but my response was anything but. I went postal.

"We will not leave Jack at home!" My husband's words had picked open the fragile protective scab, laying bare all our undiscussed fears. This was a defining moment for me; I remember it even today, with technicolor clarity. This was that day I decided that Jack would do everything his twin sister did. My son would not be left behind!

Pete saw it as an inconsequential day trip to the beach; one in a sea of many; no big deal. He did not realize he had tripped a wire that activated something deep within me. As I reflect on that moment, I may have sounded determined, but the stronger emotion at play within me was fear. A part of me sensed that I was on an edge, a precipice, which, if I inched out any farther, might result in me tumbling headfirst into an abyss from which there would be no return. On the face of it, all that lay in the balance was one more lazy beach afternoon. But I saw Pete's request to leave Jack behind as a slippery slope. If Jack wasn't "strong enough" or "hearty enough" to make it to the beach, what else was he not good enough for? What else could he not handle? What else would we be protecting him from?

I could not go down that path. If we walked out of the house and down the street for an afternoon at the beach, I would be betraying my son. I felt that if we did this now it would be too easy to come to the same conclusion tomorrow, and the next day, and the next. A precedent would have been set. It would be convenient next time to judge this or that as too difficult for Jack and that he would be safer, more comfortable, or better off, if he was left behind. And worse, we, his parents, might come to believe that this was all true…that Jack, in fact, was better off left behind.

Outwardly, I was that uniquely scary mix of offended and angry. My momma bear claws had come out and I was sharpening them for a fight. I gathered up Livie and handed her to Pete. I woke Jack, too roughly perhaps, showing Pete and anybody else around that "my kid can handle it." I snapped him into the Baby Bjorn carrier strapped across my chest and set out for the beach, pushing an empty umbrella stroller, Jack's weak cry reverberating. For him it was a cry of discomfort at being awakened abruptly; for me it was a battle cry.

I can't fault my husband for his frustration. The sleep deprivation alone that comes with having one baby, born on time, was enough to throw most couples for a loop. But this was not that. This was a multiple, premature birth to first-time parents. Objectively this was not just a lot, it was beyond a lot. Was lack of sleep the culprit, or was it more complicated? This pregnancy had certainly changed both our lives. I feared that Pete felt that this was not how "it was supposed to be." He had not let himself bond with Jack for fear of losing him. But I had bonded fiercely and knew that such unequal treatment of two babies who until very recently had shared the same amniotic space, feeding and growing together, could not be good.

That unsuspecting morning reached a fevered pitch with my declaration: "Jack will do everything that his twin sister does." Just as Jack had an "awakening" at the dinner table months before, it was my turn to be "woke." I now saw the fight I had ahead of me.

Chapter 6

DIAGNOSIS-
SCHMIAGNOSIS

*The quest for certainty blocks the search
for meaning. Uncertainty is the very condition
to impel man to unfold his powers.*

—Erich Fromm

MONTHS SLIPPED BY IN A HAZE of feeding, changing, bathing, and reading and rereading board books containing an average of 2.5 words per chunky page. About the time that Jack's state-funded developmental intervention services had run their course and were terminated, we passed that year and a half mark where I settled in to just being "a mom"—a mom doubly blessed with beautiful twins. Jack, with God's help, his own curiosity, and our baby boot camp exercise regimen, learned to sit up. While his sister was experiencing all the world had to offer on two legs, Jack pulled around the floor using only his arms, his legs dangling unceremoniously behind.

Unless we held him or propped him up against a handy end table or ottoman, the domain he surveyed consisted of toys spread out on the floor, base boards, door jambs, and dust bunnies—all the world that existed at ground level.

Like any self-respecting middle-class mom of multiples, I ferreted out and joined the local twins club of the San Francisco East Bay. This was Mecca for mothers of multiples. It served as command central for swapping everything from birthing "war" stories to general parenting tips, and it was a marketplace for trading all manner of plastic baby stuff. I tried to ignore the oblique glances I got from other mothers who detected a difference between Jack and Livie. It registered with them that something was "not quite right," but most were too polite to say anything. Then there were those moms who were unhampered by the constraining yoke of sensitivity. A few women outright asked me what he had… "Is it cerebral palsy?" "A muscular condition?" Knowing they were just trying to decrease their uncertainty, attempting to file what they saw into a familiar category did not take the sting out of their seemingly unending queries.

In addition to regularly scheduled twins' club festivities, Jack and Livie had another "extra-curricular" activity. Because they were not only multiples, but premature ones to boot, they were part of a preemie follow-up study. This involved quarterly visits to a satellite office adjacent to the Neonatal Intensive Care Unit where they had called home for all those weeks. Our usual visits went something like this: I would pack up the twins, bottles, rattles, blankets, and all, make the 40-minute drive, strolling them into a waiting room scattered with babies of varying ages. We would be called when it was our turn; the nurse would perform the ritual weigh-ins, measure ups, and temperature checks. Then the doctor would eye each baby one after the other, asking a few perfunctory developmental questions. I liked these visits because they involved pleasant professionals saying good things about my kids. Even the environment was refreshing. This was no sterile Intensive Care Unit with machines whirring and haggard parents looking all-the-more yellowed under fluorescent light. The entire office was designed to resemble a cozy living room with its dark paneled wainscoting and brightly colored play area located an appropriate distance from the wing-backed chairs and fruit-infused water dispenser, where parents were encouraged to lounge. All this warmth may have been a cunning attempt by hospital executives to appease ex-NICU parents who were still carrying around a healthy dose of hospital PTSD.

If it was, their plan worked. The vibe felt more scholarly than medical. Appointments were upbeat, and each concluded with vague, non-threatening pronouncements like, "Boy, they are getting big" and "Everybody is coming along quite nicely." The whole experience was just the right mix of positive and inconsequential, and then as quickly as we had arrived, we were on our way to shop and stroll a bit in town before returning home. Compared to entertaining two toddlers with pots and pans on the kitchen floor and mopping spit-up, our preemie follow-up study appointments felt like a spa day for this overextended working mom.

By this particular visit, I am no longer the mom of 16-month-old twins; I am now a six-month-pregnant mom of 16-month-old twins. Like so many parents of multiples who had trouble getting pregnant the first time, we were floored when the double line again appeared in the pink pregnancy stick window. However, we quickly recovered. After premature twins, the unexpected had become the norm. "It's Tuesday, of course there is another baby on the way." So now, even with my protruding belly making our entourage increasingly spatially challenged, the twins and I were experts at navigating preemie follow-up study appointments. Sometimes our visits included two shots of Respertal, a preventative strengthener for tiny lungs. But other than a little poke per baby, there was nothing scary here. Plus, I felt like I was doing a good deed by keeping these appointments. No one would have noticed if we dropped out of the study, but I was infinitely thankful for my babies, and I figured that the least I could do was give back a little by contributing to the body of research on premature births.

This particular sunny morning, Livie, Jack, and I are rolling into the building and up the elevator to Dr. Stuart's office. The twins are outfitted in a brand-new triple stroller we purchased in anticipation of baby number three. Dr. Stuart, a young new doc who I had never met, was now presiding over the follow-up study. An expert in fussy toddlers, his nurse wasted no time commencing with the weigh in. We set one and then the other on the scale with the cheery stuffed giraffe looming over. The giraffe's sole purpose was to hold a squirming toddler's attention just long enough to get an accurate weight. Invariably the nurse exclaimed…wait for it…"They are getting so big!" I reveled in this, the ultimate compliment for a preemie mom.

"Yes sir," I puffed up, "I do have big babies." Then we were ushered into the examination room. Dr. Stuart lifted one twin and then the other onto the padded examining table. This new guy followed the same protocol as old doctor Griffin. He poked, prodded and peered into eyes and ears, as he asked all the expected developmental questions. I checked the wall clock; at this rate, it would not be long before we would be on our way, with the doc reminding us to stop in downstairs at the lab to get the recommended RSV shots. "Remember, preemies are susceptible to pneumonia until age 2," he'd called out as we whisked out the door, just one step away from an unfettered day of shopping and strolling.

Only this appointment did not unfold as planned. Dr. Stuart took special interest in Jack. His growth was "off the charts." Even with his persistent low tone and delayed development, he was already towering over his twin sister. He was as tall as a three-year-old. "Jack's size is highly unusual given that he started out with the preemie disadvantage," the doctor mused audibly under his breath.

Okay, this is starting to not be fun. I was reminded of my protective posture back in the NICU surrounding all things "Jack." I was transported back to our NICU days where every query or comment by a medical professional could lead to a new test being ordered or IV inserted. As if no time had passed, I was back on my guard. Pete and I had considered Jack's height a point of pride. Stature was the one area where Jack had caught up with and lapped his peers. This was a good thing, and the one that everyone commented on: "Jack is such a tall boy." I too, grew a little taller whenever someone made this observation. I hoarded these comments because, for me, they meant that people were noticing his height rather than his developmental lags.

Today, my heartbeat quickened with each question. "Had Jack teethed early?" Come to think of it, he had. Inexplicably at 4 months, teeth had started erupting through tender pink gums. *What was wrong with that?* From our perspective it just meant Jack moved through that parents' nightmare crucible in short order. Dr. Stuart set Jack down for some cognitive tasks. "Touch the bell," "stack the blocks." Jack was passing with flying colors, or was he? What was this guy fishing for? He had not taken nearly this much time with Livie. Finally, mercifully, Jack was dismissed. Now Dr. Stuart would put Livie in the hot seat and take her through the same set of "baby school" tasks. This must be the new guy's routine, I comforted myself. But he didn't call Livie up. Instead, we were all dismissed and told by the helpful nurse to return to the reception area.

Dutifully, I locked Jack back into the stroller with Livie and rolled our pint-sized posse back into the waiting room that now had lost its cozy feel. Ten minutes took the form of forever. The nurse ducked her head back into the room and followed up with, "Can you stay around a bit, Mrs. Winking? The doctor wants to see you one more time." The old guy, Doctor Griffin, had done little more than listen for tiny heart beats and tickle tiny feet before sending us packing.

Having spent much of my twenties at a state university pursuing an academic track, I lit on a likely explanation. Suspiciously, I thought, "Was this guy working on some obscure research project and needed one more data point? That must be it; he was young, probably looking to publish." We waited even longer.

After an indeterminate number of minutes, which my mind morphed into hours, we were ushered back into Dr. Stuart's office. "Mrs. Winking," he said unceremoniously, "because of Jack's unusually rapid growth and persistent developmental delays, I suspect that he has a syndrome." His tone was roughly that of a grocery store clerk helping me locate the olives on aisle 11. Not the tenor you would expect to accompany the bottom dropping out of your world. *There*, he had said it, the dirty S-word. I began my career as a special education teacher. I knew my syndromes: Down, Williams, Fragile X, Willie Prader…all involved significant developmental delays, mental retardation and, in some cases, devastating health complications.

All of the oxygen had been sucked out of the room. I wanted to take my babies and get out, not hear what he was saying. This was all so incongruent with the day I had imagined for us when my feet hit the floor that morning. If I could just rewind roughly the last 30 seconds, I could exit the medical building and resume the carefree day I had planned with my twins. After all, we had important work to do, there were people at the mall waiting to comment on how adorable these two were, bouncing along in the triple stroller with their matching outfits and tiny sunglasses.

Jack had seen scads of doctors, for Chrissake, he *was* a preemie, I thought. If there was a syndrome to be found, any one of the army of esteemed medical personnel who attended to Jack would have caught it. *Mr. New Doctor, I'll tell you why a syndrome has not been detected…because there isn't one*, I railed silently. I had it figured out…this guy Stuart was cut from the same cloth as Dr. Friedrich, another basic research type, looking for "zebras" when there were none to be found.

I wanted to run, but I was rooted to the Berber carpet. Stuart was still talking. Focus on, "what was coming out of his mouth, something about foreheads?" Now I forced myself back into the room, back into the interrogation. This guy was actually rattling off a textbook list of symptoms.

"Jack has a broad forehead," he said. I had never liked to show my own. My mother once told me I had a forehead "that you could paint a sign on." That was precisely why I had sported a thick set of bangs since the second grade, which could double as a barometer for how reliably they spiraled up like uneven springs with a rise in humidity. I rarely unveiled my forehead, but this was "go time," and I had to protect my child.

To deflect the arrows now directed toward Jack, I lifted my auburn fringe. "See, I have a big forehead too," I announced matter-of-factly, as if this revelation would put an end to the insanity. The brilliant doctor was detecting simple heredity, not a syndrome.

He barely acknowledged my defensive move and was not deterred from his list. "Jack has a long face," he said.

Again, I offered, "So do I." He has a pointy chin. He has large, wide-set eyes. Now his observations were coming at me in rapid-fire succession. Reeling from the craziness of it all, I checked out again for a few seconds. My thoughts drifted to the sanguine, big foreheaded porcelain figurines of my youth, circa 1976. Relying on humor to defuse discomfort was a familiar tactic of mine.

"Doctor, are you saying my son has "Precious Moments" syndrome?"

Dr. Stuart continued, unamused. I was terrified but realized now I had to hear more. We had dismissed Jack's developmental delays as nothing more than a variation on the typical continuum. No one had connected the dots to a diagnosis. The doctor was still talking, but now I needed answers. My mind breezed over the physical characteristics he described. A pointy chin, wide-set eyes, and high forehead I could handle. I was interested in attributes that altered or shortened lives. I desperately needed to know, "Is this fast-growing, big foreheaded, pointy-chinned syndrome life threatening? Does it count mental retardation among its scourges?"

I flooded Dr. Stuart with questions. "Is it degenerative? Is it hereditary? Does it cause learning problems?" He said he could not confirm all the indicators of Sotos syndrome.

Hold up. Dr. Stuart had the gonads to tell a pregnant woman, hormones on fire, with 16-month-old twins perched in a stroller, that he "did not fully know" the answer to whether the sentence he just pronounced over my child would harm him? He continued by saying the syndrome was rare and he had not exhausted the research in the area.

"What?" He was still talking, but it did not matter; by now Dr. Stuart's voice had taken on the rhythmic nasal quality of the teacher in every Charlie Brown Special, "Wha wha wha wha, wha wha." He had lost me at, "I don't fully know" and now he was wasting precious time. At this point, I had dismissed polite conventions like "thank you" and "goodbye" as counterproductive. As he continued to speak, I had already pointed the stroller in the direction of the door and was careening down the hall into a conveniently positioned elevator, leaving skid marks on Dr. Stuart's tasteful, steel blue Berber.

This was fall of 1999 and the Internet was barely a thing. Today, we live in a world where we make dinner reservations, find a date, buy groceries or a new grill, and track our kids' exact locations with a few clicks and a swipe on our phones. We forget that Siri and Alexa were not always at our beck and call waiting to satisfy our every informational whim. Still, though the Internet was not even close to the intravenous feed of minutia that it is today, I knew I needed to get home, fire up my personal computer and find out what this Sotos thing was. What would this new word mean for Jack's world, my world?

Chapter 7

SOTOS

*What's in a name? That which we call a rose by
any other name would smell as sweet.*

—William Shakespeare

BACK IN THE SAFETY OF MY HOME OFFICE, away from Dr.
Stuart's questioning, I scanned the computer while the twins napped.
Quick as you can say fear, I typed S-O-T-O-S S-Y-N-D-R-O-M-E.
The Internet showed pixelated institutional-looking photos of what
appeared to be youth with disabilities. Ahh, this was an image taken
from a textbook, it had to be old. What year was it from? Now to
the text...

Sotos syndrome is an overgrowth syndrome, characterized by
rapid growth in the first seven years of life, pervasive low tone in all
the muscles of the body causing developmental and physical delays.
Because of rapid cell growth the subject is at risk of tumors on the
abdomen and kidneys. Physical characteristics include broad forehead,
wide set eyes, high arched pallet, long hands and feet. Central nervous

system manifestations are frequent. Delay in the attainment of milestones of development, walking and talking and, in particular speech, is almost always present and clumsiness is frequent (60 to 80%), as is low muscle tone (hypotonia) and lax joints. Intellectual disability is present in 80 to 85% of the patients, with an average IQ of 72 and a range from moderate to borderline mild intellectual disability. Fifteen to 20% may have normal intelligence. Seizures may occur in 30% of those affected. Some brain abnormalities (enlarged ventricles) may occur. Individuals with Sotos syndrome can also experience behavioral problems that make it difficult for them to develop relationships with others.

My eyes flickered across the screen, not pausing to honor grammatical niceties like commas and periods. I saw no mention of degeneration or death. Breath returned to my body. The first hurdle cleared. Now I rescanned the list of symptoms looking for something that was not a dead-on match with what I knew to be true of Jack. This would be my child's "get out of jail free" card, the way to escape Dr. Stuart's prognostication. Finding none, I tried another tactic: dismiss the whole unfortunate incident. Rationalizations flooded my consciousness, providing a welcome numbing that took hold like a powerful drug. Jack was on a ventilator much longer than most pre-term babies—that explained his limp extremities. His developmental delays were easily explained by prematurity; all he needed was more time. In fact, he was already gaining ground. Furthermore, he lived for over two months in level 3 and 4 NICU's and was poked and prodded around the clock; something as catastrophic as a syndrome could not have passed unnoticed under the watchful eyes of the neonatal staff. This university-type MD had it wrong. He didn't even wear scrubs or a white lab coat, how could he know more than practicing physicians?

But rationalizations, like all narcotics, wear off with time, leaving pain and nagging doubts. A few days later, when I calmed down, Pete and I brought Jack back to see Dr. Stuart. He was gracious enough to not comment on my unceremoniously rude escape from the building. He walked both of us through the litany of symptoms again. When he saw that we were still not convinced, he offered that the only definitive diagnosis of Sotos syndrome was through a bone-age test. This test involved an x-ray of the bones in the hand that could conclusively confirm the rapid cell growth, the underlying hallmark of the syndrome. Pat rationalizations no longer offered a salve. There was no relief, we *had* to know.

As fate would have it, the test took us back to familiar territory, Oakland Children's Hospital, the closest medical institution where the x-ray could be performed and interpreted. We trod to the hospital with Jack and Livie in tow. Out of the NICU for over a year now, we had a bittersweet reunion with the place where Jack's little body had undergone so many indignities. This was the place of endless pricks, IV's, catheterizations, ventilators, operations, and cannulas. I would like to say any lingering PTSD had worn off by then, but it hadn't. In my dark imaginings, the smiling doc who meets us in the examining room is not a smiling doc at all, but Dr. Friedrich, who, sensing that something is amiss, captures Jack and readmits him as a permanent resident in this sanitized society ruled by the White Coats. But we had moved on, I reassured myself…Jack was just a kid now, like any toddler. Okay, he was not toddling as surely as other kids his age, but he was still a toddler, nonetheless. Children's Hospital was so "last year," now relegated forever to a history we did not identify with any longer.

Happily, this visit involved no physical trauma. Jack lay nicely on the table for the painless hand x-ray and was offered the obligatory post-test reward. The options included a sticker catering to the nutri-tionally aware parent or a sucker for the exhausted-give-him-what-ever-he-wants types. Jack got his sucker, and we were on our way.

Back in the rhythms of life with 17-month-olds, it was easy not to think about the test. Could we just not return to learn the results? Could we just let Jack be Jack? Could we forget that the whole Dr. Stuart syndrome-fixation-thing was ever a thing? Kind of like how that optional teeth cleaning, or dermatology skin check appointment just falls off the calendar into oblivion. Tempting… was not return-ing even an option? Unfortunately, not for us—we *had* to know.

Nearly a week later, back at Children's, we sat in leather-bound chairs in the office of the geneticist, Dr. Jacobson, whose job was to give news to confused, overwhelmed parents. Our guy got straight to the point. Yes, in fact, the x-ray showed that Jack did have all the markers for Sotos syndrome. The genial genetics doc went on to explain the array of therapies Jack would need to address delays.

"You will want to get him physical therapy and occupational therapy to remediate muscle weakness, speech therapy to address communication delays," he began, "plus educational support to address any cognitive delays…and he will definitely need ultra-sounds every six months until he is at least seven to detect the tumors that are common with Sotos."

I marveled at how this doctor could maintain this light, matter-of-fact exterior as he pronounced a life-altering sentence over another human being, someone's child, as if he was ordering a sandwich with all the fixin's or describing upgrades in a new tract home, "…and you will want the granite countertops, the slow-close drawers, the brushed nickel bathroom fixtures, and definitely, the distressed hardwood." My mind wanders. I force myself to dial in again. I hear Dr. Jacobson say that he personally would like to follow Jack's progress: "Could we return in four months?" And finally, "Would we be willing to participate in a long-term study of the syndrome? Because it is relatively rare, we have a small sample size." Pete and I just listened.

I am the consummate rule follower. I never put trash in the slot that is designated for recyclables. I don't pull into the handicapped spot, even for a moment. I feel appropriately guilty when I don't rehang all my unwanted items when hastily leaving a clothing store dressing room. Participating in the Genetics study was what the doctor recommended. It was what was expected of grateful parents who, although shattered and dazed, were in some measure thankful that a credentialed professional had provided them with an answer, an explanation for the gnawing differences they saw in their child. It was what a rule-follower would do. But on the other hand, I could not see the upside of tethering Jack—for who knows how long —to a genetics practice where professionals wanted to study symptoms, collect data, and essentially put him under a microscope. On the other, "other hand" I was grateful. We now had an explanation for why Jack never seemed to outgrow the delays we had chalked up to premature birth. The fog was lifting. The diagnosis explained why back in the NICU Dr. Friedrich, with his brooding brows, would not leave Jack in peace. Our son had a syndrome, and it had a name: SOTOS.

The label meant everything and nothing at the same time. Everything because it explained the limp muscles, difficulty feeding, low tone, fast growth, and the fact that our kid was still not walking a full six months after his twin. But it also meant nothing, because having a name for this collection of characteristics did not change anything. Jack was still the same goofy-smiled little guy we adored.

A diagnosis neither erased Jack's reality nor made it worse. Today, "Sotos" was just another four-letter word, but what significance would this word take on over a lifetime?

Rule follower, yes, but I am equally a pragmatist. I mentally battled these two competing natures. We were supposed to return. We could contribute to advances in medical research. I felt guilty... the genetics doctor was a nice man who had answered all our questions. He had given us a reason. In the final analysis, and I believe in my child's best interest, the rule follower in me shut down and let the pragmatist take the wheel. This guy and his rare syndrome genetics study had nothing to offer me or my son. He was not prescribing a pill, ointment, or treatment that would make our son's syndrome disappear like a case of eczema or a nasty ear infection. Jack would come before my slavish adherence to rules. No, this was not for my kid. In my mind, this good doctor had outlived his usefulness upon diagnosis. This day, we discarded Dr. Jacobson, Genetics Associate MD, like a shabby prom date.

I realized that a diagnosis (this big hairy audacious thing I had feared) was nothing more than a group of letters that make up a word that was attached to a list of symptoms. A collection of little realities. Put them all together and would you have a whole child? No. Paste them edge to edge in paper doll shape and you wouldn't even have half a child. Where is the sense of humor, the killer crooked smile, the impossibly long lashes that women would kill for, the gentle empathy, the unyielding stubbornness, and the way he leans in headfirst against you because he is so tired but is determined to stay awake because the story is just too good to miss. I had come to know all these beautiful complexities in my child, and I knew the genetic doc's laundry list of characteristics did not begin to tell the story.

They wanted us back in four months. I realized that I needed a road map to help my child succeed, not a quarterly or even semi-annual iron-clad reminder that my child did not meet all the specs for a "normal kid" blueprint. As Pete drove and the twins dozed, lulled to sleep by the continuous motion of tires against asphalt, in my mind, I was already saying "yes" to the physical therapy, "yes" to the occupational therapy, "yes" to the speech therapy and "yes" to the tumor screen, but "no, thank you very much," to the genetics study. This study, I was convinced, would do nothing more than shine an unforgiving spotlight on each aberration from the "genetic normal," and would ultimately file them and my son into a stifling box labeled "Sotos syndrome."

It was a fledgling idea birthed that day on unsteady legs, but it is one that has held true over time. For me it answers, once and for all, the question: What is a diagnosis worth? It turns out that for all its scientific rigor and precise language, a diagnosis is only as useful as the information it gives you to improve daily life for your child.

I have come to realize that while it is a catastrophic event in the life of a parent, the diagnosis itself is a neutral event for the child. All a diagnosis does is provide an explanation and a name for a collection of observable or testable conditions that are detected within a child. Jack was the same kid he was before the genetics doctor offered the conclusive results of the hand x-ray. The act of proclaiming the words, the bestowing of a label, would change nothing. My fatal flaw would not be so much the diagnosis as it would be falling prey to limiting beliefs about my son because of that diagnosis. No, my Achille's heel would be what I would allow to change (or not) within me in terms of how I viewed my child. After all, I was the most influential person in Jack's life and what I did had the power to create seismic shifts when piled up over the course of his lifespan.

I could not allow the weight and formality of the diagnosis to kick me into "sheeple" mode, such that I was grimly buying into each prognostication associated with the syndrome. If I let this little word cause me to become fearful, overly protective, or limiting, then Sotos would take on outsized proportions in my kid's life. It would become a 5-letter "dirty word." I didn't want to live in denial. However, I also was not about to swallow every characteristic, indication, and limitation, hook line and sinker. In fact, just the opposite was true: *my kid was a kid first* with a complicated personality, interests and preferences. He had much more in common with other kids than he did with a collection of clinical attributes.

Chapter 8

EXPECTATIONS

Effort creates aptitude.

—Lauren Resnick, Lauren Resnick Learning
Research Development Center

AS WE MARINATED in the steamy California traffic on the way home
from Children's, this extrovert turned inward, consumed by my own
thoughts. I barely acknowledged my husband beside me or the kids in
the back seat. I had escaped into the extraordinary tale of a man from
California I had never met but who fascinated me. At the time he was
just starting a non-profit called World Vision for the Blind.

The man was Daniel Kish. As a boy, with the help of his mother,
he challenged the line of what was possible for blind people and then
obliterated it. In 1968, at only thirteen months, Daniel lost both of
his eyes due to cancer.[4] As Daniel tells it, his mother, Paulette, made
the decision to treat him as if he was a regular kid. He was a curious
little guy who loved to climb. He started by scaling the sides of his
crib until he landed on the floor. When he climbed, his mother's

reaction was to let him keep climbing. When he set out to explore first his house and then his neighborhood, she let him explore. When he mounted a bike and kept on pedaling down the street until he ran into a steel pole, her reaction was to let him keep riding. Over a bruising and eventful childhood, it came to pass that Daniel was a blind boy who rode a bike, navigating through town on his own, using a tongue-clicking technique he perfected that uses echolocation. As an adult, Daniel guides sighted hikers through dense forests. Literally, the blind leading the sighted! Daniel attributes much of his extraordinary story to his mom's beliefs about him and what he could do. Blindness was definitely part of his story, but he proved to himself and the world that it did not define him.

This inspiring account had all the makings of a TV docudrama. I could still hear the closing credits soundtrack reverberating as my thoughts meandered out of Daniel's triumphant story and crashed broadside against my own. The landing back into reality was jarring and sharp-edged. My own story was so messy, fragmented, and uncertain. No docudrama here, and definitely no triumph as far as the eye could see. We now had the diagnosis. As if it were a morose, but essential grocery list, I had, against my will, memorized the listing of Sotos characteristics. But what should I expect from my kid? How could I make sure that this thing did not rule his world? Daniel's mom had certainly not let the commonly accepted profile of what "blind people can do" dissuade her.

I retreated into my thoughts again. For me, expectations were at the root. I wondered: are they good or bad? Would they be a trap or a triumph? Are expectations hobgoblins, follies of the mind that inevitably knock us on our proverbial cans and leave us demoralized…or are they our best hope?

I have a dear friend who makes the case that expectations, if not outright bad, are, at the very least, dangerous. Her indictment of expectations goes something like this: "Expectations typically lead to dissatisfaction, so let go of them." She points out that before she was "expectations-free," she would bemoan her adult sons canceling plans for a long-awaited visit home, forgetting her birthday, or choosing to spend time with a girlfriend over time with her. More often than not, when she entertained expectations for her sons' behavior, she would be left frustrated and despondent. It was only after she let go of expectations that she became content in her relationship with her boys.

But in truth, what worthwhile endeavor does not serve up a healthy dose of dissatisfaction, difficulty and even heartache? Contrary to my friend, the WAY I see it, much of what we humans are up to, from sustaining friendships to creating art to changing careers, is fraught with pitfalls. Upon reflection, most of us would agree that, in the end, each of these pursuits is well worth the gut punches they invariably serve up. Moreover, it is precisely their ability to conjure strong emotions of joy, and even pain, that elevates their worth. Pain be damned; in my view, expectations are not just unavoidable, they are everything. In fact, expectations make the world go round; without them we are resigned to malaise. Why get out of bed if we are not looking forward to something?

Perhaps the argument is not whether expectations are good or bad, or whether we should have them or not; because like it or not, they are out there lurking in our subconscious, just waiting to entice us. Rather, it is how we *use* our expectations that holds the most promise for children, and particularly for children whom the world has judged as "less than."

Experts have a lot to say about expectations. Research-based popular books like *How Children Succeed*,[5] *Mindset*,[6] and *Grit*,[7] all address facets of expectations. In *High Expectations Teaching*,[8] Jon Saphier writes, "Smart is something you get, not something you are born with." He says that if he can teach teachers to believe this, children will achieve. If it is important for teachers to believe that their students CAN, how much more critical is this mindset for parents—who literally breathe their lifeblood into their children?

As an educator, I had been taught that intelligence and ability are not fixed quantities, a myth long perpetrated by a lucrative IQ testing industry. In fact, we don't just win or lose in some great cosmic lottery. While it is true enough that some of us are born with greater quantities of raw material than others, in the end our ability is molded by what we DO. For example, my statuesque friend who was graced with long, lithe fingers may have an easier road to excelling in classical piano, but that does not mean that with work hard I can't become a solid, or even accomplished piano player.

What we DO matters. I had cut my academic teeth on the idea that "Effort creates aptitude," a concept pioneered at University of Pennsylvania's Learning Research Development Center.[9] Simply put, this means that what you put in determines what you get out. If you subscribe to this world view, low expectations are an effort killer and, without effort, one cannot impact results.

But did I even believe my son to be capable? And, just as importantly, why does what we parents believe even matter? I retreated again, this time into an account of a particularly tenacious group of scientists who spent a lot of time with rats.

At this point you are thinking: back up the truck, what can parenting possibly have to do with rodents? As it turns out, a lot.

Research first undertaken in the 1960's proves that how we feel about rats affects how rats behave. Come again? At first blush, it sounds far-fetched that a person's thoughts could affect the behavior of a separate, unconnected organism. But it turns out this research wasn't some hocus-pocus, spoon-bending side show. It revealed a truth that may be considered mundane, and yet also profound. Rosenthal and Fode (foot note https://www.storming.com/results/2016/02/06/robert-rosenthal-and-maze-smart-rats/) showed that what research assistants *believed* about rats affected something concrete: the rats' behavior. This is how it went down: Scientists got a group of research assistants together. Half of the assistants in the group were told that they were each assigned a smart rat. The other half were told that they were assigned a dumb rat. Those who thought their rats were smart petted them more, talked to them with a positive tone, and treated them more gently than the research assistants who believed they were in charge of dumb rats. These differences in caregivers' beliefs translated to their behavior toward their rats and actually increased the "smart" rats' ability to run mazes and also increased their acuity in finding food—arguably important skills if you happen to be a rat. Of course, in reality, none of these rats had any more natural ability than any other rat—they were all just rats. The only explanation for the consistent patterns seen in the high performing rats was found in the messages they received from the words and behavior of their caregivers.

My brain toggled from rats back to humans. So, if we *believe* our kids are bright and capable, we will *behave* as if they are, and as a result their performance will improve. Intriguing for all of us with kids, but for those of us raising a child with special needs, this research should give us real pause. What you *think* your child *can do* actually impacts your child's performance over time.

Reader, if you are a skeptic, now is the appropriate time to ask: "Come on, how much can our beliefs about a person actually change their behavior?" Believing my child can fly will not make a pilot. If my child has Down syndrome, I can believe in him until the cows come home and it will not erase a chromosomal abnormality. If he is paralyzed due to a severed spinal cord, my beliefs will not mend tendons, bone, and ligaments. This is true, but I believe "curing" misses the point. First, curing implies that our children are the problem, are wrong, somehow defective.

Within the autism community, the deaf community and many other ability communities, there is a sustained movement that argues that difference should not be confused with "wrongness." Autism advocates point out that the autistic brain does not think "*wrong*," it merely thinks *differently*. The deaf community reminds the world that vocal communication is only one way of getting one's point across and is not innately superior to American Sign Language (ASL). We love our children for all their exquisite uniqueness. We want them to live their best lives, while embracing their uniqueness, and at the same time, we want them to *never* be constrained by negative beliefs, feelings of helplessness, or fear.

No, I could not focus on "curing" my child. Nor did I think high expectations were a miracle antidote for anyone's child. Putting aside the need to "cure," I returned to the question of how much can be achieved with positive messages sown over the totality of a young lifetime? It turns out, *a lot*. Leading mindset researchers are proving that the possibilities are expanding as we learn more about how particular beliefs impact outcomes… "as we understand how one person affects another person, the line of what is possible can actually move."[10]

I recalled how Daniel Kish described his own theory that the psychology of one person becomes absorbed and translated into the physical reality of another person. It made me think that expectations, those often unspoken, private thoughts we all possess, are extremely powerful agents that lead to subtle and not so subtle behaviors. So yes, we need to tell our kids that "they can do it," but telling them is not enough—not by a long shot. It is the faint, recurring, and sometimes insidious messages, positive and negative, that our children get from us and the world around them that impact their ultimate success.

All these musings on that endless drive home led me to a radical idea: *What if* I acted as if my child was not limited by Sotos? I extended the thought: *What if* others acted like their children were not limited by autism, developmental delay, Attention Deficit Hyperactivity Disorder (ADHD), Down Syndrome, fill in the blank, you name it?

What if we believed in our children and their innate capacity to achieve despite the labels pronounced over them? What could happen? Could we parents move the line of what is possible? Could I move the line for my child?

Chapter 9

RUNNING
THE GAUNTLET

Hard work beats talent if talent doesn't work hard.

—Tim Notke, High School Basketball Coach

AS ANOTHER YEAR PASSED, Pete and I settled back into life, he commuting to the south bay area and me with a 20-month-old on my hip trailing two 3-year-olds while squeezing in part-time work. We collided with one another as we juggled kid duty. There were play groups to be played, twins club meetings to attend, diapers to be changed, baby food to be mushed, and naps to be taken.

I was increasingly dogged by the feeling that I was not going to get away with just engaging in the typical machinations of life with pre-schoolers. A joyous orbit through which passed play time, snack time, park time, nap time, more play time, and finally plop-the-kids-in-front-of-a-movie-to-get-some-peace time. Jack's needs were greater. The stakes were higher for him. Seemingly mundane kid pursuits like crawling into a packing box, pulling out toys, and turning door handles took on gargantuan proportions in my mind. Inactivity and inertia were the enemy.

Jack was at his best, good natured and mild mannered, when propped on the couch listening to a story or lying prone in front of the TV watching the adventures of *Arthur the Aardvark* or *Caillou* on PBS. But I knew he needed to be moving. He had to practice over and over the things that other toddlers mastered effortlessly. Even if he could not be successful on his own, he had to try. I feared that if I did not make him try, he would come to think he couldn't.

Well after other toddlers' cruising turned into running, Jack's gait had remained halting. He locked his knees in his joint sockets and kept his arms not exactly straight out at his sides like a balancing tight rope walker, but more in front of him. The term that the developmental interventionist used for this was "high guard." It was a protective stance that allowed Jack to steady himself. His unusual posture prompted his grandfather, never one to be hampered by a filter, to call him "Frankenstein boy," mocking the monster-like way his arms were extended. The comment might have been dismissed as a joke, but knowing that this was the only way Jack could get around sucked every bit of humor out of it.

I was again reminded of Daniel Kish's mom as she recounted memories of those voices who sought to impose low expectations on Daniel. "How could she let her blind son ride a bike down a hill?" To which she responded, "How can I not?"

The difference between my Jack and Paula's son was that Daniel was an innate risk taker, an extreme explorer of his environment... and Jack was not. Jack limited his curiosity to the world within his grasp. He would position himself near cabinet doors and explore things at his level, but he was no dare devil. He LOVED books and seemed to melt into the stories that his dad, grandpa, or I would read to him. "More books." He was always asking for more books.

On unsteady bearings, he would toddle over and lean into strangers if a story was being read anywhere within earshot. He also loved toys that felt safe for him. Toys that allowed him to sit or lean, so that his strength or balance were not challenged. Wooden coffee table-height train tables were a favorite because they were solid, immovable and Jack could ground himself by resting against the side, giving him enough stability to extend an arm to roll an engine or coal car along the track.

But movement was hard; it took effort. At the playground Jack would prefer to sit in the sand and watch the grains sift through his fingers, a pastime that caused more than one mom, turned amateur diagnostician, to ask if he was autistic. He much preferred stationary pursuits to going down the slide, orbiting on the merry-go-round, or climbing onto the various primary-colored platforms that overlapped one another to create a playground climbing surface. The mock swinging bridges that other preschoolers scrambled across were treacherous for Jack as they confounded his already-compromised sense of balance.

He needed to be pushed to do these things and push I did. Although Jack did not like it and tried to avoid activity at all costs, he also had a resolute sense of humor, which I appreciated and took as my license to press him even harder.

Half-open doors were hidden hazards for Jack. Like the time he fell through the back door flat-faced onto the greying wooden porch planks right in front of me and a gaggle of Livie's friends who were playing in the yard. "*I dropped in to say hi,*" he mumbled at floor level, delivering the line like a pint-sized, self-deprecating stand-up comedian. The girls, bedecked with glittered crowns and bedazzled wands, did not hear him. His speech was not clear and they were caught up in their princess fantasy, but I heard. Silently, I chalked one up for Jack in the game of life. He was not yet four and was destined to fall *a lot*. This attitude would serve him well.

But good humor would not erase genetics. I told myself that each slide, set of stairs, or swinging bridge was an opportunity, a hurdle to clear. Instead of fun romps, our days more resembled a death march through play structures across the greater California East Bay. I did not let myself dwell for too long on my real reason for each playground conquest. Each one a hurdle, but what were they leading to? Proof of what? Normalcy?

I knew that my ninja mom sense of urgency did not exactly match the relaxed pace of the other park moms and stay-at-home dads. These folks viewed a park day as a time for sharing finger food neatly apportioned in individual Tupperware containers, trading gossip, and sharing endearing stories about their little ones' latest capers, which usually involved creative or unorthodox use of the toilet bowl, toothpaste, or the family pet. I was no dummy. I recognized that I would make other parents feel uncomfortable if I came off like a developmental Nazi in yoga pants. So, I tried to adopt a laissez faire exterior and always came armed with my own sharable plastic container of carrots and hummus. Besides, I liked to socialize as much as the next girl.

Even with this social camouflage, I am certain that the other parents thought me frenetic. I could only engage in small talk for so long, then I would gravitate to the playground, guiding (read cajoling) Jack to "play." All the while vaguely aware of the fact that I was revealing my desperation that my kid show he could do things that other three- and four-year-olds did effortlessly…as if to prove to the world that he was not "slow" or, God forbid, "special." I was perpetually directing my kid's life, like an overzealous traffic cop, waving cars on at the scene of an accident—*Move along, there is nothing to see here.*

Relax, all of you expert detectors of deficit who are fitted with developmental sonar designed to sound off at the slightest anomaly so you can stealthily move your kid away. We would not want your kid to catch the disease or appear to be defective by the mere fact that they, he or she, are associating with the "different" child: "There went little Johnny's prospects for early decision at Harvard; he was caught playing with the slow kid."

I felt a need to prove that my son could do what other kids could do with ease, that he was worthy, "normal." But when I was honest with myself, perhaps the person I was most trying to convince was me. If I dug deep inside, I had to admit I had my ledger. In it I kept track of each slide, nylon tunnel, and ball pit that Jack conquered. Ziplines were the worst and a prized trophy in my register of 'typical.'

I don't mean those ziplines that career through the trees, 100 feet high in a canopy of green. I am referring to the pint-sized ones that popped up in parks and playgrounds in the early 2000's. These suspend a kid a foot or two off the ground over a forgiving bed of sand or rubber tire pieces. It was on these contraptions that I was probably at my most embarrassing. The upper torso and core strength needed to suspend oneself by the arms even on these mini ziplines is considerable. But for most kids, the laws of physics are in their favor because of relatively short stature and low body weight. There is simply not that much mass to hold up. But for Jack the task was nearly incomprehensible. The muscle contractions needed to perform the feat were beyond him. His arms did not curl into taut 45-degree angles and he couldn't draw his knees up toward his chest to glide above the sand. Instead, when I positioned his hands on the handles straddling each side of the metal cording that was the zipline, his arms hung lax and his legs splayed out limply. Even so, I would coax him over to the contraption that, for him, was little more than an instrument of torture. I would tell him he would love it, will him with the sheer strength of my enthusiasm to try hanging on. He would resist, but it was not long before he realized he was no match for his wild-eyed mother's resolve. Jack then resigned himself to slide a few feet with me firmly holding his torso, supporting him from beneath lest he drop.

I knew this feat was extremely uncomfortable for him. I knew he would prefer his safe spot on his bottom snug in the sun-kissed sand, sifting grains or sorting rocks. But I could not bear for him to miss out. I did not want him sitting on the sidelines, losing an opportunity. But being left out devastated me, not him. From Jack's perspective he was just fine surveying the world from his sandy perch: ziplines and suspension bridges, no thank you very much.

At these moments, I worried for two reasons. First, I was concerned that opting out would leave an indelible mark which, over time would result in Jack coming to believe that he was not capable. Second, I knew that young children developed their brains by physically exploring their world. For children, "not doing" has not only physical consequences, but cognitive consequences as well. This was something I was not willing to risk, and my fears far outweighed the discomfort of making him try. The concern that shrouded everything was that Jack would come to see himself as disabled. This complicated assortment of thoughts flashed through my consciousness as I surveyed each unsuspecting piece of playground equipment.

At the park, every slide, monkey bar, or tree became an opportunity not just to exercise those slack muscles, but also served as a test. As I look back now, a part of me knew that it was more than a little foolhardy to put my son in situations well beyond his reach, where I knew he would likely fail, or where at best he would only approximate the movement with a whole lot of support.

Right or wrong, I shuttered feelings of putting my child in uncomfortable, unsafe, or embarrassing situations to the recesses of my mind, where I could make them virtually disappear. I convinced myself that Jack needed these experiences, that to miss any opportunity was to succumb to the diagnosis. I also felt that he was falling farther behind each time other kids were mastering feats that he was not. Seeing other three- and four-year-olds on their thirtieth repetition scaling up the slick surface of the slide while mine sat on the ground was a painful reminder of the opportunity clock ticking, and of developmental gaps widening. For me, it was essential to put Jack through this gauntlet of play structures, rock formations, ball pits, bounce houses, and staircases. Not doing so, I had decided, would be more comfortable in the short run, but deadly in the long run.

I was aware that other mothers thought it was curious how I shepherded Jack through every playground like it was part of a preschool cross-fit regime. I knew they wondered why I chose to trudge through these obstacle courses instead of observing from a safe distance, cool drink in hand…"Is she a helicopter mom, too involved, controlling, neurotic…or perhaps she herself is in training for some extreme sports competition?" If they only knew how

I wished I could be like them, vacillating between a delightfully shallow conversation about where to get cute knock-off handbags, while offering only a cursory glance in the direction of where the kids were playing. Unlike most moms, my greatest fear was not that Jack would get hurt on the playground. In fact, that would be a point of pride, it would mean that he was moving, pushing his limits, joining in. No, my greatest fear was that he would remain contentedly on his bottom in the sand.

Chapter 10

SAFER, BETTER OFF, MORE COMFORTABLE

That which makes us most human is our ability to enjoy our successes by having the ability to "own" our own failures.

—Chris Lyons, Disability Rights Attorney

TOO OFTEN, I would return from a run to the grocery store or an afternoon out with friends and see Jack propped up on pillows in front of the television like a juvenile King Tut, while his sisters played together, engrossed in some toy or another. Anyone who has ever been a babysitter may simply chalk up the scene I have described to making the job easier, minimizing activity, mess, and chaos. But I disagree, because if that were the case, all three kids would have been set up in front of the TV. When I would ask, "Why isn't Jack playing with the girls?" I would invariably hear some version of "I just thought it would be easier for Jack." "I figured it would be safer." "Jack looked tired, so I popped in a movie for him."

I found that whether it was a teenage babysitter or an adult in charge, the response was the same. The person was not being lazy or selfish, their response came from a place of compassion. I have no beef with compassionate caregivers, but I was concerned about these compassionate souls' impact on my son. I wondered what messages Jack was receiving and what neural pathways were being etched by these repeated attempts to "help" and make things "easier" for him. Was he learning that if he came off as tired, fatigued or worn out, he would get what he wanted…cushioned entertainment with no need for exertion?

Over the years, this matter of the dangers of unsolicited help has gotten me thinking about an exchange on a bus, a ski bus, that is. My girls were young teens when we boarded the bus joining the masses of powder worshippers, our puffy neon gear creating a stark contrast against the white all around us. They slid into two of the few open seats on this huge natural gas-powered people-, ski-, and snow-board-mover. Seeing what they viewed as an elderly couple standing while balancing their skis, helmets, and goggles, my girls got up and offered them their seats. (Their mama had raised them right!) Even as the pride swelled in my heart, I could predict what was going to happen next, like watching a collision in slow motion. The couple gave each other a knowing glance and, without attempting even an obligatory smile, they dismissed the girls with a curt "No thanks." This couple was part of that curious species indigenous to Colorado. If you have spent any time in the Centennial State, you know them: ruddy, athletic types wearing their wrinkles like a badge of honor for a life of 14ers scaled and trail races run. They saw themselves as extreme sportspeople, not the frail, 60-somethings in need of accommodation that my daughters assumed them to be, fooled by their silvery hair. I get it; in my 50's now, if I were in their ski boots, I would have felt the same way.

And yes, I was proud of my girls for stepping out of their all-encompassing teenage force field of self-absorption to register the existence of beings of another generation. But, because of my line of work, I was interested in this exchange for another reason. I juxtaposed the situation of the indignant ski couple with what happens every day with kids (and adults) with disabilities. The difference was that here the skiers could say, "No, thank you very much," and turn down the offer of help. What the couple was in effect communicating instead with their clipped "no thanks" was: "Don't you put that on us; we are more than that. Do not assume we are incapable." Specifically, in the case of these sporty seniors, the message was, "We are mature athletes, not an elderly couple in need of help."

We humans are an obliging species. We see someone who we judge to be having a hard time and we want to make it easier for them. This noble human emotion spurs us to open the door for the elderly, to grab the elbow of a person with a visual impairment, or to reach something off the high shelf at Target for someone using a wheelchair.

There is nothing wrong with offering a helping hand. Such gestures are a hallmark of our humanity. They connect us as brethren on this planet, one to another. Polite offers of help are just that, polite offers, as long as we have the option to respond with an equally polite "no thanks," should we choose. The ability to say "No thanks" is something the vast majority of us never give a second thought. However, those two words are not taken for granted within the disability community. In fact, being able to make these kinds of simple choices is a big part of what is called "agency"—that is, the ability to impact your own environment. Helping becomes a self-reinforcing quagmire when a person doesn't have the "agency" or the will to say, "No thanks."

When people don't communicate in standard ways and they can't or don't turn down help, they experience others offering, filling in gaps, finishing sentences, supplying things, making choices, and completing steps for them…assuming they can't hear, can't walk, can't lift. Can't, can't, can't. The cycle is self-reinforcing because, over time, these young children, teens, or adults come to believe that they "can't" or are "unable."

Not acting, because you have come to believe that you are not capable or that your actions will not make a difference, is called *learned helplessness.*

Of course, there is a bright line of distinction between the critical supports that people with special needs require and *what they have been conditioned to think they require.* There are many personal care, academic, and physical tasks that people experiencing disability legitimately need support and accommodations to complete. Each of us, whether experiencing a disability or not, as the song says, "get by with a little help from our friends," and there is absolutely nothing wrong with that.

Learned helplessness refers to a very real phenomenon where a person does not attempt certain things because they have been *taught or conditioned* over time to believe they can't. Some may say, "Wait a minute, there are things that I don't attempt to do, and as a result someone else does them for me—and I don't have learned helplessness."

True. Evidence the dance that happens between couples when one pretends they don't know where the gas pump is inserted and another feigns being completely baffled by laundry to avoid these tasks. Most of us can recognize ourselves in harmless interpersonal farces like the one described. The difference, in these cases, is that there is agency—we are choosing to ignore something in an effort to get someone else to act on our behalf. (And that is a completely different problem for a completely different book.)

No, I was concerned about the truly crippling phenomenon that is prevalent within communities that have been judged as "different," and most immediately I was on the lookout for signs of it in my own son.

Jack wasn't in a wheelchair, he wasn't non-verbal or blind, not even close. But, I had seen the negative effects of well-meaners over-helping, and was hyper-aware of making sure that the insidious effects of learned helplessness were not creeping in and choking off my son's choices and agency.

Although I was hypervigilant, I did not encounter many problems with close friends or family imposing help or limiting choices for Jack. They took their cues from me, they knew Jack's mama and trusted me (at least at some level). They may have wanted to help, ease the burden, or make things more comfortable for Jack, but they followed the program, at least in my presence, even if they thought me a little careless, overly nonchalant, or even irresponsible. They dutifully followed the leader. Those unfortunate few who thought they knew better and tried to help, to make things easier, or "safer" for Jack, pretty quickly encountered a resolute look from me or they were interrupted with a "He has got that." Those close to us soon learned "it may not seem right that the kid who is unsteady on his feet is carrying two gallons of milk, but just humor the wacky lady and go along with what she says." While I am sure that my behavior toward Jack prompted more than a few raised eyebrows, the owners of those perplexed brows took their lead from me. If I let Jack struggle uncomfortably long to push the plastic straw into his juice box, or if I allowed Jack to teeter on unsteady legs across the uneven surfaces, they cringingly allowed it. When I handed him an obviously too-heavy cooler or tote bag full of park paraphernalia and walked away, with Jack groaning, family and friends scratched their heads and assumed, "I guess she knows what she is doing." Frankly, even if they thought I was dead wrong and hurting my kid or putting him in danger, they went with it. In America, it goes without saying, that unless there is obvious abuse, we don't parent each other's kids—at least, or especially, in front of them.

Our situation may have appeared a little curious at times but, I reminded myself, it was nothing compared to what Daniel Kish's mom must have experienced. Imagine how many well-meaning safety hawks she had to dismiss as she allowed her blind son to get back on that bicycle!

The real land mines lay in situations where I was not present, in the great beyond where I, as mom, did not wield absolute power. The world is filled with serial helpers, safety bees, and people who are just plain uncomfortable with children and adults who register in their consciousness as "different." Granted there is a virtuous quality to each of these motivations. The motivation for the serial helper is compassion. The safety bee avoids danger. Even those who approach people who are "different" with skepticism are activating a primitive protective response within themselves. From the perspective of the doer, this is all perfectly rational behavior. From my perspective, it was behavior that was simply unhelpful to my kid, and could even cause damage, especially if he were exposed to it systematically over time.

As sure as the sun rises, the helpers and well-meaners would begin to move in, filling the spaces where I was not involved to mediate expectations…all of them with the ostensibly positive motive of making something easier for my son. These were good people, trusted babysitters, teachers, scout leaders, and other parents who became uncomfortable seeing Jack struggle. They saw him navigating the room, bearings awkward, arms out at half guard; they saw him topple over, they saw him tiring, fatigued by the work of moving his body through space. They saw a knot tying or cooking task that they judged to be too challenging. These "first responders" predictably came to the rescue.

This pattern of underestimating reared its ugly head throughout Jack's childhood. People would make decisions for my kid, not giving him the option to say, "No thanks, I want to try this myself." Teachers served up the "easier" questions, not requiring him to answer if he did not respond immediately. When making Mother's Day gifts, scout leaders cut out pieces for him, to save him from having to manipulate the "dangerous" scissors. PE teachers looked the other way, allowing Jack to sit out or quit early.

In all these cases, others made decisions for Jack, in effect taking away opportunities to try, struggle, learn, and feel the sense of accomplishment that comes with cutting out and attaching the antler on the reindeer yourself…even if they end up a little crooked and look more like cauliflower than six-pointed racks. For me, it all went back to that day at the shore…*wouldn't he be safer and more comfortable and more content at home propped in front of the TV?*

My answer to all of these is, *probably so.* Jack *would* be safer if he was not left unceremoniously dangling from a zipline. Certainly, he would be more comfortable with all his toys within arms' reach.

He would much prefer watching TV lying on his side with a pillow cushioning his head than being forced to lie on his stomach and hold his head up in his hands. If not much was asked of Jack, no one would have to hear him whine when the task became taxing. But I had made up my mind long ago: I did not want easy, safe or comfortable for Jack, because with that would come loss of agency. I feared that he would be helped too much and would begin to believe the negatively seductive lies behind the kind gestures: "I can't do this, I can't do that—but someone else will do it for me." Helping Jack may have looked prettier in the moment and may have made him more content. It certainly would have caused me to embarrass myself less. But if life were a Candyland board game, I knew each space on the path marked "easy route" was a breeding ground for learned helplessness.

I could not risk letting Jack internalize that he was "less than." I concluded that it was not only okay to be less comfortable, less safe, in fact it was quite possibly more desirable and in fact, therapeutic. I saw it as the way out of a lifetime of limitation for my kid. Therefore, I vigorously pursued discomfort for my son.

Do I wish I would have done it more subtly, less embarrassingly? Yes, but I would not change the way I parented to save him discomfort or frustration. (Son, please don't hold it against me when you write your tell-all book.) I felt that the experience underlying every awkward moment was sending him all-important messages of "I can" and "my mom and dad believe I can."

My kid had a syndrome, if I wanted him to escape the limitations that accompanied that diagnosis, I felt I could not afford to play it safe. There is dignity in making all kinds of choices and having all kinds of experiences. Preempting opportunity because of fear of failure or embarrassment can ultimately rob a person of their dignity. I wanted to keep all options open for Jack. Even if it was painful, inconvenient, or embarrassing at the time. I was determined not to have the specter of learned helplessness creep in and put my kid in a deadly holding pattern, waiting for someone else to "do" for him. I feared this was a pattern that had the potential to impact him for a lifetime.

Chapter 11

STEPPING OUT OF THE COMFORT ZONE

Any idiot can face a crisis—it's the day-to-day living that wears you out.

—Anton Chekhov

THAT DAY IN THE IMMACULATELY PANELED geneticist's office, I was blindsided, overwhelmed by the sheer volume of jargon, information, and recommendations. So numb that I barely registered the slim white pages being pressed into my hands. It was only when the twins were safely ensconced in their car seats that I noticed that I was clutching four separate prescription orders, one for occupational therapy, one for speech therapy, one for physical therapy and a fourth, a standing order for tumor ultrasounds. Dr. Genetics talked a lot. Some of his talk I could dismiss, I knew my child better than a guy who was riffing off a brief introduction and a translucent greyscale x-ray of my kid's phalanges, carpals and metacarpals. The talk felt clinical and surreal at the same time, something weighty but vague, like a drama playing out on a TV screen. I could turn it off. But these four slips of paper were real. They were concrete documentation that all was not well and that there was work to be done. So, like all parents of children with delays, we immersed ourselves in the work of researching, identifying and scheduling therapies.

Initially, helpful, in-home technicians came and manipulated Jack's arms, legs, hands, and tongue. They offered him rewards for holding up his head and upper chest while lying on his tummy, grasping a block placed on his right side with his left hand, following a block with his gaze, blowing bubbles, and licking a dab of peanut butter off the roof of his mouth. As he grew, the home visits morphed into little sojourns to offices, gyms, and cheery playrooms awash with floor to ceiling murals of fanciful fairies, exotic jungles, and dark forests.

In these spaces, Jack would lie on his tummy in a nylon swing suspended from the ceiling, attempt to balance on uneven surfaces, reach out one arm and then the next while perched on a large ball, and try to push a cotton ball across a table by blowing through a straw. I watched every move the therapists made and listened intently to their words. I took note of how they were coaxing and cueing Jack to perform these feats that challenged balance, strength, cognitive processes, endurance and body awareness. I wanted to learn their trade secrets. What was magical about these exercises and activities. Would they make my son "typical"?

I had pledged to myself that he would do everything his twin sister did. I wondered how many of each of these individual gyrations it would take to get to "typical." Could success be quantified? How far across a table does one have to blow a cotton ball to speak intelligibly? How long does a child have to swing through the air to make the necessary neural connections to seamlessly move their body through space? How many times does a child have to cross the midline with his hand to improve cognitive processing speed?

Jack was already behind the eight ball. Because of his low muscle tone it was fatiguing to move his limbs against gravity. He tired quickly. His unsteady gait and lack of endurance created practical obstacles that barred him from exploring his surroundings. Ask anyone who has a kid, and they will tell you that kids learn by doing. Jack was missing important experiences that other kids were having in the regular course of playing. If he was sitting or, worse, lying prone while other kids were exploring, he was losing ground just as they were gaining, widening the developmental gap even farther. This was the quandary that I puzzled over as I drove the therapy circuit with Jack and the girls in tow. Was 30 minutes two times a week enough to transform slack muscles? Double that, would 60 minutes a week allow Jack to leapfrog over missed developmental building blocks? What could 90 or 120 minutes a week achieve over time?

As I put the car into park in Developmental Therapy Associate's parking lot and began liberating the kids from their car seats, I mouthed a silent word of thanks for Claudine. She was probably my favorite of all the occupational therapists we had encountered. In her late 20's, with cascading ringlets of dark hair pulled off her face by the brightly colored woven scarfs that were her trademark, Claudine was a force to be reckoned with. I contrasted her style with other therapists who kept the work within Jack's comfort zone. They would push some, sense that Jack was getting uncomfortable and back off. Playing it safe, I called it. If they did not ask too much, Jack remained a smiley little guy and they felt liked; it was a winning proposition.

I appreciate that these practitioners were attempting to maintain a delicate balance. Staying close to what the child can already do even has a name. The practice is what developmental experts call the "zone of proximal development"—keep things close to where the child is already functioning and incremental gains can be made; veer too far in either direction, that is, make things too easy or too hard for the child, and the therapy loses its effectiveness. I get it. But let's just say this: to the mom who just loaded three crying kids, toys, and snacks and drove the whole gang across town, these upbeat, yet tepid, therapy sessions did not feel like a win. I was counting on therapy to help Jack catch up and recover lost ground, not just maintain the little he had as his peers whizzed by.

So yeah, what I liked about Claudine was that she worked Jack hard. She was not afraid of taking him out of his comfort zone. Always positive, she would push through his protests, whining, and stubborn refusals and get him to do one more repetition, go a little farther, try just a little harder. I also liked that she was a straight shooter. At the conclusion of one session when Jack was three, Claudine told me something I would never forget. "Be aware, Jack will plateau where he is." She went on, and the next part piqued my attention, "...unless he is constantly challenged."

"Unless," she had said. In that one little preposition lay the hope I craved, a possible escape route for Jack. Current circumstances were not static. Ground could be gained if we were ever vigilant about increasing Jack's mental and physical endurance, strength, and stamina. Perhaps the scourges of Sotos syndrome were not stamped on this kid in indelible ink. But still the question remained: how much effort was necessary?

I took her words to mean that doing the minimum and

lackadaisically taking opportunities as they came would not do the trick. This would require a monumental effort; the relentless, hang-in-there-day-in-and-day-out, break-a-sweat kind of effort. Still for me her words reverberated with hope, things could improve.

When it is your child, you are constantly thinking, scheming, and dreaming about how to help him or her, how to improve the odds. In my case, I was puzzling about how to raise him with the expectation that he would achieve the same as other kids. I did not possess the MD credentials of Drs. Friedrich, Stuart, or Jacobson, but it was not hard to take Claudine's advice and piece it together with information I collected from other therapists and practitioners. Over time, I cobbled together my own personal theory. It *was* an intuitively plausible but not scientifically proven theory that went something like this:

> It is generally true that muscles strengthen with use. The prob-lem of muscle weakness, then, is a problem of exercise and use. If we could figure out how to strengthen muscles, each of those tiny unnamed muscles, Jack could perform within range of his peers. Following this line of reasoning he could catch up.

Of course, I knew this was not the only complication. There were a whole host of other complications arising from Sotos, including developmental delays, slower cognitive processing speed, behavior problems, even learning disabilities. But as a preschooler, it was the muscle weakness that was keeping Jack from exploring, learning, and competing with his peers. This would be my path forward.

An intriguing theory—I patted myself on the back… but where to start, given that the practical problem was that the syndrome caused pervasive muscle weakness throughout the trunk, arms, legs, hands, and even mouth. All Jack's muscles were slack. That included the miniscule ones in the fatty center of the palm that allow children to grasp a crayon, and even those in the mouth and throat that govern chewing and sucking. It also included the large muscle groups in the arms, legs and torso that help us climb out of a pool, run, balance so that we can lift one foot and balance on the other to kick a soccer ball or aim a bow just before we let an arrow fly.

I was out of my depth here; knowing the location of *quads, lats,* and *glutes* was close to the extent of my anatomical muscle knowledge. What is "lat" short for, anyway? Even if I could point out where they were, I did not know much beyond these shorthand terms lifted directly from the outdated step aerobic workout classes of my 20's.

Armed with this knowledge (or lack thereof), I held fast to my working theory. Jack needed to exercise his muscles as much as humanly possible. I unscientifically tried to calculate— if it took the typical infant 50 repetitions to lift his head while lying on his stomach, how many had it taken Jack? 100, 500, 1000? He was now holding his head up while on his stomach, but even with the added support of cradling his head in his hands, the position was difficult for him and he avoided it like the plague.

Was repetition and strengthening the answer? Not fully trusting myself on the subject, I tried my theory out on another trusted professional, this time a physical therapist.

"All Jack needs to do is exercise each muscle group enough to catch up to his peers, right?" I asked my question in the affirmative, as if I could get the answer I wanted through a mix of careful phraseology and sheer strength of will. Her answer was supportive and matter of fact as she explained that it was not that easy. "You cannot discount the collective impact of all the missed building blocks that have created and continue to create holes in Jack's development."

It was not a ringing endorsement of my armchair theory, but I was not surprised. I had suspected she would give some weight to developmental constraints. We would not adopt our fourth child for two more years, but I would come to know intimately the wages of early deprivation on developing minds, and how even years of course correction cannot totally make up for trauma and lost experiences. However, like a pit bull with a bone, I clung to my theory and pushed forward, stubbornly discounting the parts that did not match with where I wanted to go.

As the theory calcified in my brain, I began thinking more intentionally about therapies overall and each session specifically. What were the goals of each visit? Was the session focused on a foundational skill like trunk strength, which could improve functioning across multiple areas, or did it target a specific isolated skill like clicking the tongue to the roof of the mouth to make the hard C sound? Did the therapist have specialized techniques or custom equipment, like the nylon suspension swing, that made in-office practice more effective than what we could achieve improvising with an old-school metal swing at the park? Even with ongoing therapy, how much additional concentrated practice would be needed at home? How could we simulate therapy at home and in the community as we went about the regular course of "doing life?"

The more I thought about it, the more calculated and miserly I became with our time. If we had to drive 30 minutes or more to another town to access the therapy, what was Jack missing by sitting inert in the car for an hour or more, round trip, and was the benefit of therapy worth the lost time?

But there was more on the line than just calculating time, opportunities, and logistics. As Jack got bigger, I also became concerned about how he viewed the act of going to therapy. Of course, he had seen specialists since we busted him out of the NICU at five and a half pounds. Therapy was his 'normal', so maybe he thought nothing of it. But I also knew that he had two sisters, a twin and a younger who he saw were not marched through a weekly regimen of therapy sessions. I wondered how long it would be before he sensed these differences and what he would make of them, and how they might shape his beliefs about himself and his abilities.

To make good on my theory, I made a point of getting to know the therapists and often stayed and "hung out" during Jack's sessions. I knew that these adults were conveying positive messages. They reinforced the behavior they wanted to see. Their talk and tone of voice showed that they believed in Jack. But I still wondered about their actions. It was subtle, but insidious. If a therapist let Jack off the hook too easy, would he surmise that the adults around him thought he could only handle so much? Then by extension, would he come to believe he could only do so much? Granted, I knew I could not control everything. I'd like to think I did not become obsessive about it (I may have). However, I did not want to discount any negative messages that Jack might get from prolonged or watered-down therapy.

At the same time, I knew it would be naive and not good for my kid in the long run to abandon critical services for fear of creating dependence or altering his beliefs about himself. There was a balance to be had and it made me intentional and even ruthless in scrutinizing each service that was offered. As Jack grew, rather than rejecting therapies I sought to leverage them. I came to view all supports through the lens of their function given the goal of maximum independence for my kid.

Chapter 12

[PRE]SCHOOL
DAZE

Children need a flood of information, a banquet, a feast.

—Eric Jensen, *Teaching with the Brain in Mind.*

WHETHER THEY CONSIDER IT A GIFT or a grind, some parents get to be home full-time with their little ones; others have to manage a complicated childcare dance while working all day, and still others fall somewhere in between, filling in the puzzle with part-time babysitters, willing grandparents, or nannies. Regardless, there is something about the magic age of three that makes most of us seek out a preschool to challenge or socialize our kids or just give ourselves a little well-earned freedom. I was no exception, but since I worked part time, preschool was a welcome break, not a childcare necessity.

I was not in the market for an academic preschool, a selective institution for budding prodigies. I chose a sunny co-op preschool with the lyrically playful name, Kinderkirk, which was run by a neighborhood church. I romanticized it as the perfect place for my kids. I could push the twins (with Rosie, our third, along for the ride) up to school in the triple stroller for a morning of homemade play dough, sand table, circle time and snacks with whimsically delicious sounding names like "ants-on-a-log", "Ritz cracker spiders," and "mini-fruit pizzas." I dreamed of Jack and Livie being ushered into their classroom on the first day, hand-in-hand, tiny vinyl backpacks bouncing on their backs, with me trailing, snapping photos, a little misty. However, my bubble was burst by the early intervention diagnostician whose judgment was that Livie fit into the playful, fun (aka. regular) preschool and Jack did not.

Since his diagnosis, Jack resumed early intervention services through the state of California Regional Center. So far, the services included occupational, physical and speech therapy. When Jack turned three and no longer qualified for services from the Regional Centers, like all parents of kids with delays, we sought help through the public schools. I was aware that the "price of admission" to a host of school district services was having Jack sit for a new round of evaluations. No longer would a medical diagnosis of Sotos syndrome prompt support. Having a medical problem in and of itself does not entitle a child to help from an educational standpoint; in order to get help, he or she has to have a challenge that impacts learning. Jack would have to be categorized and sorted to determine eligibility for services, which would be laid out in an Individualized Educational Plan (IEP) tailored specifically to him.

This meant going through a complete battery of psychological and developmental assessments that would make the block stacking and picture pointing tests that Dr. Jacobson performed in his office look like a cake walk.

As a teacher and evaluator, I was no stranger to evaluation. I had administered these tests with their alphabet soup names: the Kaufman Assessment Battery for Children – II (KABD-II), Differential Ability Scales (DAS-II), the Social Communication, Emotional Regulation and Transactional Support Model (SCERT), and the Woodcock Johnson Early Cognitive and Academic Assessment (ECAD). But now for the first time, I was looking at them from the other side of the desk.

Their names alone can make a parent's head hurt, but what the tests boil down to is a collection of tasks that children do in a certain order while the test administrator observes and rates their performance. They assign a score that corresponds to a particular ability, skill mastery, or functioning level. Just like their medical cousin "the diagnosis," psychological and educational ability tests spit out "a label" that helps to count, capture, categorize, or describe the child we see before us. They allow us to wrap our heads around behavior and can be comforting because they give us tidy language. They reduce ambiguity for frustrated parents; the unknown being almost always more frightening to humans than the known. However, just like the medical diagnosis, an educational label is only as good as the practical information it provides.

No matter what high expectations I held or what strengths Jack possessed, the fact is that much of a preschooler's "tested" potential shows up in his or her motor ability (stacking blocks, balancing on one foot, speaking clearly, holding a crayon with a tripod grip, etc.). None of these were Jack's strong suit at the time. The diagnostician who tested Jack assigned two relatively innocuous labels: "developmentally delayed and other health impaired."

This label was Jack's ticket to services. In terms of learning programs, the best fit the district had was a multiply handicapped, pre-school classroom at the public school a little less than a mile from our house. The special education team recommended five hours in the class Monday through Friday, which sounded like a lot to me. As an ex-special education teacher, I knew a thing or two, certainly more than the average parent. However, in spite of, or maybe because of that experience, I didn't want to dismiss these practitioner-experts too quickly. I was determined not to be the parent in denial. Maybe there *was* something I was missing. Perhaps I could not see through the positive smoke screen of the high expectations jihad I had been waging.

I reminded myself of my own mantra that a label or diagnosis is only as useful as the independence your child gains from taking advantage of the services it affords. From that vantage point, the multiply handicapped preschool offered some obvious positives. It ran every weekday from 8:45-12:30 and afforded a lot of time for catching up. In addition, all of Jack's services, occupational therapy, physical therapy, and speech therapy would be provided during the preschool day. This eliminated the need to shuttle from one therapy appointment to the next and created a veritable one-stop shop for the developmentally delayed, if you will. On top of it all, this class was free—something Kinderkirk wasn't. While I still worried about the messages it could send Jack about his capabilities, I had to set my fears aside. I reasoned that if there was some synergy to this integrated education and therapy approach that could accelerate progress, I wanted Jack to benefit from it.

I agreed to give the special class a try, but my "yes" was qualified. Jack would only attend Mondays, Wednesdays and Fridays. Holding fast to my conviction that Jack would do everything his sister did,

I enrolled Jack in the multiply handicapped preschool *and* in the regular neighborhood co-op preschool with Livie. Conveniently, since the neighborhood preschool offered a Tuesday and Thursday morning class, Jack could squeeze in "regular" preschool two days a week while still attending the public school, multiply handicapped preschool class on alternate days. Kinderkirk was all about playing and socializing, while the special education class was designed to address the well-articulated goals and objectives written in Jack's IEP. Being the maximizer that I am, I satisfied myself with the rationalization that this arrangement was perfect. Jack would not be missing any opportunities his sister was getting, he would just be getting more—a double dose, if you will—of socialization, movement, and learning!

At the same time, I was just fine with two mornings a week of school for Jack's twin sister. This plan fit nicely with my personal and professional philosophy around preschool. I had always believed that preschool should be all about finger painting, story time, and creating masterpieces with too much glue and uncooked macaroni, with a little bit of counting and letter identification thrown in, as long as it did not get in the way of the fun stuff. My own work in schools had shown me that barring a specific learning disability, kids read when they are ready, so I did not feel the need to rush the process with an uber-academic preschool.

It only took a couple of weeks for me to confirm that Kinderkirk was my kind of school. It was the kind with more "pre" and less "school" and it was a co-op to boot. The "co" part in co-op meant that parents participate, help with centers, story time or snack time, in exchange for reduced tuition payments. It is great for anyone who wants their kids in preschool, but still wants to see what they are up to once in a while, sort of a harmless kiddie surveillance program.

The school was so close to home that even as a working parent, it was easy for me to show up for my co-op days two mornings a month.

Being the laid-back place that it was, Kinderkirk teachers welcomed both Jack and Livie those Tuesdays and Thursdays. I had only taught special education preschool one short summer during college, but I had a pretty good bead on the range of behavior that was generally expected of typical three-year-olds. Each time I arrived for my co-op shift laden with teddy bear shaped graham crackers and sliced-up apples, I was able to spy on my kids benignly and legally. Jack was slower to get to the centers, still walked with his hands out in front of him, avoided tasks that required movement or balance in favor of activities where he could sit or lean, and more often than not, played by himself. On the other hand, he was a champ at story time and never caused any trouble. Most of all, this plan met my all-important condition: Jack was in school with his sister.

We enjoyed this rhythm for three months. The kids went to school and I did my obligatory co-op time, hanging out at the sand and water table, helping with activities, hanging up artwork, and serving snacks. I say obligatory, but no one was twisting my arm. Yes, these hours were a basic requirement of a cooperative preschool- -parents and teachers "cooperating" to care for and develop little people. But for me, it was a joy watching these kids who moved so easily; who so effortlessly held their paint brushes with a perfect tripod grasp; who ran, jumped, and otherwise cavorted on the playground with coordination and confidence. It made me smile to see them mixing with my kid for whom those skills were still a mystery. When Jack was at Kinderkirk, he was truly one of them, a regular kid; halting, slower, and sometimes trailing behind, but still one of them.

Even so I would torment myself, 'Come on, this is preschool, kids are sitting in sandboxes, splashing in water, and painting with fingers. In preschool there is a wide berth given to "difference." But what about in 1st grade, 5th grade, and high school, where requirements were exacting, the margin between a passing grade and a failing one was razor thin, and the tolerance for difference was slim? These were my thoughts in darker moments, but for now, my kid was folded into the loving embrace of Kinderkirk and all was right with the world.

At the same time, I was dying to see what the school day was like in the multiply handicapped pre-school classroom, but there was no parent involvement option that I could see. The classroom was generously staffed with a teacher and an aide for a small number of students. There was no co-op structure and parent volunteers were not necessary or encouraged, as far as I could tell. On Mondays, Wednesdays, and Fridays, I loaded three kids in their car seats, stepped out to drop Jack off at the classroom door, put the car into gear and headed home or to wherever the day was taking us. Then I returned with the girls at 12:45 for pick up. I had seen some of the other parents dropping off their kids. As far as I could tell, none of them seemed to be chomping at the bit to volunteer. The goings-on in the classroom were a mystery. I wanted a window into this black box. I comforted myself that I was not the helicopter type. I did not need to be there all the time, I just wanted to know what my kid was doing after Livie, Rosie, and I waved good-bye.

As it turned out I was about to find out. I got a call about three months into the program. Jack was displaying some behavior at the special education preschool. The teacher just said "behavior," not bad behavior, but I knew that is what she meant. I was a little confused.

Jack could put up a stink if he was required to leave a toy or activity that was comfortable for him, but other than that, he was a pretty easy-going little dude. So, I asked. The teacher replied, "Jack is leaving activities and crawling under the tables. He is going over to the teacher's desk and touching things that he should not be touching." But cheerily, as if to negate all the juvenile crimes she had just leveled against my kid, the teacher added, "But he returns to the group pretty easily when redirected, there is nothing to get too worried about."

I like to think I am not the anxious type; however, when you tell a mama that her kid is screwing up but not to "worry" about it, you have just kicked the maternal worry apparatus into high gear. Also, the teacher's account of Jack's behavior was far afield enough from his typical *modus operandi* that I was curious and needed to see for myself what was going on. After all, I reasoned, he was spending most of his "learning" time in the multiply handicapped preschool class—three times as much as he was spending in Kinderkirk with Livie. This school was an investment. He was logging over 15 hours a week there, a lot for a kid who needed volumes of practice in deficit areas and did not have a lot of time to waste.

I wanted to get into that classroom but without appearing like I was checking up on the teacher. I had not shared much of my background, but the school district staff knew that I was an educator, and as a teacher, I was well aware of the uncomfortable vibe that ensues when there is even the slightest appearance of a parent pulling rank on a child's teacher. Trying not to cross this unspoken line, I made all manner of reasonable ploys to get invited. I offered to read to kids, to wash toys, to make copies, but nothing worked. Finally, after making other arrangements for the girls, one day at drop-off I indicated that I had to stay for the morning, feigning that I was without a car.

I announced that I was going to be around until dismissal anyway, so I might as well lend a hand, and then planted myself on the bench pushed against the stucco wall just outside the classroom door. The prospect of having me loitering outside the classroom all morning was just too weird. The teacher, while not exuberant, took me up on my offer to help. I was in.

The teacher did not assign me specific tasks like at the co-op preschool, but I busied myself with the honest, but humble work of sanitizing toys that were spilling out of brightly colored bins. When I could sanitize no more, I spied a pile of construction paper bumble bees and a stapler piled on top of a file cabinet. I noticed that a few of the bees were "buzzing" on the bulletin board. Eureka! I seized on the incomplete task and settled in stapling bumble bees onto a bulletin board masquerading as a flower bed. I felt useful. Impaling insects on a corkboard would be one less thing waiting for this teacher at the end of a hard day, and it allowed me to observe without sitting there with a clipboard in hand like an efficiency expert or, worse yet, an overzealous mom on a mission.

As I continued to fumble with the bumble bees, I followed the rhythm of the classroom. I counted bodies: eight students, the teacher, and an assistant. It was obvious from the interactions I witnessed that the teacher was kind, and the children were loved and treated with respect. If that was all I was looking for, I could have walked out satisfied, chiding myself for worrying in the first place. But it wasn't. I wanted to see what was expected of the students and hear the messages they were getting from the adults around them.

The teacher signaled for the children to gather for story time. I had always looked forward to story time when I volunteered at Kinderkirk, in part because afterward the kids would create something related to the book that was read. At Kinderkirk, the teachers read big books with illustrations as students sat in a circle on shag carpet squares that ringed the teacher's chair. They read whole books, with colorful language tumbling out of the teacher's mouth as kids listened, some fidgeting, some enthralled.

Now it was story time in this classroom and here again kids were gathering. In the multiply handicapped preschool classroom, the teacher sat on a rocker with five three- and four-year-olds flanking her on shag shapes scattered on the floor. Two students had their wheelchairs pulled up so they were tightly aligned with the circle, and one student sat in the lap of an older woman who appeared to be her dedicated assistant. (It turned out she was a third adult in the classroom, no wonder they weren't jumping at my offers of help.)

I have always been a sucker for a good story, so I gave the bumble bees a reprieve. As the teacher opened the first page and held the book high for all to see, I moved into the circle, sitting cross-legged behind a couple of students. I listened. The teacher picked out two to three words from a half page of text and offered them up to the children.

"Farmer sows seeds," she said, pointing to the picture. Story time at both schools featured big books and carpet squares, but as she continued, I began to see that this was where the similarities ended. She may have these kids fooled, but I was a reader; she had nothing on me. "Farmer sows seeds" came out of her mouth, but even from ten feet away I could see that the text went something like this, 'Old Farmer Brown went out to his field with his precious seeds clutched in his hand. Stiff and old as he was, he bent over and made a little hole in the dirt with his finger, then he carefully dropped in a single seed, He hobbled two steps down the row and made another hole with his finger and dropped the next seed in. His back went "creak" as he tried to straighten up. He lifted his hand to shelter his eyes and looked up. "It looks like rain, tsk, tsk, tsk," Farmer Brown thought, "It was an angry sky."

The teacher made a sweeping panoramic motion with the book and then turned the page. Next, we heard more words… "the seeds grew." These were offered in place of the sentences on page two. Wait a minute, now the book lover in me was getting frustrated. Farmer Brown and his precious seeds had more going on than this. Where's the beef? However, there was no relief. The teacher uttered another phrase and pointed to the picture as the book was splayed wide open and flashed to the entire group. One time, I think she even skipped a page, but no students took notice, so sparse was the storyline. This went on for nine or ten more pages, and then with a glance at the clock, the book abruptly ended even though there looked to be about five or so pages left unread. Students were then assembled for a bathroom break without any of us ever finding out what happened to Farmer Brown, his seeds, or what I assumed to be his nasty case of lumbago. I felt robbed. We never learned what it meant to "sow," what it felt like to "clutch" with your hand, what the seeds grew into, or why Farmer Brown cared about what he saw in the sky. If this truncated story "telling" took the place of story "reading" each day, I began to surmise why Jack was losing interest and crawling under tables. This was only my first day of story time and I wanted to crawl under something!

As the morning continued, I could not help but be drawn to other contrasts between the co-op preschool down the street and the special education class I was witnessing. The next thing I noticed was the sparing use of language. Communication was short, clipped, and used the minimum number of words necessary to get the message across. When the teacher wanted something, she often paired the word describing the desired object with the word "get" and pointed directly to the object: "get ball," "get book," "get doll," "get car." She did not say, "Please bring me the yellow monster truck," just "get car," even though you did not have to be a gearhead to see that what she was pointing at was clearly a truck. These stingy sentences have been called "telegraphic speech" in the special education vernacular. I knew this to be technique for uncomplicating language to get students with all kinds of cognitive processing delays to "hear" important words.

Further, I noticed that kids in this class waited…a lot. They waited as much as they learned and played. Students waited for the teacher to get activities ready, waited while individual students were taken to the toilet. As opposed to the routine in the church preschool classroom where kids independently joined centers set up throughout the room, these students waited to be summoned to specific activities and then waited some more while pre-fabbed materials were doled out student by student. The classroom was not set up for children to take the initiative; it was set up for children to be "served-up" a predetermined set of activities and experiences. These were organized, highly qualified special education teachers and staff. I was not experiencing a lack of structure, in fact, the environment was highly structured. It was just not structured for kids to independently create, play, or perform. Kids in this class were not expected to initiate; they were expected to wait and comply.

This day a picture began to emerge. It took a few more days of volunteering for me to realize that this Cliff Notes version of story "telling" regularly took the place of story "reading" each day. My kid was crawling under tables because he was not stimulated by "farmer sows seeds." He was wandering over and turning on the computer because he was curious. In my mind, time was a precious commodity for Jack, and I was convinced that this special education preschool class was not the right place for him.

My decision that this was not the classroom for my kid is in no way a rebuke of special education writ large. None of the exchanges I observed represented "bad practice" or "inappropriate teaching." There are plenty of children who have benefitted from instructions provided only with "necessary words," or children who behaved best when story sessions were abbreviated, or who were more successful when materials were prepped for them. I might even advocate these practices with specific students, if used with the goal of successively increasing reading time, complexity of language, and independence over time. There was no doubt that the teachers were professional, loving, and kind. There are scores of effective special needs preschool classrooms out there where individual children are getting just what they need. However, in my opinion, partially read pages, conversations devoid of articles, adjectives, and adverbs, and being helped to complete activities was precisely what my kid did not need.

I have always contended that children with delays need more, not less. Three-year-old Jack didn't need isolated words, but an abundance of sentences. He needed to listen to and digest whole stories, not the teacher's short-cut version. He needed to be challenged, to be given problems where some information or supplies were purposefully missing so that he had to initiate and create. He needed to be expected to persevere through and complete tasks and not have his learning preempted because of the schedule or convenience. Above all, he needed to explore, move, and learn. Jack did not need practice waiting, he was already great at that, as it did not challenge his slack muscles. Granted, he was still receiving various therapies over the course of each week in 20- to 30-minute segments, but that was not enough. What was Jack missing during the roughly 15 hours and 45 minutes a week that he was in this class while other children were out there learning, moving, and problem solving?

While I was sure that this was not the right classroom for Jack, I was not indignant about it. I was and still am monumentally grateful for the kindness and acceptance extended to my son. The teacher and assistants genuinely liked Jack, and although it is hard to say "no" to help graciously given, after nearly a semester, I got the school district on the phone. I explained to the early childhood special education director that I wanted to remove my son from the preschool class and a meeting was set.

When the appointed day came, we all sat with our knees pulled up under us at the miniature kidney shaped table; the special education teacher, one of the therapists, the early childhood special education coordinator, and me. They were all skilled, intuitive women. I could relate. I was one of them in another life, sitting behind a primary-colored kids' table across from a strung out, confused or particularly militant parent. Behind their patient expressions, I thought I detected a patronizing tone, a version of "this poor woman is in denial, she doesn't know what her child needs." But I did not want to play the part of the entitled, demanding parent; I wanted to be a reasonable adult who spoke rationally and prevailed on behalf of her child, while allowing everyone in the room to save face.

"I want to take Jack out of the class," I said. To their credit, they listened respectfully. There was some inferred awkwardness as I attempted to sidestep judging their teaching methods or their professional assessment of Jack. But I had to put up with it, because I knew

I wanted my kid out and they were the people who were going to make it happen. Very respectfully, but without ever fully agreeing with me, they finally gave me, and Jack, our walking papers.

I felt the breadth of our disconnect when the district early childhood special education coordinator stopped me at the door as I was making my exit. I could tell she truly felt she was doing me a favor when she gently informed me that she would write the exit paperwork conditionally, so that I could re-enroll Jack easily and without further evaluation if I realized I had made a bad mistake. "Bad mistake" were the words she used. *Thanks, I guess*, I thought, *but Jack and I will take our chances out on the road.* As I saw it, just having to make his way through an unpredictable world for those five hours a day, three days week would provide Jack with at least as many challenges, interactions, and opportunities as he was getting in the multiply handicapped preschool class.

Maintaining high expectations for my son involved choices and intentionality; if Jack was going to catch up it would happen on purpose, not by accident. Even if they were not directly damaging to him, environments that lacked challenge were at minimum a waste of time, and extra time was a luxury Jack did not have. It was true that because we quit the special education preschool class, we had to increase time spent driving to various therapies. But those alternative days were also filled with play dates, park dates, and excursions to ball pits and bounce houses where I had more control over the challenges and messages my child was getting from the world around him.

Difficult decisions like these were eclipsed by days of joy and laughter. Jack continued to play and learn at the co-op preschool with Livie on Tuesdays and Thursdays throughout that year. The next fall, he and Livie welcomed Rosie to the Kinderkirk family and all three got to make shaving cream finger paintings, splash around the water table, paste pastel tissue paper on butterfly cut-outs, push Thomas the Tank Engine around a wooden track, sit upon shag carpet squares and listen to stories, and randomly stick colorful letters to a magnetic board. It was a great gig for three- and four-year-olds and it was even a better gig for their mom, who loved every minute of it.

By May, the preschool calendar was spent, and I was searching for summer fun that would allow me to recoup a few precious hours of peace in a day otherwise dominated by the machinations of three preschoolers. For this, I relied on that final refuge of the preschool parent, vacation bible school (VBS). These church camps were a welcome refuge, places where a stressed-out mom could drop off not one, but three preschoolers and be sure that they would be fed, played with, and loved—no strings attached! I had run the VBS circuit the year before with Jack and Livie, jockeying weeks across churches to score almost a month of me-time as my kids listened to Bible stories, learned Bible songs, and made Bible crafts. (I am confident that a merciful God has long forgiven me for gaming the sacred VBS system.)

This summer I had enrolled Jack, Livie, and Rosie in *Roar!* Bible Camp at our local Catholic Church. This week-long program was a favorite of discerning moms because it boasted three hours a day of God-given peace and sanity, as opposed to the 2 ½ hours offered by other church camps. I dropped the kids off for their third day of camp, offering a silent prayer of thanks to the patron saint of VBS and was shortly thereafter meandering through nearby boutiques, as one does when they know their freedom is precious, but short-lived. There was no point in driving home only to turn around again for pick up. I was absentmindedly enjoying the guilty pleasure of window shopping when I heard the shrill caterwaul of fire engines. I turned from the windows to see not one but two hook and ladders screaming down the street. Not being overly paranoid I briefly registered that the engines were headed up the main thoroughfare in the same direction as the Church. I mused that if they were headed to the Church, chances were that one of my kids was responsible.

With only fifteen preschoolers enrolled in *Roar!*, it did not take a math genius to figure out that my three represented a full fifth of the likely suspects. I quickly dismissed the thought as coincidence and returned my attention to shopping. After all, I only had a sweet 40 minutes left before this Cinderella turned back into a haggard, 30-something mom of three. After savoring every bit of my non-kid time, I arrived at the church a couple of minutes late refreshed and ready to resume my maternal duties. However, I found both entrances were blocked by the two engines that had passed by earlier. Seeing no sign of smoke or fire, I immediately breathed a sigh of relief. Probably some smart-aleck middle school kid pulled the alarm. Sure enough, when I reached the grassy spot near the playground where the teachers and the kids were seated cross legged while the firemen made their obligatory inspection, I learned that this was not the work of a smart-aleck middle schooler, it was *my kid* who had done the deed. Thankfully, the church volunteers had a jovial attitude toward the disruption Jack created; these were the lazy days of summer and no critical learning had been interrupted. The teachers and kids filed back into the classrooms to get their backpacks and water bottles, no harm, no foul.

The amiable summer program director graciously explained that Jack had tripped the alarm as their tiny group of preschoolers was being paraded single file through an outside hallway. I feigned an appropriate mix of surprise and disapproval as she informed me, but silently I knew what had happened. The false alarm was the result of Jack's tendency to run a hand along the wall to stabilize himself. Because he was so tall the hand that hugged the wall likely hit the fire alarm. He may have grasped it to steady himself, and like any preschooler he did so not knowing that pulling it would signal an alarm causing all manner of havoc. They didn't routinely teach 4-year-olds about fire alarms because they were not within preschoolers' reach. But this wasn't true of Jack, who at age 4 was now as tall as an 8-year-old.

Chapter 13

DON'T BELIEVE EVERY[ANY]THING YOU READ

The optimist proclaims that we live in the best of all possible worlds; and the pessimist fears this is true.

—James Branch Cabell

YOU WANT YOUR POWER RANGER, *you'll have to get it*. Still armed with my theory, I remained obsessed with providing Jack with opportunities. Every minute in his chair, on the couch, or in front of the TV became the enemy. I made a game out of putting the things that he wanted out of reach, so he had to work to get them.

Having a theory did not insulate me from doubts and fears, those parasites of the mind, which alternately whispered and shouted, "You can't," "You're wrong," "It is no use," or just plain "Give up." The Internet is a sure food source for incubating doubt. As much as

I knew I should stay away, I was equally curious about what various authoritative websites had to say about Sotos syndrome and its prognostications for my child. Even as I craved information, I resisted for fear of facing soul-crushing truths that I would not be able to erase from my conscious mind. I played a schizophrenic game of "I am looking, I am not looking." But too often I gave in to curiosity, scanning websites for pearls of wisdom. What should I expect? How did other children fare? I mined the webisphere for descriptions that did not square with our experience, proving that Jack was unique and surely not in the same category as the forlorn-looking children pictured on screen. There it was again:

Sotos syndrome is characterized by a distinctive facial appearance (broad and prominent forehead, sparse frontotemporal hair, down slanting palpebral fissures, malar flushing, long and narrow face, long chin); learning disability (early developmental delay, mild to moderate intellectual impairment); and overgrowth (height and/or head circumference ≥2 SD above the mean). These three clinical features are considered the cardinal features of Sotos syndrome. Other features include communication and behavioral problems, hypotonia, advanced bone age, cardiac anomalies, cranial MRI/CT abnormalities, joint hyperlaxity/*pes planus*, maternal preeclampsia, neonatal jaundice, renal anomalies, scoliosis, tumors, and seizures.

This litany of clinical characteristics did nothing practical to help my child; but I knew each reminder could cause me to believe or expect things from him. Although I actively resisted the natural impulse of looking to these descriptions to confirm what I was seeing, I found this type of knowledge, the kind originating from an authoritative source to have an insidious, seductive, and reductionist pull to it. The times that Jack came home from preschool clutching pictures that he created that were far simpler and less detailed than those made by either of his sisters—was this iron-clad proof of decreased intellect? When he gave up on a puzzle, was this the obvious sign

of the learning disability that had been predicted all along? I had to resist this tendency to judge, or each activity or game intended to be fun would be reduced to some kind of a high stakes, Sotos syndrome acid test.

One research article that I read on the official Sotos syndrome website provided data about technology use by effected children. The conclusion of the small study was that children diagnosed with Sotos have "fixation" with television that led to behavior problems. Remember that this was 2003 and the Internet was relatively young. Today I am sure this study would have been extended to all the hand-held miniature versions of TV screens that sustain life today—the IPad, tablet, and smart phone. Today, the culprit would surely have been labeled "screen time." In any case, the conclusion of this study did not ring true to me.

You did not have to be a super sleuth or eminent scientist to gather ample evidence that Jack liked screen time, just like all kids. Sure, Jack would resist, cry, or whine when we turned off the television, when we removed him from the desktop computer, or when I closed my laptop. But it did not add up, there was nothing inherent in Sotos that would cause a "screen" obsession. I decided that it was not that children with Sotos had a fixation with TV, but rather that the parents studied had a problem saying NO to their children with regard to screens.

While I had smugly proclaimed the premise of the article flawed, there was a nagging logic to it. All-over muscle weakness, lack of coordination and sensory awareness make daily activities and active childhood play fatiguing and fraught with peril. So yes, Jack was definitely on-course for a "fixation" with the television as predicted. Anyone who has binge-watched Netflix knows the lure of "chilling" with a good story that requires nothing more of the viewer than passive attention. We all have pestered our kids to get out and play and turn off the tube, the IPad, or computer screen. This was true for my other kids too, but neurotypical children have more options, and play is not fatiguing, it is fun. There are not as many hazards in the environment. For Livie and Rosie and the other neighborhood kids, exploration was adventurous, not arduous. They did not have to deal with the hindrance of moving slack muscles against gravity, unsteady balance, and the ever-present sense of failure that comes with always falling behind other kids.

For Jack and many children with special needs screens, food, or other comforts serve as security blankets. They become a substitute for challenge and exploration. Every parent has used the TV or iPad as a babysitter, but for Jack, I feared it could become a surrogate for living life.

Because pervasive low tone was a main characteristic of Sotos, I knew that inactivity was deadly. It was safer and more comfortable for Jack to lie on his back in front of his favorite cartoons or even adult programs like Oprah where he could relax, unchallenged. No doubt, the same is true for all of us, it is more comfortable to put our feet up and settle in for a few episodes of Game of Thrones or Downton Abbey than it is to trudge off to cross-fit, run a mile, or walk the dog. When we choose to challenge ourselves with one of these activities, at least part of what goes through our minds is, how doing so will make us healthier, happier, stronger, or fitter.

Focusing on potential benefits makes us feel good in the short term. The act of "doing" releases endorphins which make us truly feel better. We get into active routines which have long-term benefits that motivate us to "go" and "do" even when we do not want to.

That's the grown-up psyche, but what of a child for whom movement is taxing or defeating? He knows nothing of long-term benefits, endorphins, or the virtues of a "no pain, no gain" attitude. There is no problem with a little TV for typically developing kids. But every moment in front of a screen was robbing Jack of precious muscle development that he needed. I surmised that if he needed 50 or 100 times as many repetitions as the typical child to master a movement, then every inert moment in front of the TV while his twin sister and playmates were out exploring was digging out a deeper hole from which Jack would have to climb. Screens, wherever they cropped up, became another enemy.

We cancelled cable and never reordered it until Jack was out of the house. When possible, we avoided places we knew were dominated by screens, like certain restaurants and even some neighbors' houses. I remember incurring grandma's rebuff, "You kids had TV when you were growing up and it didn't hurt you." *Yes Ma*, I thought, *but for this kid a relationship with the TV has totally different stakes.*

Our house was not a loveless place devoid of the comforts of TV, but when we allowed it, it was offered to the whole crew after a full day of activity. For Jack I tried to use screens in ways that promoted strength and balance. Not nearly as fun as reclining on his side, head facing the screen, I flipped Jack on his tummy, so that if he wanted to physically see the picture, he had to lift his head and trunk and balance his head in his hands. Legions of kids naturally fall into this posture and watch TV effortlessly for the length of an entire show. But for Jack, it was a feat of core strength that amounted to benign torture. I would lie next to him modeling how it was done. We would bribe him to stay on his stomach a couple of minutes at a time, always seeking to increase his endurance. What was easy for us was extremely taxing for Jack, but still this sweet boy hung in there. Before long, his head would get too heavy and his arms, shoulders, and torso tired…soon he would give out under his own weight and turn onto his side.

Even as I hated taking the fun out of watching TV for my child, I had the long view in mind. These precious core strengthening opportunities which promised such a powerful reward could not be squandered.

So, we continued, a cable-less family, adhering to our TV moratorium. Over time, it became easier to enforce as there came to be virtually nothing on network television that would catch a child's attention. Movies remained a treat reserved for evenings only. At the end of the day, we would put on a Disney movie to give everyone a well-deserved break. But ever the task master, if I came into the room, it wasn't long before I was coaxing Jack on to his tummy for a few more precious moments of strengthening.

Chapter 14

SLIDING DOWN A BANISTER AND OTHER CHANCES TO BE TAKEN

My mom raised me as if there were no limitations on where I could go or what I could do. When I look back, I realize she raised me like a white kid—not white culturally, but in the sense of believing that the world was my oyster.

—Trevor Noah, *Born a Crime*

MY MOTHER-IN-LAW ONCE TOLD ME, being a parent makes you a hero, in spite of yourself. My correlate is: being a parent of a child with special needs takes you to places you never thought you would go.

I was an enthusiastic student; I made it my business to study the moves that each physical, occupational, and speech therapist made as they moved in and out of our lives. The more I learned, the more I was sure that Jack was being confined by the arbitrary limits of time and opportunity. The way I figured it; the math just did not work out. Jack was only with the physical therapist 35 minutes weekly, and with the Speech and Occupational therapists for 40 minutes each weekly. How could such meager practice overcome gaping holes in Jack's strength, processing, and development? What difference could an hour and change per week possibly make?

This was akin to the person seeking to lose weight by only counting points assigned to the foods he ate during his hour-long Weight Watchers group meetings. If Jack relied solely on programmed opportunities offered by the therapist, I feared he would always remain behind. Surely the time between scheduled appointments was at least as important as the time with the therapists. I was reminded of the fact that time spent sitting strapped in a booster seat driving to and from appointments was longer than "therapeutic time." Of course, all of these skilled therapists encouraged practice between sessions and, consistent with their recommendations, we were working at home. Still, for me the tick of the opportunity clock was deafening. I was dogged by a nagging sense that I had to do more to find and leverage naturally occurring opportunities to build strength, balance, endurance, and confidence in my young son.

It occurred to me that curiosity had played a prominent role in past success. Livie had long been toddling around. I should have been jubilant, but instead, I remember feeling downcast. Jack was not even close to walking. I reflected on my single-minded stubbornness the day I dragged Jack to the beach, proclaiming—possibly too loudly—the statement that would become my anthem: "Jack will do everything his sister does!" I believed he would. Yet while his sister was walking, he was not even able to pull his knees under him to get into a crawling position. It was in this position on the kitchen floor that Jack encountered the dishwasher door I had left down. With three little ones, I was not the most conscientious of housekeepers. (Full disclosure, even with no little ones around I remain a less than conscientious housekeeper). Fascinated, Jack began to pull on the door's edge that lay flat just a couple of inches above the floor. Noticing, I had begun leaving the dishwasher door down on purpose—the shiny metal beckoning him to check it out. Before long Jack was dragging his whole body up and onto the dishwasher door. From that vantage point he could see into the yawning white cave of dirty dishes. Jack saw it as fun, and I saw it as an unequivocal success. If curiosity could bait him to scale the few inches up onto the inside of the dishwasher door, and pull his entire body weight up onto the door, what else could it get him to do? Ironically, although Jack never achieved the typical "all fours" crawling posture, natural inquisitiveness was powerful enough to trick him into pulling himself onto the dishwasher door.

I kept my eye out for other developmental gems. One day, while jockeying kids, I glanced over and noticed Jack grabbing onto the banister leading up the stairs. Seeing potential in this new fascination, the next time I saw him heading toward the stairs, I seized my opportunity. I lifted him so that he was lying on his tummy straddling the banister, one arm and one leg dangling from either side. Holding my breath in anticipation, I shadowed my hands around him hoping he would use his arms to inch himself up. Exhale, nothing. He lay there with a tepid grasp on the railing, then became restless and began to protest. That was enough challenge; he wanted off.

The bottom of the stairs proved to be too much of a challenge, possibly because Jack could not see the payoff. Still, I wanted to see if curiosity might overcome his tendency to avoid movement that taxed his strength.

The next time I lifted him onto the banister about one third of the way up the stairs that ascended to our second-floor bedrooms. The house had an open floor plan, with an open staircase, the outer edge of the banister dropped off into the abyss with the family room and the kitchen on the main level below. I gingerly spotted him, holding on from both sides as he slid a few feet down the banister.... Wheee! Jack giggled and flashed that killer smile as he skimmed down the slick surface. This was the fun part. Oh, how I wished we could just remain in the fun part.

"If you want to slide down, you have to climb high," I tempted him. Would the thrill of going down be enough to get him to use his arms to pull? The wooden spindles that held up the banister provided convenient hand holds, but the angle was wrong and did not provide enough stability, so he ended up gripping the banister itself, moving hand over hand. I shadowed his long, slight body, moving one of my hands over each of his small ones, willing him to put one hand in front of the other to inch up the banister. When he made a bit of progress, I would move my hands away letting him slide down again a couple of feet. There was the "Wheeeee!" again. Sometimes he would only manage to pull up a short distance, but that effort was enough to earn a mini ride down. Jack and I would repeat that routine over and over again.

This became a game and after a few months, it was something he approached on his own. Nearly a year later, he would walk up the stairs and pull himself on to the banister and slide down. He had built the strength to pull himself up onto it and sometimes with help, sometimes on his own, he got into a straddle position on the banister. He would ride down a few feet at a time. *This* was an unbridled success, my kid was climbing and sliding! To the consternation of safety moms, I encouraged it. It was a point of pride for me. Was it possible that my kid was becoming a daredevil?

The week my extended family and their kids were visiting from out of state, I remember my sister-in-law's alarm at seeing Jack precariously perched on the banister, body flat in army crawl position hand over hand pulling up and sliding down. This scene gave way to a mix of alarm and confusion as she saw me going about my business in the kitchen, seemingly oblivious to the chaos and looming danger. "I would never have let my kids do that" she wondered out loud, helpfully trying to lift Jack off the banister, or at least doing her best to spot him gymnast style.

What would she say if she knew that I was not only aware that Jack was climbing but also had taught him to do it? I am embarrassed to say social convention caused me to acquiesce lest she think me a "bad mom," negligent and endangering my child's life. Not only was I not insisting on safety, but I was giving a neon green light to reckless behavior. That day I called out, "Get off the banister, Jack." I did this from the kitchen below where I was prepping dinner. Now Jack was bewildered too. Mercifully, he did not "out" me, but his expression seemed to say, "but Mom, you like it when I do this, you even put me on the banister sometimes and make me." This all-around weird exchange conjured complicated feelings within me. First, I thought, what a coward I was. Why had I not explained my theory, stood up for my belief that scaling banisters was good for this kid, a kind of super-charged physical therapy. But of course, I knew why I had not explained my role in legitimizing the sport of banister scaling in my home. Secretly, I reveled in the thought that others might see Jack as an explorer, a little stuntman, caught up in the throes of "typical" boy behavior! I knew too well that what we were witnessing was an isolated event rather than business as usual for Jack, still I welcomed any ventures that took him out of his comfort zone. "Viva la Typical!"

I love my sister-in-law as if she was my blood sister; she is Jack's godmother. We purposefully chose her for the role in part because she lost her third child at birth a few years before the twins were born. She was always tender and patient with Jack. She "got" this miracle of fragility and fortitude at a gut level that others could not quite comprehend, possibly because she had experienced that same aching mix battling it out in her own devastating experience. But all empathy aside, in this particular moment, she was witnessing a child, a physically precarious one at that, suspended well above the ground on a thin railing, with only a couch partially covering the hardwood floor that lay below. This kid was working without a net! And inexplicably the ringmaster of this crazy circus didn't seem to care. What my sister-in-law did not know was that any apprehension I had about skinned knees or (God forbid) broken bones was measured against the relative benefit that each repetition was providing in terms of strength and endurance. What she saw as risky, unsafe and undisciplined, I saw as potential, practice, and opportunity; another precious chance for Jack to build tone, strength, motor planning, and muscle memory.

What of Jack's confusion when I reprimanded him and demanded that he dismount with just the appropriately calculated amount of insincere indignation? I feel bad that I befuddled my kid to save face with another adult. Again, not one of my proudest moments, but I knew I could fix it with Jack. He would forgive this moment of motherly derangement. Just as sure as I was about that,

I also knew that I would have my kid back on the banister as soon as the out-of-town company left.

As parents, at some level we all know what is best for our kids, but sometimes fear gets in the way. I am reminded of the resolve Daniel's mother Paulette had to allow him to get back on his bike after he hit that pole.

I knew instinctively that Jack needed an environment that constantly invited practice, persistence and repetition. I rationalized that risking, what I optimistically estimated was the relatively small chance of a broken bone, was worth the skill, strength and confidence that could be built. Honestly, in my prayers, I brazenly dared God, "you gave him a syndrome, you would not be cruel enough to give him a broken bone or a concussion as a kicker." Jack was building strength while having fun. The allure of the slick wood and the downward slope of the banister fooled him into practicing the same skills he was presented with in physical therapy sessions but in an even more advanced and challenging way. The whole experience dialed up the motivation quotient too. He resisted the contrived practice at physical therapy, but this banister game was pure play! You go, Jack.

I thought about the pros and cons of risk. When you have a kid with special needs, you can't risk playing it safe. Safety and comfort are not friends of progress. More often than not, they encourage the status quo and regression.

Instead of focusing on deficits, I sought to capitalize on something that Jack had going for him that all of us instinctively possess in varying degrees. He may have been slow, uncoordinated, and tentative in his movements, but above all he was a kid, and at base, all kids are curious. It was fascinating to see how curiosity seduced him out of his comfort zone and invited challenge.

Jack saw these games as fun and I saw them as unequivocal wins. If curiosity could bait him to pull himself onto the dishwasher door and scale the banister what else could it get him to do? For me, the lesson was: when curiosity knocks, indulge the heck out of it. Distressed dishwasher door hinges and a wobbly banister (both of which we had) were a small price to pay for progress.

Chapter 15

OVEN MITTS AND ALPHASMARTS

*I am not in denial. I'm just selective
about the reality I accept.*

—Bill Watterson, *Calvin and Hobbs*

JACK AND LIVIE WERE NEARLY FIVE and Rosie was three and a half, when we picked up stakes and relocated from beautiful and crushingly expensive California to also beautiful but relatively affordable Colorado. A career change for Pete was the official reason, and it certainly would be cheaper. At that point we had three kids but soon it would be four. Will would come along before the end of our first year in Colorado. But he would grow in our hearts through adoption and not in my belly, so he was not even on the radar at the time of our move.

The unofficial reason for the change was that I was missing my family monumentally. My parents were absent from too many of the kids' milestones for my liking. A life in Colorado still amounted to a 12-hour drive between us and my hometown in Illinois, but at least each trip would not involve a cross country air excursion for five.

We marveled at the dueling beauty and peril of a summer snowstorm as we navigated icy roads over infamous Donner Pass on the way to our new-to-us rental home in Northern Colorado. It was crazy to me how both existed in equal measure on this slick highway originally etched by wooden wagon wheels.

Over time we invested the profits from selling our overpriced California property in a five-bedroom house with a big yard and nearly unlimited open space that could accommodate a Slip-'N-Slide and super soaker fights in the summer and sled riding and snow fort building in the winter. This was a large lot, the likes of which we certainly could not have afforded even if lots that size existed in the Bay Area.

We relished the wide open spaces of this western place that wasn't quite California but could maybe prove to be even better. It felt good to us, like we were home. Colorado was our sweet spot; we boasted that it offered that rare combination of a healthy west coast lifestyle with a "ya'll come" midwestern attitude.

Putting down roots in Colorado had meant another round of finding schools, testing, doctors, and therapists. I wish I could say that Jack's preschool experience was different this time around. In fact, it amounted to a variation of the California drill. The integrated special education preschool where Jack would be guaranteed speech, occupational and physical therapy services did not have space for Livie or Rosie. Outnumbered by our kids, pragmatics kicked in. We opted to forgo the special education preschool and put Jack in a regular church preschool with both of his sisters. The simplicity of having all three kids in one school felt like a warm blanket on a cold night. Unfortunately, we enjoyed less than a year in this preschool Zen place before kindergarten and all the demands of "real" school intruded.

Absentmindedly enrolling our kids in the neighborhood public school was a luxury that we did not take for granted. Jack needed occupational therapy, physical therapy, and speech therapy. Since, like most families, we did not have the unlimited resources necessary to pay out of pocket for these services, again we contacted the school district. To receive services, Jack would have to be evaluated, labeled, and placed. Once again, the judgments of others threatened the quality and rigor of Jack's school experience.

After a particularly rigorous testing session, administered by a caring, well-meaning diagnostician, the label "developmentally delayed/health impaired" was bestowed on Jack. We were just a year or two shy of when the label "Pervasive Developmental Delay" or PDD came into fashion. PDD has become a catch-all category given to children who don't tidily fit into other defined categories such as ADHD, autism, cognitive delay, etc. Had PPD been the coin of the realm at the time, I am confident that it would have been Jack's label, but given the state of categorization systems at the time, developmentally delayed/health impaired was what was served up.

This label came with an Individual Educational Plan (IEP) and various services designed to address Jack's specific delays. Speech and occupational therapy would be offered by therapists at the regular elementary school. We would have to seek physical therapy outside the school day and pay for it with private insurance. By law, only the teachers, administrators and therapists at the school were apprised of the label and the special services that Jack received. Of course, parents and kids could wonder and conjecture all they wanted, but labels were not common knowledge.

With that behind us, Jack was off to kindergarten with his twin sister. He had a label, special services, and continued to move through the world on unsteady bearings holding his arms out in front as partial guard to steady himself. Even so, I felt that same visceral sense of hope that I had at Kinderkirk. Jack was in (sigh of relief). He was good enough, passed inspection. He was accepted into the public Kindergarten with all its gloriously fully functional, non-labeled children. I connected with a couple of other moms with boys, suggested play dates and "voila," kindergarten friends appeared. That is how Jack met Sam, an athletic, confident little guy who lived a few streets down. His mom and I hit it off right away. It helped that two of her kids were the same ages as three of mine. From these roots commenced a friendship that connected our families for years.

Jack and Livie's teacher, Mrs. Hayden, was an amiable silver-haired woman with a Mrs. Santa Claus feel about her, who behaved as if she was unaware of Jack's differences. Or, if she was aware, his deficits simply did not play into her calculus of relating to children. She truly loved all the little people assigned to her without regard to what diagnosticians, psychologists, and standardized tests said about their potential. Later in the year, I learned that tragically Mrs. Hayden's son had committed suicide and her daughter, adopted from Armenia, experienced a severe form of autism. No doubt she had plenty of her own to say about the labels and judgments of this world.

Livie thrived in Mrs. Hayden's class and Jack moved with the current created by the 24 other little tadpoles swimming along in Kindergarten Room 101 not distinguishing himself in ways that would call into question the appropriateness of his placement in the class. There were songs to learn that assigned every letter of the alphabet its own unique persona: 'Leo the Lion Hearted L, Dora the Darling D, etc', there were counting games, and big books to listen to and little photocopied books to take home. Mrs. Hayden's classroom may not have been the bastion of cutting-edge educational methods, but it felt gloriously uncomplicated, probably because it conjured some of my own kindergarten experiences.

In the midst of all that loving and learning, we ran headlong into what I would call an "expectations problem" with the Occupational Therapist, Mrs. Kelly Marshall. It became increasingly clear that I did not agree with the messages I felt were being communicated to my kid about his ability. Occupational Therapy is a noble profession populated by individuals dedicated to helping people, young and old, improve their ability to participate in activities of daily living. They are experts in deconstructing and reconstructing the fine movements and sensory functions that we depend on every day to get the "job" of life done, hence the "occupational" part of occupational therapy. They enable older people to maintain their driver's licenses and assist stroke victims in regaining their ability to eat, drink, and cook. In schools, they help kids with feeding, holding a pencil, writing, balance, and coordination.

In kindergarten, Jack spent a large portion of his time with his fingers in his mouth. Not all his fingers, mostly just the index and middle fingers of his right hand. We never received a good explanation. It was likely a sensory deficit, a building block missed as a baby, possibly a hold-over from his underdeveloped suck reflex. I tried mightily to cue, cajole, prompt and prod him to keep his hands in his pockets, thereby giving his digits a safe and hygienic place to reside until he needed them. However, Jack would have none of it; he continued to keep those two fingers in his mouth. Mrs. Marshall, OT, tried numerous remedies and incentives to get Jack to stop, but to no avail. I knew that it bothered some kids and made Jack look "handicapped," but we could not get him to stop. I also knew that Mrs. Marshall's professional patience was being challenged every time she entered the classroom and saw Jack munching on his digits.

Everything came to a head when she requested a meeting. There, she wasted no time informing me that Jack's fingers-in-mouth behavior was repellent to other children and spreading germs. All the while she is talking, I am thinking, "you are telling me my kid is grossing people out, not great, but this I can handle." At least she was not saying that he couldn't learn. Furthermore, she went on, for hygiene reasons as well as to finally extinguish the behavior, she was going to require Jack to wear oven mitts in the classroom.

This hit me like a record being scratched on an old-fashioned player. I had worked way too hard to ensure that Jack tracked along with his twin sister to have everything undone this way. In the kitchen center where kids played house, I could buy it, but even in the whimsical landscape of a kindergarten class, a kid wearing oven mitts at his desk screams "I am different!" Mrs. Marshall was the expert; I was not an occupational therapist. I acknowledged her training and experience, but did that mean signing on to subjecting Jack to what amounted to juvenile humiliation? My mind raced, had Jack met his match in public kindergarten? Had he topped out here, were his issues so significant that I would have to raise the white flag and surrender? Did my theory of raising my child as if he was capable not hold up when exposed to the harsh light (and judgment) of kindergarten norms? Was this behavior so far afield from what was expected that it could not be tolerated? I had not sorted everything out, but at that moment, I was sure of one thing: my kid was not going to wear oven mitts at school unless he was putting a kiddie soufflé in the little wooden oven in the play kitchen corner!

The "oven mitts" intervention was introduced on a Friday. I remember feeling dejected, defeated and "done in" that weekend. I also remember that, like all flawed (read human) moms, I took it out on my kid. Saturday morning, Jack unwittingly made the deadly mistake of walking out of the bathroom with his fingers in his mouth. Fear took over and I could no longer see my sweet boy for the amazing creation that he was, I could only see Mrs. Marshall back at school on Monday applying the final solution: Operation Oven Mitts. I went postal and screamed at Jack, "what is wrong with you, don't you know you have to keep your hands out of your mouth, or they will make you wear oven mitts?" I vividly remember Jack's quiet voice, "Mom, you worry too much." That from my son, snapped me out of crazy long enough to consider what he said. Out of the mouths of babes. He was right, I *did* worry too much. My relationship with Jack was more important than anything the system could do to him. I scheduled an impromptu meeting with Mrs. Marshall on Monday and summarily rejected the oven mitt remedy but did concede to putting a bad tasting substance on Jack's fingers to create a gastronomic deterrent.

Fast forward a year to first grade, and a new teacher who was not nearly as loving, wise, or intuitive as Mrs. Hayden. The twins had a new classroom teacher but the constant for Jack was Mrs. Marshall, Occupational Therapist, and past prescriber of oven mitts. In terms of pace and competition, the difference between kindergarten and 1st grade was pronounced. The stakes were now much higher. The lyrical rhyming songs still echoed in the background, but now they were muffled by academic demands. Little sight word lists, math work sheets and spelling lists started showing up. The expectations for performance had risen, particularly in writing. In kindergarten, Jack got away with his closed fisted grip on the crayon, paintbrush, and pencil. The creations that kindergarteners produced with these tools were expected to be inventive, experimental, fun, and a little off the rails. But now in the space of barely three months, from the end of May to the end of August, these children-turned-students were expected to write sentences complete with punctuation, make paintings, and color within the lines.

Having a history with Jack, our occupational therapist had already reached some conclusions about his potential. Stoked to the gills with PTSD from my last private meeting with Mrs. Marshall, I reluctantly joined her for another meeting conducted in a makeshift semi-circle consisting of small chairs positioned just so in the back of a vacant classroom. Just like last year, she cut to the chase. (You had to give her points for brevity.) Having observed and assessed Jack and having worked with him over the past year, it was her professional opinion that Jack would not learn to write with a pencil, or if he would, it would not be an efficient way for him to produce academic work, rendering it untenable. I had to admit Jack could not hold the pencil with the typical tripod grasp that most kids had mastered at three. In that moment, I reflected on the way his pencil stuck way out in front of his hand angled in the opposite direction. This position, I supposed, was a way for him to stabilize it in his hand. I also reflected on the fact that many of his letters were largely indecipherable. All this I had to admit was true that day. But that did not mean he would never learn to write with a pencil; of course, he would.

Her proposal was dangerous. Just her voicing it amounted to heresy given my stubborn belief that Jack would do everything his sister did. Numb now, as I was in the office of the Geneticist all those years ago, I sat quietly and attempted to focus on the actual words coming out of her mouth. The solution she posed to Jack's inability to write was to teach him to use a keyboard. I parroted back to her what I thought I heard just to make sure that I was not missing something.

"So, you are giving up on teaching Jack to use a pencil to print or write and are having him write on a computer?" I imagined Jack doing his work sitting at one of the desktop computers in the room while the other kids sat at their desks, pencils in hand. This seemed wrong, he was a first grader, for God's sake, not a temp wearing a headset at a call center.

Not a computer exactly, she offered, "Jack would be using an *Alphasmart,* a piece of adaptive technology that kids use to write and even communicate if they are non-verbal. It is a portable keyboard with a digital display above it. Kids type and their work is displayed right above the keyboard."

"It is portable and set up for little fingers," she offered perkily as if she was a used car salesperson determined to get me into a slightly used Ford Fusion with some carefully worded selling points. At first blush, one might not find much to quibble with. In fact, some parents might even see replacing pencil writing with what amounted to keyboarding as a plus. Even I could recite the potential virtues of this "skills swap." The logic goes something like this... Handwriting is going the way of the Dodo bird. By the time kids are in high school or even middle school, they are doing all their work on a laptop anyway. Keyboarding is a job skill that everyone needs. It gives kids a head start on the future. Technology is a universal good, right?

This easy rationalization focused on the central role of technology in life. It did not even touch on arguments around increasing motivation, which was another compelling angle. Dumping the pencil in favor of something that looked like a computer also paved the way toward the path of least resistance. Show me the kid who does not love immediate gratification. Getting to push buttons and receive instantaneous feedback for your effort is what makes technology so seductive. How do you pit the *Alphasmart* with all its bells and whistles up against a stick of lead covered in a wooden shell painted a ubiquitous shade of mustard? Like every kid I have ever met, Jack loved computers. With equal measure, he did not love the discomfort his undeveloped hand muscles felt when they were taxed by balancing a pencil over the length of an assignment. I was doing the calculations in my brain…if we chose the *Alphasmart*, my kid would be happier, more comfortable, and a lot less frustrated. However, I instinctively knew that if we went that route, there would be no going back. Jack would be the "special" kid who did his homework on the adaptive keypad because he could not learn to write like everyone else.

My head was pounding…what was true? I knew that it was true that today Jack could not write with a pencil. There was one other thing I knew was also true: if he was not required to learn to write with a pencil, he never would. If we made this "skills trade off" on this day in first grade, we would be giving up on his potential to learn this skill. Once we had agreed to the technological solution, no matter how expeditious or sexy it was, Jack would likely never write with a pencil. Because while "typical" kids might prefer the computer, they could also pick up a pencil, pen, or marker and create whenever the spirit moved them. They already had the skill, using the computer was a choice. By going the adaptive technology route, that choice would be outside of Jack's grasp—no pun intended.

My mind wandered to pragmatics: technology is not fail-safe. What is that much-used adage? "Technology is great, when it works." What happens when it is not working or readily available? People need to know how to light a candle when the electricity goes out. People need to know how to read a map when Google is down, and people need to know how to write, period. I fast forwarded 10 and then 20 years and imagined, if Jack did not know how to write, how would he leave a note for his roommate to pick up milk, or sign a Valentine's Day card for his girlfriend? How would he endorse his paychecks or sign home mortgage papers?

Mrs. Marshall was the credentialed professional in this arena, but it just did not sit right with me. I again reminded myself of what I felt was a universal truth about human muscles. They strengthen with use and atrophy without it. So, I thought, it is true that what Jack is doing *now* does not look like writing, but that does not mean that he will never learn to write. What I did not know then was that, in my desperation, I was channeling the power of a growth mindset, which is the subject of a wealth of research today. In Carol Dweck's book,[11] this is called the power of yet. It wasn't that Jack could not write; it was that he could not write YET!

Jack was of the generation they called "native" to technology. It was the air that kids of his age breathed. I knew he would learn to type even if it meant hunting and pecking the letters; that was not my worry. What he needed to do was write. I mustered some pluck and I challenged Mrs. Marshall again. (By now she must have liked me as much as I liked her.) "No," I said, "we don't want to exchange the pencil for the *Alphasmart.*"

"Jack will learn to write," I pronounced with all the resolve of Scarlett O'Hara letting the world know she would never go hungry again. Mrs. Marshall was nonplussed, assuming, I guessed, that I would come to my senses in time.

But time did not change my mind. I set yet another meeting with the Special Education team, which included Jack's 1st grade teacher, Mrs. Marshall, and the special education district representative. During this meeting, I formally rejected the *Alphasmart* as Jack's primary means for writing, but I did not reject the tool wholesale. While I did not want it to take the place of handwriting, I was not above using it strategically as a reward. The idea was that the keyboarding tool would be the carrot at the end of the writing stick, so to speak. In Jack's Individualized Educational Plan (IEP), we proposed that he would use the *Alphasmart* for a few minutes to retype his spelling words, but only after he wrote them with a pencil. The same could occur with other class work...if he completed the handwriting task, he could use the *Alphasmart* to recopy the work if he desired and if time allowed. This way, I reasoned, we maintained the goal of conventional writing but added the powerful motivator of access to technology. Our agreement was not so different from the garden variety parental trick of allowing TV after homework. Nothing revolutionary, but what was important to me was that we had not closed any doors, not traded Jack's long-term potential for the expediency of what looked like an easy answer for him and his teachers. The team agreed to using the *Alphasmart* only to reward conventional pencil usage. Mrs. Marshall agreed too, reluctantly.

I'd love to end this chapter with a tried-and-true fairytale ending: "and Jack wrote happily ever after," followed by a biblical-sounding revelation, "and his Teacher saw that it was good." But unfortunately, believing in your kid is a long-term proposition, not just a series of quick fixes strung together like a candy necklace.

I had won a battle of principle. Jack would not be allowed to skip writing and printing exercises. He would not be told by anyone that he could not write. Importantly, he would not get the message that he was "less than" in this area. But the practical dilemma remained of how he was going to learn to write and who was going to teach him. His classroom teacher did not have the specialized skill or the time to spend teaching one child to hold and use his pencil. Mrs. Marshall did not have the will to do it, partially because her ego was bruised by what must have seemed a rejection of her technology proposal. But she also did not have the time; she was only assigned to work with Jack 30 minutes two times a week and had other goals to accomplish. There again the problem of frequency of practice and repetition reared its head. Jack needed concentrated, consistent practice to master what other kids were learning incidentally.

I searched for a solution to ensure that Jack would learn to print and write legibly. I found a program called *Handwriting Without Tears*.[12]

I'll admit it seemed outdated to me even 13 years ago, but I was determined that Jack was going to write with a pencil and there was no "Printing Without Tears" program that I could locate. When I brought this information to the school district, I learned that Mrs. Marshall knew of the approach. (By this time, we had had so many run-ins that we were on first name basis…a relationship was blooming.) I was disappointed that she had not offered it as an alternative. If she was unwilling or unable to give it a try, why had she not recommended another specialist who was trained in the approach? Assuming I was on my own, I searched and eventually found a hospital-affiliated program where a trained therapist offered one-on-one instruction in *Handwriting Without Tears*. It is true that many have consigned handwriting to the same fate as the woolly mammoth, and that many school districts have ceased to provide handwriting instruction all together. However, I had not selected the program so much for the skill of handwriting per se, but because I was betting that it would provide Jack with desperately needed practice in holding a pencil and would provide him with the repetition necessary to build the numerous miniscule muscles in the hand that must work in concert to govern writing. I reasoned that this handwriting workout, sustained over time, would give him the strength, muscle memory, and endurance to manage a pencil for purposes of communicating and taking notes, whether it be with printed letters or classic cursive.

So, on top of the speech and occupational therapy services provided at school and the private physical therapy we drove to after school, we began a pilgrimage to the hospital each week for *Handwriting without Tears*. In retrospect, I cannot say that the instruction was particularly inspiring or the approach revolutionary. I would call it structured, methodical, and disciplined. However, it did serve two purposes. First, it signaled to Jack that the adults in his life believed he could master the skill of using a pencil (or pen) to communicate, just like all the other kids in his class. Second, it set up a routine that held Jack and us accountable for regular repetitive practice of each of the micro-movements that we all execute mindlessly every day when we pick up a pencil to jot a grocery list or scribble a reminder to ourselves on a Post-it note and slap it on our computer.

Life is a series of little decisions, many made unconsciously or with extraordinarily little thought. We could have avoided acrimony with the therapists and special education staff and at the same time appeased Jack by replacing a frustrating and physically fatiguing task with a piece of technology that was made all the more attractive by its availability, ease of use, and the fact that the "pros" had recommended it. Again, I was reminded of the tantalizing siren song luring us toward the "easier," "safer," and "more comfortable" route for our son. We could have taken the off ramp and chucked the writing expectation in favor of the *Alphasmart*, but at what cost? How would Jack's life be different now? Despite how frustrating and laborious the task was for him, would he have taken an interest over time and forced himself to learn on his own?

Or would he have internalized that he was not capable, that he was "different" or somehow less than as he watched his classmates writing spelling words, sending notes, and authoring poems, pen in hand, while he was limited to producing all his work on the peculiar device that displayed only a few sentences at a time? We will never know for sure. However, I maintain that this holy war I waged with the therapist to ensure Jack's right to learn to use a pencil was based on something infinitely more important: the belief that the messages we send our kids matter. These messages shape how we treat our kids and ultimately what they think they can do. The writing quest was part of my stubborn and unyielding belief that Jack would have access to all the opportunities and experiences that his twin sister had. Equally important for me was that Jack knew that we expected him to write.

Chapter 16

THOSE NEXT 15 YARDS

Luckily my parents were pragmatists, not poets.
They knew that ignorance and fear are matters
of the mind and the mind is adaptable.

—Daniel Kish

HIGH EXPECTATIONS DOES NOT MEAN head-in-the-sand blind optimism or living in La La Land. Is it foolish to hope? I thought a lot about how it is that parents of children with differences can maintain unbounding hope in the harsh glare of reality. Perhaps the "how" is secondary. We do this because we must. On the edge of each small success lies the come-hither promise of the next. The 1950's Russian psychologist Vygotski identified a learning principle he termed "zone of proximal development." Back then it made waves, now it is a staple in undergraduate human development classes. The basic idea is that we can grasp that which is close to where we are currently. Try for something too distant, too ambitious, and we fail discouraged. But identify that which is directly above or adjacent to where we are, and we will seek it and achieve.

For me the power of "next" was the precious fuel for my expectations. When I first saw the light in Jack's eyes at the dining room table, I thought what is the next object of interest those eyes will capture? When he lifted his head ever so slightly, I dangled the toy a little higher, imagining how he could lift an inch or two more. When he grasped a pencil whole-fisted, we made a pencil grip out of two elastic hair ties that forced him to hold the pencil back between his thumb and forefinger. Typical progression for kids without developmental delays, modest and expected by the world's standards, these were substantial accomplishments for a child with Jack's delays. Planting my feet on the path and training my gaze on the next anthill rather than the mountains that loomed in the distance was how I nourished hope. Focusing on the mountains would be enough to break anyone.

My husband and I learned to ski as adults in the Colorado Rockies. Anyone who has skied Colorado knows these are not bunny hills. The way down starts at twelve thousand feet. To us, not particularly athletic 30-somethings clinching our knees, making wide turns, our skis locked in classic pizza formation, the base looked impossibly distant. It was a place we would never reach. That day we shared a lesson as that was what we could afford. I listened intently, hanging on to every word the ski instructor said as we stood poised over the vertical expanse that lay between our tottering skis and the horizontal security of the base below. His words burned in my conscious brain as I made my way down the mountain. "Don't look at the base," "keep your eyes fixed 15 yards ahead, and when you reach that point, look toward the next 15 yards." And so we moved from the impossibility of a 12,000 foot summit to the gloriously flat terra firma below by allowing ourselves to visualize only a stingy 15 yards at a time. That is how I think it is with hope.

Hope is the "what could be," and it feels good to dwell there. But how does one reconcile the euphoria of hope, the great "what could be," with the razor-sharp pain of "what is," the oppressive reality of the moment? It is true that parents and young children's fortunes are intrinsically intertwined. They meet their friends because we take them on play dates, we are friends with the parents of kids that our kids play with. We eat the food they leave on their plates and we often fall asleep with them in our arms; essentially, we do life together. It takes years for a child's sense of individuality to develop. In fact, until about seven months of age a baby is not even cognizant that he is a separate being from his mother. At six years, Jack's experience and mine were still co-mingled.

I cannot presume to say what Jack felt, but this was my reality. Kids at school (and their parents) are looking at my kid funny because he walks with his arms out to balance. He is rarely invited to birthday parties because they sense a difference (unless the birthday child is Livie's friend and they politely include her twin). The lack of muscle tone in his mouth makes my kid's speech slow and sometimes difficult to understand. He has to work hard to enunciate each syllable. By the time he gets a thought out the kids around him have moved on to their next youthful fascination. He often repeats what other kids say because the processing time needed to come up with a unique response is a luxury he does not have. The trained specialist at school is telling me that Jack won't learn to write. He can't hold the bat for T-ball. He tires so quickly that he gives up and hangs behind on the field, not even getting near the soccer ball, and he can't lift himself out of the swimming pool. That was the unvarnished truth of the present and it was a demoralizing place for me to live.

I don't know that I was cognizant of it at the time, it may have been self-preservation on my part, but it was too painful to reside solely in the present. I had pledged to not give up on my kid, but back then I could not articulate what I was doing. With the benefit of reflection, I can now unpack the goings on in my head. I was holding two competing ideas sacred at the same time, one that I feared and one that I indulged. The first idea: 'what it is'. My kid has Sotos syndrome, every muscle in his body is flaccid. His speech is not clear, kids walk away from him, he does not have the muscle strength to blow out birthday candles, he doesn't hold a pencil correctly, and the school district wants to place him in a special education classroom. And the second idea: "what it could be." Although all of this is true today, what could the future hold? What might he do tomorrow, next time, next week, next year? After all, I had seen his eyes open, his head lift, his curiosity coax his torso into the open dishwasher, his body inch up the banister. Holding fast to these data points, the sky was the limit.

I am not a peddler of snake oil or a faith healer, even though I believe that faith is inextricably linked to hope. High expectations will not cure Down syndrome, ADHD, autism, cerebral palsy or, even Sotos syndrome. My child's condition will always be part his story, but it does not need to define him.

I can predict critics of my stance: "Yeah, all of this is great for you, your goal was to raise your kid as if he had no disability. But my child faces challenges that won't put her even close to striking distance of "typical." What then?" As a teacher of students with severe and profound disabilities, I say with confidence that no matter what a child's specific circumstance, parents are always better off believing *and* behaving as if their child "can" rather than "cannot." The promise of expectations research haunts me "as we see how beliefs affect human behavior, we don't know how far that line can move."

I think about others, parents of children with all manner of "differences". I want to ask: "What is the next 15 yards for your child? Is it forming the sign for 'all done'?" Is it making eye contact? Is it signaling the need to toilet? Or is it attending to a half page of math problems? Believing and acting as if your child can achieve will send positive messages to your child. These messages will help her become the most capable child you know, who by the way, also happens to have autism, ADHD, intellectual delays, a learning disability, Down Syndrome, you fill in the blank.

Chapter 17

PULL-OUTS

He will take your breath away
Stop you in your steps
Fear he is a liar

—Zach Williams

THE TWINS WERE NEARLY HALFWAY THROUGH 1st grade when I learned quite by accident that Jack's label had "bought" him more than just the standard fare of speech therapy and occupational therapy prescribed in his IEP. It happened to be Scholastic Book Fair season; which I often thought would have been more aptly named the Scholastic Stuff Fair because kids were at least as enthralled by its unicorn pencil fidgets, squishy animal-themed erasers, and furry bookmarks as they were with the books themselves. I was just inside the main entrance to the school building assembling a cardboard display. Venturing down the primary wing in search of scotch tape, I noticed two small desks in the hall facing one another. As I approached, I noticed that in one of them sat my son and in the other the special education teacher. Weird, I thought, and I made a mental note to ask Jack's general education teacher, Mrs. Mullen, what was going on. When I ran into her that same day, she explained that Jack was receiving one-on-one, pull-out instruction in core skills.

"What kind of core skills?" I queried.

Mrs. Mullen expounded, "At this particular point of the year, our skills focus is on identifying blended sounds (part of phonemic awareness) and number relationships."

It sort of says it all in the name. With a "pull-out" service, a student or small group of students are pulled out of the classroom to receive customized help. This is contrasted with a "push-in" service where the support provider comes into the classroom to work with a child or small group.

My expectations antennae went up. Curious, I wanted to know exactly what "goes down" during pull-out time. I made sure that the next time I volunteered I would again happen upon Jack in the hallway. My privileged book fair worker status offered legitimate cover for me to unobtrusively observe (read surveil). What I saw this time was an instructional aide arriving at Jack's 1st grade classroom and ushering him out into the hallway, where they sat at the same two small desks facing each other. The aide presented cards showing individual letters and letter pairs (sh, ou, oi, ow) and Jack was supposed to make the blended sounds and find words that possessed those sounds. Then she showed him cards with numerals on them and Jack had to make number sentences with colorful, interlocking cubes.

What's not to like, right? This setup was akin to having a personal tutor for my kid without having to pay for it. It could even give him a jump on the other students. Quite tempting since I was all about finding stolen opportunities and extra time for the repeated practice that I believed Jack needed. I was uneasy because, in theory, there was absolutely nothing wrong with this supplemental service. Show me a first grader who could not benefit from a little extra time devoted to reading and math foundations?

I emerged from my covert position at the book display, and continued down the hall, feigning that I had accidentally happened upon the scene. I asked how things were going, and then threw out the offhand comment, "This is great, actually Jack's twin sister could use this kind of practice", musing out loud that Livie could benefit from an extra helping of phonics instruction.

The aide took the comment as a joke because, of course, she could not; these services were for students in special education. But I was not kidding…Livie could have really used some dedicated 1:1 time as evidenced by the letter we had received the week before, informing us of her ailing reading scores.[13]

The fact that Jack was getting this help and his twin was not illustrated what I saw as the capricious assignment of this service. Jack struggled mightily compared to his sister in almost every area: forming words, cognitive processing time, coordination, balance, speed, strength, endurance, and making friends. However, in the world of reading and pre-reading skills, he was not particularly behind. Yet Livie, who was slow to read, was not eligible because she was without a label. Since he was a toddler, Jack had preferred the sedentary pursuit of listening to stories to physical activity. As it turned out, those early years sitting on the living room rug with books strewn around him had paid off. Ironically, here was an arena where Jack was not lacking, but still he was being treated as if he was.

I was obviously no stranger to special education, but this was my first shot at "doing school" with a kid of my own who had been labeled by the system. I knew that the label assigned to a child allows him, by law, to a free and appropriate education, in the least restrictive educational environment, governed by a plan customized just for him. That plan, the Individualized Educational Plan or IEP is written with parental participation and is designed specifically for the child. However, Jack was in the public school system, and "systems" by definition, are built to work best for groups and not individuals. A system for one is a bit of an oxymoron. Schools in the United States have to serve lots of kids, that is why we call them school "systems."

Depending on the school district, various diagnoses and labels carry with them a range of services and supports. In an IEP meeting, a program or a suite of services may be suggested for a child because experience, best practice and even research has indicated that these services or programs work well to address the needs indicated by that child's label or diagnosis. These may include therapies, counseling, assistive technology, special programs, clubs, academic practice, adaptive physical education or even an entire classroom, as in the case of Jack's multiply handicapped preschool class.

In this case, it felt to me like, along with Jack's special education label, the powers that be threw in some additional basic academic services, "free of charge." It reminded me of those obscure TV channels they bundle with the expanded cable plan. Sure, they are nice to have if you don't have to pay for them, but did you really want ESPN 8 and the Home Shopping Network? Did you need them, and what other pursuits are you missing out on when you tuned in just because these channels were there?

I thought it perverse poetic justice that after working so hard to secure an additional service for my kid, (the handwriting training), I now found myself on the other side of the extra services fight. I now felt I needed to advocate to get a support removed. Let's be real, a half hour or forty minutes in the hallway, media center, or tucked in an empty room immersed in letters and numbers wasn't going to change the trajectory of humankind. After all, he was in first grade, not medical school. But still, I was preoccupied with what Jack was missing during that time, and the messages he might be taking away from this segregated, one-on-one time.

All instructional time is precious, and I felt an aching sense of urgency for my kid who was behind in so many areas. I perseverated on what he was missing when he was out in the hall practicing consonant blends, vowel diagraphs, and basic addition and subtraction. It was a confounding balancing act. My goal was to raise Jack with the expectation that he was competent and could, with effort, achieve anything he wanted. On one hand, Jack was likely enjoying all that extra teacher attention, and he may have even been gaining confidence from the positive feedback he was receiving for performing in an area where he was relatively strong. However, the other side of this opportunity see-saw revealed what Jack was not getting during his pull-out time. Unless the rest of the class was freeze-framed for those 30 minutes, he was missing something. I was pretty sure that I would rather have him learning alongside his peers than sitting in the hallway, regardless of what the activity was, unless the class was spending that time in a darkened classroom passively watching a Disney movie. (A pursuit for which, neither my son nor virtually any other child needs additional practice.)

I learned that Jack's pull-out time had effectively scheduled him out of a portion of the reading and social studies academic block. In addition to missing the group academics, he was cut off from any student-to-student interactions that naturally occurred during that time. This pull-out service created yet another concrete way in which Jack was separated from his "typical" peers. I knew that anything which set Jack apart from his peers sent messages I did not want him getting. Because I looked on his delays as impermanent, I conceded to him being separated, if necessary, for services that backfilled actual delays, but I was not willing to have him set apart for the mere fact that he had a label.

I formally asked that the pull-out time be removed from Jack's IEP. There was no fight; the request was inconsequential. No rationale was required; I did not have to muster a passionate case like the one I had made to get access to writing instruction. The team simply complied. While the special education case manager seemed a little perplexed at my insistence, she said, it was "no problem" to drop the service off Jack's IEP.

Special education reforms over the years have resulted in some changes, but it generally remains true that services flow to your child from designated labels. Although every school district is different, ours was quite willing to provide a variety of services based on the label they had assigned Jack. Removal of Jack's hallway pre-reading and math drills was insignificant in the eyes of the special education pros, but it was important to me. Although I was relatively new at being on this side of the desk in parent-teacher communications, in this mama's brain a lesson was crystalizing. Just because a service was offered, it did not necessarily follow that I should accept it.

I made myself a promise from that day forward: I was going to scrutinize every service, support, or special opportunity that flowed from Jack's label.

Services make sense when they are based on goals, not labels. Services mattered in terms of the end game I envisioned for Jack— that is, the short- and long-term goals I had for him. It required me to visualize where he could be in five years or ten years, and as an adult. For example, the *Alphasmart* was an accommodation provided as part of the service plan recommended by a skilled occupational therapist. Some parents may have viewed it as a win, a golden opportunity, "my kid is going to use this special tool that will make his schoolwork more manageable." However, I envisioned Jack taking handwritten notes in high school and signing on the dotted line for a car loan as an adult. Viewed in this light, the *Alphasmart* went from being a convenient support to a dangerous compromise that threatened the end game I sought for my child.

The same was true of those daily letter and number drills. Pull-out academic support was a service that, at face value, was beneficial, or at least not harmful. Again, what 1st grader could not benefit from a little extra practice in the letters and numbers department? Don't look a gift-horse in the mouth, right? Here lay the exception to this widely accepted piece of pop-wisdom. When I stared down this horse, I did not like what I saw. I envisioned Jack connecting with other kids and moving through the grades as a full member of his class. Given the goal, this pull-out service thwarted the end game: it set Jack apart from his peers. It was, in fact, no gift at all.

I was familiar with those who have confused inclusion, that is, children with special needs learning alongside "typical peers" with keeping a child in the classroom at all costs, even in cases where is it unclear how the child (or his peers) are benefitting. Inclusion for the sake of claiming that your child is in the regular classroom represents a wrong-headed understanding of the concept. I am not advocating dumping children in classrooms with teachers who are unprepared to meet their needs in exchange for the privilege of saying that they are "included". That most certainly does not yield positive outcomes for anyone. What I am advocating is making decisions about each service or support offered given the end game or "vision of capable" a parent has for their child.

I argue that when it comes to special education services and therapies, more is not always better. In fact, quite the opposite is true... more may actually turn out to be worse. When I weighed what Jack was getting during those hallway drills, the benefits did not outweigh the costs. I arrived at the conclusion that the value of the specialized service did not justify him missing opportunities. I saw precious group time and socialization with classmates as not worth sacrificing at the altar of extra teacher attention and academic practice.

I am a teacher and I respect teaching above all professions. All my kids have been blessed with more creative, inspiring teachers in their school careers than I can count. Rather than a critique of special educators or special education in general, I want my experience to serve as an anthem for parents. "Walk alongside the professionals in your child's life, but never forget that you know him or her better than anyone." Just because a label or diagnosis entitles your child to something—a specific service or support—it doesn't necessarily follow that you need to take it. Don't accept a classroom, or sign on to a program, intervention or therapy just because it is served up.

In this instance the decision was easy. Given my vision of capable for Jack, dropping the reading and math pull-out was a no brainer. But the choices that would present themselves would not always be so cut and dried. Time is a limited commodity. All decisions must be made based on the goals parents have for their child and must be balanced with the time he or she has to get there. I knew that my goals would likely need to be adjusted as Jack grew.

This realization took me back to a classroom I had worked in years earlier and a set of parents who had initially wanted their son Jorge to learn to read fluently and for pleasure, that is, to achieve what teachers call "academic reading." By the time Jorge got to me as a 9th grader, they were unsure. Now they were focused on him participating in the community, eventually finding a job and working. Their goals for him had changed. Because time and resources provided by the school were necessarily limited, I helped them make the decision to abandon academic reading for what has been called "survival reading" or reading for community independence. This is the kind of reading we do to order at a fast-food restaurant, use public transportation, or find the appropriate bathroom. Services changed as did goals over time.

Parents of kids with special needs are met with a mind melting number of decisions: Should I keep her in one-on-one physical therapy or put her in a cross-fit class? Should she be in "friend's club" after school or join a Brownie troop? Should my child receive pull-out algebra support at school, or should he instead go to a commercial tutoring service, or do both? The answers to these questions depend on parents' goals for their child. As I reminded Jorge's parents, they know their child better than anyone! All our kids who have been identified as having a "special need" are people first. They have complex personalities, specific preferences, and unique motivators. Knowing our children well and keeping our vision of "capable" in mind is the wisest counsel through this labyrinth of choices.

Chapter 18

DIY THERAPY

*You need to have sufficient courage
to make mistakes.*

—Paulo Coelho, *Brida*

WHILE OTHER KIDS WERE AT SOCCER PRACTICE, swim trials, or dance class, Jack was with me in the car trekking to our local youth clinic for physical therapy, or to the Masonic Center for speech therapy. Before he was eight, he had been through at least six physical therapists, three occupational therapists, and just as many speech therapists. At physical therapy, Jack was prompted to walk on uneven surfaces, directed to focus his eyes on targets, and required to raise one leg and then another while balancing on brightly colored balls of various sizes. While speech therapy focused on the slack muscles in Jack's mouth and tongue.

*My tongue can be a paintbrush, paint the roof with me; my
tongue can be a clock, tic toc, tic toc; my tongue can be a lion's
tongue, move it up to make a grrrr; my tongue can be a dog's tail,
watch me wag my dog tongue back and forth and side to side.*

Speech therapists were particularly preoccupied with the fact
that Jack could not lift his tongue to the roof of his mouth. Tongue
pointing was a very big thing.

*There were also numerous soft palate and lip pursing exercises to
be done.* Occupational therapy focused on small muscle groups—
those that allow us to squeeze, grasp, twist, and pinch. These simple
movements, when performed in concert, allow kids to paint masterpieces, write stories, tie shoes, zip zippers, shoot water guns, and
complete hundreds of tasks we take for granted every day.

*In addition to all this scheduled time with professionals, we worked
at home on core stabilizing exercises...we blew through straws, rolled
snakes with dough, and stretched rubber bands over nails pounded
into plywood to create our own DIY peg boards. We even installed a
heavy-duty hook in the basement ceiling and attached a triangular
bar for Jack to hang from, essentially creating a mock-up of those
playground ziplines that had confounded him so. This way he could
work on core strength, supporting his body weight, and drawing his
legs up toward his chest-all the requisite skills necessary to pull off a
successful zipline glide. Despite best-laid plans, it turned out his sisters
commandeered the contraption as a gymnastics bar for doing cute flips
and penny drops. Eventually, just like the therapy exercises,* over time
this at-home practice became contrived, and for Jack, felt like work.

Seeking to leverage the precious "time between" scheduled therapy sessions, I scanned the environment for tasks that automatically

work the multitude of small muscles that needed strengthening. I turned to a mix of feigned and real requests for help to create practice opportunities. Every time a jar or can needed to be opened (and lots of times even when one didn't) I sat it in front of Jack saying I needed help from my strong boy. He would battle with the jar or can opener, but because it seemed like I assumed he could or should be doing these things, he did them.

Garlic crushing served as another convenient source of practice. Although my German heritage has its own culinary traditions, we are a family held together by Italian meals, recipes in which countless garlic cloves are a mainstay. My husband's father is Sicilian, and his mother schooled me in delicious Italian specialties like pasta with broccoli and anchovy, ricotta stuffed shells, and spaghetti sauce Sicilian style with short ribs and hardboiled eggs. Each of these requires a generous portion of garlic. If Jack was not in the kitchen, I would save the task and call him down from his room for the express purpose of squeezing the garlic crusher. I often overstated the number of cloves needed, which multiplied the practice. As a result, our family consumed an abundance of garlic and Jack got in a lot of reps. He became my official garlic crusher, and as an adult he continues to have that domestic distinction in our home.

These exchanges also served another powerful purpose. His brother and sisters, and any neighborhood kids who happened to be over for dinner or sleepovers, saw that Jack was the one I called upon to open jars, crush garlic, and take out heavy garbage bags. It created the impression at least among his siblings that Jack was "strong." I marveled to learn that it did not matter that this characterization did not exactly match their day-to-day experience of Jack. Over time we had successfully created the common expectation that their "big" brother would get the job done. It was not that Jack was performing any miraculous feats, but rather the power of suggestion implicit in my repeated requests that he do "this or that" for me, which led to the conclusion: "Jack must be strong and able or why would Mom always rely on him to open stuff, lift stuff, or carry heavy things?"

The everyday tasks of toting groceries, luggage, camping gear, and packages were strength-builders. As we went through the mundane machinations of life, I was hoping to show Jack that he was able do anything everyone else could. He was never protected or given less chores. If anything, I made a point of giving him more to lift, carry, and haul, figuring he needed exponentially more opportunities than the other kids who were born with muscle control and strength. There was inherent risk in this fearless attitude, and sometimes my blind optimism and fervor to show him that he "could" overshot my good sense.

When Jack was about seven, I remember him standing in front of the gaping yaw that was the open hatch of my mom van, eyeing the mountain of groceries for six. I pointed to two gallons of milk and said inconsequentially, "You've got this." Jack reluctantly picked up a gallon in each hand and started trudging down the sidewalk to our front door. For reasons unknown to me now, I had parked up the street from our house instead of in the driveway. I was conscious that the milk was heavy, but thought the plastic jug handles would provide sturdy handholds. I wanted to believe Jack could do it and I wanted him to see that I believed he could. I walked ahead carrying my own load of groceries, willing myself not to turn around to check on him as further display of my solid vote of confidence. That was when I heard it. A loud splat followed by a wet whoosh. Jack could not maintain his grasp and one of the plastic jugs burst to the ground, sending a narrow river of white cascading all the way down the sidewalk from our neighbor's house to our driveway. Jack was devastated and I was devastated when I saw him starting to cry.

My visceral need to avoid any suggestion that he had failed kicked in. "No worries, Jack, it's no big deal, we don't cry over spilt milk." But I feared he was not convinced. I felt all the worse because it was my overzealous request that had put him in this impossible situation. What if I would have given him something easier, safer, more comfortable to carry? What kind of mom would do such a thing? Where was my good sense? I roundly beat myself internally. Even as I mentally flagellated, there it was, that chorus in my head again, "safer, easier, more comfortable." I had definitely made a mistake, yet another miscalculation, but what if I erred on the other side, purposefully choosing the easiest tasks for Jack?

No, I would not retreat! If I started adapting and accommodating, what messages would that send, what experiences would he miss out on, and would he detect that his mom believed that there were things he was just not able to do? I convinced myself that the risks and inevitable disappointments of high expectations were worth it. I figured they, like the spilled milk now whitewashing the concrete, could be wiped away by a balance of positive, affirming, and strengthening experiences.

Or could they? I cannot say how Jack logged these experiences into his conscious and unconscious brain. What role did they play in the story he told himself? The fact is, I do not remember specifically asking how the broken milk jug made him feel. I just kept pushing forward, confident that I was right. I believed with all my being that having those closest to Jack behave as if they thought he was capable was far better in the long run than overprotection and calculated suggestions of caution; even if a few tears and a gallon of two percent had to be sacrificed in the process.

This is tough stuff because intrinsically bonded in parental DNA is the need to protect our kids from danger, embarrassment, and failure. My ongoing DIY therapies definitely produced more incidents like these, disappointments for sure. But I saw each of them as necessary casualties on the road to competence.

I am in no way advocating that families go it alone, devising their own DIY therapy regimes for their child. Discontinuing therapy, cancelling counseling sessions, or refusing services does not equate to high expectations nor does it dissolve a child's deficits. Although I admit not a day went by when I did not yearn to erase Jack's therapies and special services, like you click "delete" on an electronic calendar entry and the thing ceases to exist, as if the services and therapies themselves were the problem. If they would just go away, I could will my kid into "normal."

No, the problem is not the therapies designed to correct imbalances, improve processing speed, strengthen muscles, smooth speech, build tolerance, remediate behavior, and hone skills. Nor are the therapists the problem. Therapeutic fields are rife with caring individuals who possess unparalleled expertise, professional conviction, and heart. They have much to offer our children. However, an unintended consequence of therapies over time can be the messages they send our children. In Jack's case that was not a consequence I was willing to tolerate. Experience taught me to neither accept nor refuse a service blindly. I maintain that for the good of the child, parents need to become critical consumers of each therapy offered and have a plan for how to supplement, replace, or discontinue them over time.

With special services, more is not always better. In fact, over the long term, take it from this special education teacher: more is usually *not* better. Evidence the toll that too much helping, I believed, would eventually take on Jack. I am not saying that services and therapies are inherently bad. Just the opposite—these services often offer an important leg up that grants the child access. Services and supports can give a child a place at the table, so to speak; allow them to participate in activities, engage in important developmental experiences, or compete with their peers. In this sense, they are vital. However, I have cautioned parents to be aware that each additional service that they say "yes" to creates a scaffold that the child will have to disentangle himself from so that he can someday stand on his own.

As the primary advocate for their child, parents need to be ever on the look-out not only for helpers (aka people) who want to "do" for their child, but also for services, supports, and accommodations that "do" for their child. These can circumvent important growth opportunities and developmental experiences. Supports and services can unintentionally become ends in themselves if the scaffolding is not deliberately removed over time. I am reminded of those graffiti encrusted plank walkways surrounded by metal girding that we traipse along when our family is sightseeing in Manhattan. It is my assumption that city planners want the building facades obscured by these supports to stand on their own someday. In order to appreciate the full symmetry, strength, and grandeur of the building, the scaffolding eventually must be removed. So, too, with the scaffolds that special support systems construct around kids.

Weigh each offering in terms of what it gives the child access to, while being mindful of the artificial conditions that are forged to allow that access. For example, limiting the amount of time a child is expected to tolerate story circle may allow him to sit with peers, which is itself a reasonable goal. But be aware that he is missing important vocabulary and auditory comprehension opportunities. Not to mention, when story time is short circuited, he is not experiencing the predictable rising and falling action that makes a story "a story." Similarly, providing a child with pre-cut shapes may allow him to access the art activity, but it robs him of the sensation of moving the muscles in the center of his hand in concert to open and close the scissors. Having a child do half of the math problems may help him complete his assignment without frustration, but over time it seriously limits his tolerance for doing homework. These are tricky calculations because, although thoughtfully designed supports and services open doors for children, they can also have a crippling effect if left on autopilot.

I was an uber critical consumer of services being offered to my kid. I looked hard at what opportunities and skills the service purported to offer. If I thought he could better achieve that skill or get more authentic practice opportunities at home or in the natural course of doing life, I declined the service. Inevitability mistakes were made which I regret, feelings were bruised, and milk was spilled, but I rested in the knowledge that I was minimizing the scaffolds that would eventually need to come down for my son to make his way in the world.

Chapter 19

HEARTBREAKS
PART 1

Pretending does not make something so.

—Dorothy, *The Wizard of Oz.*

OUR CUL DE SAC IN SMALL-TOWN COLORADO was the place to party. It was full of "swingers" of the two- to nine-year-old variety, that is. Four houses hugged the bottom of our circle and in them resided a total of ten little kids. There was always traffic on the shared playset that was wedged between our homes. On any given day there were small posses of bikes, tricycles, cozy coops, and scooters circling the sidewalk. There were kickball tournaments, four-square competitions, and pint-sized Michelangelos creating pastel chalk masterpieces. I had thrown all four of my kids outside to get some peace (and a bit of work done) and had just hunkered down at my computer when I heard a knock at the door. It can't be a kid, I thought, they don't knock.

I opened the door to find my neighbor from three houses over, an esthetician married to a realtor, with three of her own high-school aged kids. It was out of place to see her on my front stoop. We were the friendly-at-a-distance kind of neighbors. Since her kids were older, we did not have much call to socialize.

I steeled myself as she spoke in a placid, I-am-just-here-to-help tone, that manages to be matter of fact and patronizingly apologetic at the same time. She started out slow.

"It's great that it's getting warmer and the kids are able to play outside, and, I mean, I want them to be able to be out there." My neighbor pauses and I think, 'No one treads across three yards just to reiterate the universal truth that "kids should be outdoors"'. This is when she revealed the real reason for her visit.

"I am always very careful, but I know that Jack is a little slow, and I just don't want him to be behind the car and not know to get out of the way when I'm backing out."

Her words hit me like a slap across the face. My neighbor betrayed all with just a single word, "slow." She thinks Jack is different, wrong, defective. She and her husband wave at us from across the yards, and we talk in smiling generalities about our kids, but they had made up their minds about Jack. Or maybe they hadn't, maybe they talk in hushed tones so their teens won't hear as they muse about what is "going on with that kid." In this moment, I detected in her voice something else: fear. She had pegged my kid as "different," he is slow and non-responsive and that makes him unpredictable in her mind.

I made a mental note. Jack and Livie are among the oldest kids in the cul de sac at the ripe old age of six. My close friend and neighbor Trish's three kids ranged in age from five down to two.

Among my own brood, Rosie was four and Will only three. Yet, this neighbor was not coming to me with her concerned citizen routine regarding little Will or Trish's daughter, who was tiny and nearly five years younger than Jack. She was not concerned that with the sheer number of kids playing out there, someone would get hurt. No, her particular worry was reserved just for Jack.

My neighbor's comments triggered a deep sadness within me. It registered, but I quickly replaced it with anger and indignation. This is stupid, I thought, Jack has Sotos syndrome, which causes muscle weakness and developmental and processing delays, but he is not deaf. I couldn't hold in my ire any longer, I interrupted my neighbor, who had convinced herself that she was justified in her public service mission.

"What do you do, Bridget?" I asked, "when the other kids are behind your car and you want to back out of your driveway?" She was taken aback by my abrupt question.

"I tell them to move." she offered, somehow still confused, not quite knowing where I was going.

"Then" I said, "tell Jack to move, too…he is not hard of hearing."

But I didn't stop there, I went even a step further, rejecting her categorization of Jack, by assuming that he was simply not following directions.

"And if Jack has been disrespectful or has not listened to you, I am really sorry, Bridget." My neighbor did not know quite what to do with this and began stammering.

"No, no that's not it…" she offered uneasily. Of course, I too knew that was not the problem, but now I found myself comfortably going over the top, with the hope that she would finally get it—she has not judged my kid correctly. I wanted her to travel back across those three yards a little less secure and self-satisfied with the box in which she had placed Jack.

This awkward moment passed quickly. The one where I subtly, or not so subtly, set my neighbor straight for assessing my son unfairly. We offered each other a couple of brief pleasantries and she was gone. However, I was not over it. Just to further set her prejudicial judgment of my kid askew, I decided to make Jack apologize. I called the kids in for lunch and while they were munching on mac and cheese with a few frozen peas thrown in just so I could call it "a healthy lunch," I told Jack, 'Mrs. Combs is worried that you have been playing behind her car and she is afraid she will hit you. You need to go over and ring her doorbell and tell her that you are sorry for playing behind her car, that you will be more careful, and that you won't do it again."

I may be judged as a bad mom, but I am not concerned at that moment that I am likely making Jack apologize for something he hasn't done. What is more important to me is that Bridget holds my kid to the same standard of behavior as all the other kids out in that chaotic circle. I want this for two reasons. First, no matter his gait, or processing speed, Jack has to learn to get out of the way of cars and now is as good a time as any for him to learn that life lesson. Second, I want to change her perception of my kid so that in any future interactions, no matter how few, she will treat Jack the same way she treats all the other little people in our fast and furious cul de sac gang.

My neighbor's comments left a wound, but it was more important to me that Jack not be subjected to differential treatment by adults, even a neighbor who, if this was a movie dramatizing his life, would be little more than a non-credited "extra." I know that there will be countless people who will judge and make conclusions about his ability or intellect. I also know that I will not be around all the time. But to the extent that I could prevent it, people minimizing my kid was not going to occur on my watch, or, if it did, as in this case, I would not allow these slights to stand unchallenged.

Jack was often prejudged and subjected to what I would call "wrong thinking." Of course, all humans judge. It makes us feel more secure if we can put tidy mental fences around things, particularly people and behaviors that we can't readily figure out. In my experience, people fall into three rough categories. First, you have the folks who offer their unsolicited assessments. I assume they are intending to make sense of Jack for themselves, but interestingly, they often did it out loud. In the case of these folks, I had to steel myself as they offered their assessments… "I assumed he has cerebral palsy" or they would say it matter-of-factly as an explanation for the unexplained "of course, because of his ADHD," as if their opinion was going to settle the matter once and for all, case closed.

Without fail these comments were followed by that familiar stab of pain. But I learned to redirect the pain to a private place because, when these comments occurred, it was my cue to go into tiger mom mode and set straight these poor souls who dared to make presumptions about my kid. I say tiger mom because rage is the emotion I mustered on the inside, but typically I responded by directing the conversation toward Jack's strengths, subtly putting them on notice that their assumptions were false.

The second type of folks were those who said nothing but who telegraphed their discomfort by avoiding interactions and excluding my kid. Finally, you had those glorious souls who got it. They sensed that I was confident that my kid belonged right where he was, and they went with it. They felt the positive expectations I had for him and they followed suit. One of them was my friend Stacy, who commented only after the writing of this book, "I thought there was something going on with Jack, but you always acted as if there wasn't, so I assumed as much." These people lightened my step. They made me almost giddy when we were together because they reinforced what I wanted to believe about my kid. They were the ones who were unafraid and curious. They asked questions like "What is Jack doing his project on?" "Is he going to be at the game?" They invited him to parties.

Vanquishing fear, for me, meant continually challenging common assumptions of what someone with Jack's diagnosis could or should do. In ways, both great and small, I made a point of encouraging activities that proved that Jack would not be defined by the circumstances of the label.

Field day was a hurdle in this regard. At school field day was just what the name implied, a day of friendly competition, of zany, Olympic-like challenges. They featured kid-inspired events like passing an orange held snuggly under the chin from team member to team member and stomping on balloons tied to each Olympian's leg until a sole victor remained standing with an inflated balloon. These unique contests coexisted with more traditional physical tests like tug of war, wheel-barrow and three-legged races. I recognized that Jack would be challenged and possibly overwhelmed by the games as they were all contests of balance, speed, coordination, strength, and endurance. However, for me it was more important that Jack saw that we believed he could do it.

I wagered that Jack would receive a far more dangerous message if we hesitated or opted him out. The message: You can't do it or, you are part of a special class of beings who don't get to try these things… was a message I could not risk. Besides, what transcended label, diagnosis, and limitation was the fact that Jack was a kid. For any kid the trappings of field day, trading a stuffy classroom for fresh air and virtually unlimited cherry and blueberry popsicles was just too darn fun to miss. With that enticement, I sent him off to school. As always, this pressed my fear button, but I encouraged him to venture out holding fast to my commitment: if his twin sister was going, Jack was too.

When the day passed without incident, I breathed a sigh of relief, happy to have it behind me. My happiness was short circuited however when a good friend mentioned how her daughter, Maddie, Livie's friend, sought Jack out on the field and took on the task of serving as his personal helper throughout the day. Entombed in my own pain, I peered out beyond my own battered feelings just long enough to "see" her. As a fellow parent she possessed her own need at that moment to have her child acknowledged. "Maddie is such a caring girl," I offered the mom sunnily. After all, her kid had engaged in a compassionate act. I just wished that it was not my son who was on the receiving end of her good deeds.

Had Maddie's support truly helped Jack participate in the sporting events, or had she come to the rescue out of her own extraordinary need to help? I would never know for sure, but regardless, I was disappointed. I don't know what I expected; maybe that the excitement and electric vibe of the day would ignite his slack muscles and he would surprise everyone with his vigor. Maybe I just wanted him to pass unnoticed as one in the small army of elementary Olympians. This is one of a hundred decisions I questioned: Did participating in field day do more harm than good? I finally rationalized that regardless of whether he stood out, struggled, or failed, he still was out there, feeling the sun on his back, experiencing the adrenaline that comes with competition. My son, just another pint-sized athlete, all of them united as the juice dribbles down their tiny chins, those popsicles, the real prize and the final conquest of the day.

Chapter 20

SHOOTING
HOOPS

You miss 100% of the shots you don't take.

—Wayne Gretsky

IF WEAK MUSCLES COULD BE STRENGTHENED, then logically
exercising them was the obvious path to improvement. Weekly,
the physical therapist focused on important foundations like body
awareness, core stabilization, balance, eye-hand coordination, and
strengthening. Jack practiced walking on a line, pointing at a target
and throwing a bean bag, and navigating uneven surfaces. By 2nd
grade, we were just going through the motions, dutifully making
the trip every week. He did his best to comply with the therapist's
well meaning, if not a little awkward, game of Simon Says. "Jack,
stand on the tilting platform." "Jack, point to the bullseye with one
arm and throw the bean bag with the other." "Jack, step between
the rings."

The therapist was creative and worked hard to normalize the exercises, to make them mimic typical tasks a kid would do. However, despite her efforts at making them fun and Jack's efforts at compliance, it still amounted to him doing exercises in a small carpeted office space in our local children's clinic where, in adjacent rooms, other children were perched on examining tables waiting to get booster shots or throats swabbed. My impatience grew. The medical setting bothered me, but I calmed myself with the thought that the therapy was targeting critical foundations of core strength, stability, and muscle memory. It was the right stuff. What was really nagging me was that it wasn't enough of the right stuff. I had long believed that Jack needed mega doses of practice, countless repetition to develop strength, coordination, and muscle memory. Reasonably, in a single session, the therapist could get him to throw a weighted bean bag toward a target maybe 10-15 times and then repeat the process with the same number of reps across exercises. At this rate, I feared that Jack would never catch up.

In my imaginings getting Jack into a sport was the answer. This solution addressed two of my concerns. First, it was "normal." Typical seven-year-olds swam and did Tae Kwan Do, they played soccer and T-ball…they did not sit in clinic waiting rooms waiting to toss bean bags and balance on platforms. Second, I had never been overly sporty myself, but I knew enough to know that when it came to sports, repetition and practice were the coin of the realm. Kids say, 'I have to go to soccer practice, I have to go to swim practice, I have to go to track practice." Something that was all about "practice" was exactly what Jack needed, I convinced myself.

Jack had participated in pee-wee soccer with his sister when we were still living in California. The sport requires stamina, speed, and coordination, but it also requires the player, even a pee-wee one, to stabilize on one leg while aiming and kicking the ball with the other one. No matter that they were preschoolers, the divide between Jack and the other players was significant. He trailed far behind, walking more than running on the field. He avoided the ball and getting into tight situations with other players challenged his precarious sense of balance. The experience spoke for itself and even I did not have the resolve to put him through that again; the gap was too great.

Now Jack was four years older and I lit on T-ball, surmising that this time would be different than the last. Here was my thinking: in T-ball there would be no one crowding him. He could hit the ball from a stationary point, and while it required speed, the bursts of running were confined to relatively short distances. Players ran from base to base but did not have to run throughout the game. I became enthralled with the idea that there was a sport out there which revolved solely around a ball sitting quietly on a peg literally waiting to be hit. I focused on the fact that baseball players run in an orderly fashion, a predictable distance to a predictable spot aptly called "base." This seemed infinitely preferable to relentlessly chasing and attempting to kick a moving target. We signed Jack up for a team and got all the gear.

Great thinking, but I could not have been more wrong. It turns out that baseball, and even its "training wheels" version, T-ball, both require a significant amount of eye hand coordination. Jack could not make his eyes focus on the ball and looked away as he swung the bat in front of him, missing the ball most of the time. The bat was awkward for him, not to mention the pressure of having all eyes on him when up at bat. To his credit, and at the urging of his over-zealous mom, Jack gave it a try. But he was frustrated and he hated it. I got the vibe from the other sports moms and dads that they did not appreciate me acting as cheerleader encouraging my kid to hang in there. A couple of the parents I knew from the neighborhood looked at me like I was a cross between a delusional simpleton not in touch with the obvious reality that this was not working, and a maternal monster who was intent on torturing her child. With all the optimism of the insane, I clung to my supposition that T-ball was a better match for Jack than sports predicated on speed and endurance. That is, until it became obvious, even to this queen of the growth mindset, that T-ball was not within Jack's reach, not yet and not at age 7.

I was torn. While I knew we had to move on from T-ball, I worried about the message that quitting would send. Finally, I agreed to raise the white flag after a few painful games. I began to realize that in my zeal to find something that would afford him regular movement, practice, and strengthening, I was violating my own belief in creating challenges that reside within a child's zone of "proximal development". Forget zones, T-ball was not even in Jack's zip code. It was producing exactly what I did not want, instead of normalizing my kid it was making him an oddity.

This particular chapter in my tale of high expectations is one that is especially painful for me to recount. I want to squirm away from these memories; put distance between them and the parent who I believe I am. Was I so blinded by my theories of normalization, my prescription of practice; so locked into my belief that high expectations were the answer that I would put my kid in excruciatingly humiliating positions? It gives me no pleasure to say this, but "you bet I did." This was my thinking at the time: "we are talking about six- and seven-year-olds playing on a recreational team; this is the time for fostering new experiences and developing preferences. I assumed that Jack would be out there with kids displaying a wide range of abilities, and I knew he was not the only kid who was trying on the sport for the first time. But even so, the chasm was too wide.

This was just one of many miscalculations in our quest to find a physical pursuit that could provide endless repetitions for Jack's slack muscles. At four, Jack's little brother Will was somewhat of a fish, so I signed both boys up for swimming lessons. I knew that heat and humidity exacerbate low tone whereas cold generally tightens muscles. In Jack's case, this generalization held true. It seemed like the cool, chlorinated water of the pool activated and tightened up his muscles. Despite the fact that the pool offered a degree of buoyancy, swimming turned out to be an agonizing workout for Jack. To further complicate matters, he did not have the muscle strength necessary to lift himself out of the pool, and so had to inch himself around the tiled edge to the nearest ladder as other kids were effortlessly hoisting themselves out of the water. Although Will advanced quickly, Jack was not improving. Swimming, it seemed was not the answer either.

My husband has unflatteringly called me a "bulldog" when I sink my teeth into an idea. Living up to my reputation, even with all these miscalculations, I was not ready to give up. I still maintained that the idea of "sport," an activity that offered practice, discipline, and repetition, was the most effective vehicle for Jack to build muscle strength and endurance, and to fill in developmental gaps.

Dejected but not defeated, I began rethinking my original proposition. I realized that I was so fixated on choosing a sport that featured less of what Jack could not do, (e.g., T-ball required less endurance, balance and speed than soccer) that I was overlooking what was pleasing and potentially motivating for Jack. Perhaps instead of being hyper-focused on my son's limitations, we could attempt to identify strengths, advantages, and potential motivators. I began to seek to match Jack with a sport that could be fun, rather than marching him through a regimen of confounding, frustrating, and defeating experiences. Up until then fun had not been in the equation for him or me.

In my 20's, fresh out of graduate school, I took a job in Boston at the New England Center for Autism. I was building a vocational program for students who had little purposeful activity in their lives. Although much of the time was spent training students in pre-vocational skills like wiping cafeteria tables and stapling papers, my favorite part of the work involved creating job matches. I reached out to numerous area businesses including Puma Tennis Shoe, Poland Springs Bottled Water, Burger King, and CGT Insurance Company to create partnerships.

The other teachers on my team and I would break down the jobs into their component parts, called "task analyses." For example, the job of bottle washer at Poland Springs involved lifting water cooler-sized plastic bottles off a palette, squeezing the handle on a metal sprayer that hung from the ceiling, spraying the inside and outside of the bottles, and placing them on a clean palette. A stocker at Puma Tennis Shoe had to stand in the backroom of a retail store and open big boxes, slide the clear plastic off 8-to-12-piece sets of athletic tee shirts, hoodies, shorts, or running pants, and hang each piece individually on a white plastic hanger.

In order to create satisfying job matches, we sought to fit these isolated job tasks with the preferences, interests, and proclivities of each student. If a student enjoyed water play, we would let them squeeze the trigger on the metal sprayer and experience the satisfaction of seeing the water cascade through the bottle, cleansing and shining its insides. If a student liked feeling texture in his or her hands, we would let them try unloading the boxes of nubby fleece, slick rayon, and cool cotton tee shirts. Sometimes in these trials we would hit upon a job task that resonated with a student.

We were in the business of drawing upon the strengths, interests, and predispositions of students, many of whom did not speak. Sometimes we leveraged predilections that would have been considered distractions or even inappropriate, such as a student going up to a stranger and running their hands over a silky shirt or furry coat. Sometimes, but not all the time, our matches transformed these seemingly quirky preoccupations into satisfying, paid work. When we got it right, our matches helped these young people become productive members of their communities and made their families proud beyond telling.

Now, as Jack's mom, I borrowed upon this experience to identify a sports activity for him. What natural proclivities could Jack draw upon in finding his match? It seemed like Jack had to put so much effort into everything. It was hard for me to watch, especially when he struggled with things that came as naturally to other kids as falling off a log; things like jumping over puddles and hanging on monkey bars.

The one thing that Jack did not have to work hard at was being tall—he just was. In the height department, Jack was a natural. Fast growth was a defining feature of Sotos, which while making him a lot taller than other kids, was also a complicating factor in developing coordination and stability. Even so, it was height that made us finally light on basketball, the sport where a tall kid has a built-in advantage. In addition, the large, ribbed ball was easier to grasp and hold on to, especially compared to a baseball, which was significantly smaller and included the impossible complication of a glove serving as an intermediary between hand and ball. Initially, I had dismissed basketball out of hand because of the need for speed. All the basketball players I had seen were fast. But while it requires running, a basketball court is significantly shorter than a soccer field. As I continued to mull it over in my mind, the plusses began stacking up. Jack wilted in heat and humidity, so an indoor, climate-controlled gym was preferable to an oppressively sun-drenched soccer field. The timing also worked—two 20-minute halves in a kid's basketball game required less stamina than an endless 2 ½ hour baseball game. There emerged an intuitive rightness to this. Basketball held promise. Jack could practice grasping the basketball even in the house and we could play catch indoors. From this idea a well-spring of hope emerged and we were off to the races, or should I say to the courts?

Jack could scarcely toss a ball more than a couple of feet in the air when I lobbied my sweet husband to buy and install a regulation size basketball hoop in our front driveway. At the time, Jack treated the basketball the same way he had the T-ball: he instinctively averted his gaze. This was true whether I tossed him a ball, an orange, or a bean bag. The physical therapist explained it as a self-preservation reflex, "If you do not have a firm foundation and someone throws something at you, it disturbs your sense of balance," So Jack preferred not to see things coming at him.

Like a sword that cuts two ways, the same syndrome that compromised his balance also offered the mixed blessing of overgrowth. In addition to the fact that most 2nd grade boys barely reached Jack's shoulder, he also scored one more win in the overgrowth department, Jack had big hands. Both could be an advantage in basketball. Even though now the network of small muscles in the soft center of his palm were too slack to tauntly pull his fingers together to grasp the basketball, those lanky hands held promise for the future.

We began practicing holding and tossing the ball. Jack was far from independent. We contemplated enrolling him in a special needs basketball league. However, a happy circumstance intervened causing us to go another way. I saw an online flyer advertising a "sports camp" offered at the local university. The camp promised a sampling of various sports and activities for elementary-aged children. Archery, kickball, flag football, volleyball, and basketball with a little arts and craft time built-in for good measure. Some parents used it as glorified day care. Moms and dads could feel satisfied that their kid was occupied in healthy pursuits at a learned institution while they were away at work. What's not to like? I was drawn to the camp because it was another way for Jack to continue sampling potential sports. As I waited in the pickup line one day, a good-natured undergraduate camp counselor reported that "Jack liked basketball." I had no idea of the basis for this commentary. Reflecting now I realize it could have just been a throw-away line, an off-hand comment meant to satisfy an expectant parent. However, at the time, I mused that if Jack could participate in this camp, then why not give the recreation leagues a go?

And so, in this circuitous way, over time Jack exchanged physical therapy sessions for basketball practice. Once in place, this exchange of sport for therapy led to others. For example, we found Tae Kwan Do to work on balance and enlisted a personal trainer to work on strength. Over the years we made a series of trades to address deficits with activities rather than with formal therapy sessions.

I am certainly not insinuating that sport cures disability. But I am confident that there are strengths within every child, no matter the disability, that can be recognized and exploited for good.

Chapter 21

JUDGE NOT...

We are learning to see, unlearning to judge.

—Richard Elmore

WE HAD TRAVELED TO RUSSIA back in 2003 and adopted Will, a sinewy ball of energy. When he arrived to take his place in the kid pecking order, he was nearly three, Jack and Livie were almost six and Rosie was a precocious five. As our family grew in the rarefied mountain air and Colorado sunshine, so did the population of our school district. Newly drawn district boundary lines dictated that Jack and Livie would be shuttled from the school they had known since kindergarten, to a new school for 5th grade, and then to yet another new school for 6th grade. All this jumping around caused us to look seriously at a school in the district that bordered ours.

There was a lot that appealed to me both professionally and personally. The school was small and housed kindergarten through 8th grade (K-8) in one building, as opposed to their current school, which boasted five classes per grade level and only went to 5th grade.

I had the K-8 experience myself as a uniform-clad Catholic school girl in the 1970's. Professionally, I had worked in K-8 schools during my time in Minneapolis and I saw firsthand that pre-teens generally did better in smaller, more accountable K-8 schools than they did in large middle schools, regardless of wealth or race.

Nationally, I had also watched with interest as the Philadelphia Public Schools and other school systems divested from large middle and junior high models and converted many elementary and middle schools to smaller K-8 buildings. Science prompted this K-8 band-wagon. New developments in brain learning showed that the young adolescent brain benefits more from security and nurture than choice and autonomy. This research backs what I already believed about tweens and young teens. Sure, big schools had all the bells and whistles and offered an abundance of course choices and extra-curriculars. But in my professional experience, kids grew more confident and secure from the nurturing offered in the relatively more intimate, family environment of K-8 schools. These virtues I valued more than the seemingly limitless course choices that were the lure of large schools.

In fact, if the fate of all middle schoolers were in my hands, and I got to pick between confidence and security and Mandarin Chinese and Biology, I would pick confidence and security every time. In my opinion, there is plenty of time for specialized courses in high school when brains are a little more mature. Finally, research aside, unofficially and unprofessionally, I would also say that middle schools always felt to me like teeming cesspools of unchecked hormones where kids could too easily fly under the radar of the adults in charge.

This, minus the part about cesspools and hormones, was the elevator speech I offered to friends when they inquired as to why we were swapping school districts. But honestly, a deeper reason for considering the change was because I thought it would benefit Jack. Even though Mrs. Marshall had moved on and we had been blessed with many gifted teachers and therapists, I remained unhappy with the sheer number of special education services Jack received within our home school district. He was in 3rd grade and had been labeled since pre-kindergarten. There were no signs of him shedding services. Those in charge had not taken the time to determine whether or not he still needed all the supports he had. Teachers and students at his elementary school viewed him as "different" despite my best efforts to will him into normalcy and the blissful invisibility that comes with being just average.

For all these reasons, we bit the bullet and committed to exiting our home school district in favor of a school in the smaller neighboring district. Rosie and Will, because they were younger, already had spots secured at Abigail Franklin K-8. If we were going to make the switch, now would be our best chance to get Jack and Livie in. Riding on Rosie's and Will's coattails with the extra boost siblings get, they would be able to enter as 4th graders. I imagined that the uncomplicated, familial atmosphere of the small school was the golden ticket Jack needed. It could allow him to escape the clutter of special services his label dictated, not to mention the stigma that I believed was being increasingly engrained over time. We filled out the paperwork, requested letters of recommendation from Livie's and Jack's current 3rd grade teachers, and both were added to the district wait list. With Rosie and Will already enrolled, it was just a matter of time until Jack and Livie would be offered a space. I just hoped it would happen before the school year started because I did not know how I'd feel about plucking them out of a classroom in which they were already settled.

I did not have to sweat that dilemma. We got the call one morning just as the lazy days of summer were dwindling. There were two spots in fourth grade and two fourth grade classes in the school. Jack and Livie would each be assigned to one of them. The kids would be given a placement test so that their new teachers would have a sense of where they were academically.

My worry that other people would view Jack as "different" was ever present, just under the surface, like that splinter in the fatty pad of your finger—you know it is there, you know it will eventually have to come out, and you know there will be pain. Of course, there would be a test. But just like their current school, Abigail Franklin was a public institution. I had even memorized the statement inscribed on the glossy brochure in small but serious black type under the freshly scrubbed faces of students clearly enjoying what they were learning. "Abigail Franklin is a tuition-free public school and does not discriminate on the basis of race, ethnicity, or disability." It was there in writing, and so it must be true.

The day I brought the kids in for a tour with the principal and to take the test, I tried to view Jack as others might see him. I was acutely aware of Jack's awkward gait, slightly out of sync movements, and the fact that he still hadn't fully kicked the oral stimulation habit of putting his fingers in his mouth. His articulation was not great, his speech somewhat lazy and slurred when his muscles tired. He often did not look at people when he spoke. Our family and others, people who knew Jack well, appreciated his goofy sense of humor and his kind demeanor. Many saw that he possessed a depth of understanding, not apparent in first impressions. It was like a rare gift not cheaply displayed, but exquisite to those who experienced it. They also knew he was a voracious reader. But, of course, the principal would know nothing of these things. I only hoped that she would be disarmed by the sweet smile that lit up Jack's whole face when it flashed.

Principal Gibbons, a pleasant older woman who appeared caring in a steadfast, rules-first kind of way, greeted us at the front doors. The tour was not overly intimidating; Franklin was a much smaller school compared to the one the kids were leaving, but still the space was new, and they were curious about the classrooms where they would be spending roughly seven hours a day. I was aware that Jack was lagging on the tour, something he did often. Was his endurance waning or was he just being noncompliant?

The tour concluded at the principal's office. The time had come for the test. Principal Gibbons explained little about it other than it was called the STAR test. (Would uninitiated parents assume from the name that this test was designed to detect academic "stars"?) I knew the acronym stood for something but for the life of me I could not remember exactly what it was. As we waited, I mused, *why the STAR test?* I wasn't trying to get them an audition on *The Voice* or get them a slab of stamped concrete outside Grauman's Chinese Theater. Who named these things? Now it came to me: STAR stood for Standardized Testing and Reporting. It was merely an achievement test that compared kids across the country; a measure that captured how a child performed on a predetermined set of tasks at the moment they took the test and nothing more. Star or no star, this thing possessed no magical power to discern innate ability within children.

Principal Gibbons ushered Livie into her office and left Jack and me sitting in chairs in the vestibule. Was she choosing Livie first because she was already more comfortable with her, or was I being paranoid? After 15 minutes that seemed more like an hour, Livie came through the closed door. She was tentative, not smiling. I had already gotten signals that she wanted to stay at her current school. Since kindergarten she had moved through the grades at Tremont Elementary without incident. She played soccer, loved Brownies, and had a reliable group of little girl friends. She had no desire to rock the boat by moving to this new school. Now her expression glared at me, "This is all your fault."

Was I sacrificing one child's happiness for the promise of bettering life for her twin? Wasn't that the subject of a bestselling book? Again, I rebuked myself for being paranoid. This was a great school and Livie would learn to love it, just as Rosie and Will had before her.

Now it was go time. Jack was ushered into Mrs. Gibbons' quarters. He was alone. I was not in the room to jump in to correct misperceptions, to provide convenient explanations, finish Jack's sentences, or fill in awkward spaces in the conversation. When Jack's 15 minutes (a 15 minutes that spanned an eternity) were spent, the office door opened and Mrs. Gibbons emerged from her office with Jack leading the way. A consummate professional, she did not offer any indication one way or another regarding how either child performed on the assessment or what she was thinking. She escorted us back to whence we came with a string of concluding niceties that I did not track and we were back to the car and on our way.

Not so bad, I thought; Jack passed. I was walking on air. I related the visit to my husband with cheery details because now with the test and its associated pressures in the rearview mirror, the experience felt warmer and more embracing, less stilted than it had at the time. Having cleared this hurdle, we mentally prepared for the move. This school required uniforms, a touch I liked, because it avoided the inevitable clothing battles that would have been in my future if we would have stayed put. I would have to get both kids the blue, white, burgundy and tan pieces that made up the dress code at Abigail Franklin. I was nagged by the fact that Livie had not warmed to the switch; maybe I could sway her with a new backpack, I thought. My idyllic vision of all four of my kids learning together was coming true. There would be one school handbook to learn, one pick-up and drop-off point, and one school at which to focus any volunteer efforts. All would be encompassed within one building, at least until high school, which felt light years away. This was a glorious simplification compared to what had become a tangle of overlapping kid activities and therapies. It felt normal.

Two nights later we got a call. It was Mrs. Gibbons asking about some nondescript form that I had not filled out in the twins' admission packet. Could I come in to fill it out? The breath returned to my body. It was nothing, an overlooked form.

"Yes, of course, I will be in." Then, just as we were about to hang up, she threw out one more question, nonchalantly, as one would toss out a used tissue. She wondered if Jack would have trouble with the challenging Core Knowledge curriculum at Franklin.

The question perplexed me. It was true that the twins' current school, Tremont Elementary, was known more for its friendliness than its rigor, but Mrs. Gibbons had the written recommendations from both third-grade teachers. Thinking I misheard, I retraced her words in my head. She didn't "wonder" if the twins would struggle with the challenging Core Knowledge curriculum; she wondered precisely if JACK would have trouble. Then I became suspicious of the pretense for the call itself, an unsigned form? Didn't the school have a secretary and admissions assistant who handled such matters?

Was "form signing" merely a rouse for a call which held another purpose. I silently recalled from memory the statement on the glossy brochure, "Abigail Franklin is a Free Public School and does not discriminate on the basis of race, ethnicity, or disability."

This was a public school. I had worked in public schools for almost 20 years. Public schools could not turn kids away, that was the law. Maybe this was her way of editorializing about what she perceived as Jack's awkwardness. A little jab, but I could handle it. I had endured worse in my son's short life and was not dissuaded. I put the comment out of my mind.

Until it happened again.

Always one to jump into the deep end with both feet and no life preserver, I had gotten involved at the school not long after Rosie and Will started at Abigail Franklin. It made sense, two of my kids were already there and I hoped the other two would soon be joining them. I had applied for a school board vacancy. This would be a good use of my volunteer hours; I would be able to devote all my time to one school. Possibly because of my education background or possibly because no one wanted the job, I was inducted into the Board of Education.

The Board conducted its regular course of business in the library on the 2nd Monday in August. After the meeting, as board members were mingling with the teachers, administrators, and parents present, Mrs. Gibbons and I found ourselves alone. When no one else was within ear shot, she offered once again, this time in person and with her always helpful countenance, "I just don't know how Jack is going to fare with our challenging Core Knowledge curriculum."

There it was again, but not over a cell phone connection where it could be mistaken for something vague, off-hand, harmless. She put it out there smiling, in brilliant technicolor. Nope, this was not an innocent comment made in passing to help prepare my kids for the rigors of 4th grade. This was prejudicial language selected precisely to let me know that Jack was less than welcome at Franklin. There was no other explanation for what I had heard this second time around. Mercifully, we were interrupted by another board member, something about the length of uniform skirts or was it future of the newly adopted Math curriculum? No matter, the interruption provided a welcome distraction as I found myself utterly and impossibly without words.

In my professional life, I had fought hard against the institutionalized racism that drove achievement gaps between black, brown, and white kids. And now it was happening to my kid, except the prejudice was not prompted by color, but perceived ability. I thought about the systematic pain and injustice that has been heaped on entire classes of people in our country since the time of slavery. I imagined that this was how landlords and realtors maintained obscenely pristine, segregated neighborhoods in the 1970's, 1980's, and 1990's. A realtor in a crisp suit offering, with kindness a little too polished, "You wouldn't want this property, the taxes are so high." Now I was feeling a measure of that directed toward my kid.

The more I thought about it, the madder I got. I ruminated on the drive home and connected with Mrs. Gibbons that very night. As I sat in my driveway, I called her out on what I saw as an illegal practice.

"Kim (I used her first name), you have come to me twice now expressing your concerns about how Jack will do at Abigail Franklin. Since Jack and Livie are twins, and since both have come with letters of recommendations from their previous teachers, and you have not expressed concern for Livie's performance, I can only surmise that you are trying to discourage us from sending Jack. Is it because of his special education label? His looks? Or simply because you do not perceive him to be Abigail Franklin material?" Silently, I wondered if it was one or a combination of all three.

Now on a roll, I started in, "I am sure the citizens of this town would be interested to learn…". I finished in my head, but she knew exactly where I was going, "that citizens would be interested to learn that their taxes were going to support a public school that is discriminating against children." With this truncated threat, I curtly ended the call, not giving her time to respond.

Those accusations, if made in public could lose a principal her job. Did she see the headlines the same way I saw them? "Parent exposes discriminatory school screening practices." This would be red meat for the school district that had long accused the school of favoring kids who could enhance school test scores. My words must have registered because hardly a day went by before I got another call from Mrs. Gibbons. There was no mention of the previous night's call, and this time she did not express any concerns about Jack falling short. This time she was backpedaling as fast as she could to put distance between herself and her earlier statements.

She led with, "Jack will be a welcome addition here at Abigail Franklin and our school will be better for having him." The rest of the brief conversation was peppered with platitudes about the high caliber of students and staff at the school.

"Okay, that's more like it," I thought. Still, I could not help but wonder about how she really viewed my kid and if her views would spill over to how she treated him. I wondered how she treated other kids with differences who dared to enter her hallowed halls. I wondered to what extent "having the right kind of student" and "test scores" motivated this woman's administrative decisions. Keeping my ear to the ground, I learned from another parent of a child with a hearing impairment that she had also endured the principal's loaded questions and innuendo about her son's ability to "make it" at Franklin.

My world view, and that of our constitutional framers, is that public schools exist to serve the public good of creating an educated citizenry. I privately wondered if Mrs. Gibbons was the "right kind of principal" for my four kids (or any of the other kids) at the school. Fortunately, as a board member I figured that I could keep an eye on her. After all, she had revised her statements when pressed and I was not about getting people fired.

As it turned out, I did not have to wonder for very long about Mrs. Gibbons' motivations, because a scant four weeks later she announced at a board meeting that she was leaving. She was giving notice so that she could assume a position as lead administrator at a private school in another state. As a relative newbie on the Board, I maintained a low profile while our soon-to-be outgoing principal made her remarks. I listened stoically as she received, in turn, each board member's congratulations, gratitude, and expressions of sorrow at her leaving. I am sure I weighed in with obligatory, if not quite enthusiastic well wishes, but I don't remember exactly what I said. I am not one to hold a grudge, and from my perspective, Mrs. Gibbons' exit was a relief. Perhaps the school to which she was relocating had a mission statement and policies that would allow her to select the students she considered most "suitable." I will never know for certain if my veiled threat to "out" her discriminatory stance was part of what prompted her abrupt move or if this was a merely the next step on a carefully planned career path.

Now, when I take the long view that only time and distance provide, I can see that Mrs. Gibbons was not a bad person. In terms of other measures of principalship, she would have been considered quite a good administrator. I believe that she truly felt she was the standard bearer in a school that had earned a reputation for being "good." Perhaps it was her feeling that my kid was just one in a long line of questionable applicants whom she viewed as paving a slippery slope toward mediocrity for Abigail Franklin--a version of "you let all these awkward kids with IEP's in and there goes the neighborhood" mindset. Regardless of her intentions, my child had been judged and sentenced based on his appearance, the suggestion that he had an IEP (she had not even seen it) and a 15-minute standardized test.

The question remained: Should such measures be allowed to be the last word in determining the potential of an 8-year-old? Here again I had seen the cruel face of discrimination cast its heavy shadow on my kid and it made me shudder. Was Jack destined to encounter all manner of *Mrs. Gibbonses* throughout his life? Perhaps, but what I knew was that, at least in this case, Jack was in…and the one who sought to judge him was out.

In the field of education, I am what some might call a learned person, armed with graduate degrees in educational psychology, and just enough school law classes to be dangerous. If this was an investment debacle, an insurance scam, or a medical malpractice concern, I would be as defenseless as a babe in the woods. But in this case, I had the bona fides and social capital to protect my kid from unfair discrimination. But what of another parent of another child who looked differently, acted differently, or learned differently? How would they fare against the likes of a Mrs. Gibbons?

What if this parent was unschooled in the fact that while principals have impressive titles, they are people first and foremost, who are fallible and can fall prey to fearful, prejudicial impulses just like the rest of us mere mortals? What if a parent's, grandparent's, or foster parent's respect for authority or reverence for credentials led them to submit to the will of a discriminatory school leader? What if the person in authority caused them to doubt their child, to believe that she was less capable, in need of protection, and/or required some different type of school environment? And then, what if, in turn, these parents, grandparents, or foster parents treated their child differently? In the short run, these kids would be successfully counseled out of schools, programs, and activities from which they may have benefitted. But one could also imagine more damaging consequences if cycles of treating the child differently continued over the long term. Fully acknowledging the limitations of comparing humans to rats, even cute rats, I am reminded of the subjects of Rosenthal & Fode's studies and many others, which showed that when caregiver beliefs diminished, performance diminished. It is not a big leap to conclude that these kids may fare less well over time because of the altered expectations important adults have for them.

This experience, and so many others, cemented my role as advocate for my son. I had to provide a buffer between him and a whole cast of characters, including well-meaning neighbors, skilled therapists, caring teachers, and high-minded principals who threatened to treat my kid like he was a second-class citizen. Furthermore, if these types were lurking about in our narrow orbit, who else was waiting out there to have their turn at shaping my kid's view of himself as different, awkward, special, slow, retarded, you pick the pejorative. I became even more firmly aligned with the growing body of research that shows that what we believe about people can actually affect who they become. If beliefs affect behavior and behavior changes people, then the beliefs and behaviors that my kid was exposed to were all-important. The stakes were far too high to think or behave otherwise.

Chapter 22

HEROES

"But what could possibly go wrong now?"
asked Harold. "FREEZE!" shouted the Chief of Police.
"You guys are under arrest!"

—Dav Pilkey, *Captain Underpants and the*
Preposterous Plight of the Purple Potty People

FOR JACK AND LIVIE, changing schools amounted to uprooting them from the place they had known since kindergarten. For me, it meant swallowing a little attitude from Livie, who liked her old life and friends at Tremont and disrupting friendships with other parents who had sprouted way back when as we all leaned together against the century-old, yellow-bricked walls waiting for our kindergarteners to emerge from their classrooms. This did not feel good, but I rationalized that in a year when new district boundaries went into effect, friendships would be disrupted, and change would happen anyway…I had just gotten in front of it. Further, I comforted myself that this move would be better for everyone. The Winking offspring were in the same school, all of them students at Abigail Franklin, learning together in their tan, navy, and burgundy regalia. This is what I had longed for, all my kids together, with all the goodness that went along with that. I imagined them high-fiving each other as they passed in the hall, looking out for one another on the playground, secretly comforted by the knowledge that their brothers and sisters were close by. I had zero evidence that those high fives ever occurred, but for me it was enough to think that we had set up conditions where they might.

Will was in first grade and Rosie was in second and Jack and Livie were placed in two different fourth-grade classrooms. Special Education staff from the two school districts talked, and paper and electronic files were transferred, enabling Jack's label and IEP to follow him to the new school.

As it turned out, it was not long before my suspicions about this school in a smaller, less well-funded school district were confirmed. The special education machinations here were newly established and less ensconced in bureaucracy. As a newish school there was not as much standard operating procedure, not as much codified support from the school district, and with fewer kids overall, there were less structures in place. To be sure, there were speech pathologists, occupational therapists, and psychologists to provide support and special education teachers assigned to fulfill the IEPs of students with labels. But there was less system oversight. Here, we were in the wild west when it came to regulation, and, absent established precedents, teachers were proceeding in their classrooms as each one thought best.

Jack's fourth grade teacher, Mrs. Grimm, was anything but. She was a spirited, blonde woman with whom I felt an instant affinity.

She was flamboyant and capricious in ways that favored kids. One day, part way through the fall semester, Mrs. Grimm tipped me off to the fact that Jack was going to receive an award so I should not miss the upcoming 4th grade recognition ceremony. This was elementary school and students were not only honored for grades, but a host of awards were also bestowed for other noteworthy accomplishments like "most books read," "math facts mastered," and "highest integrity." These accolades involved presenting each recipient with a brightly colored printed certificate accompanied by an effusive speech delivered by the nominating teacher.

Both 4th grade classes united for the ceremony. Jack's classroom hosted the event on that fateful day, and when I arrived, I found it packed with twice the usual number of students. In addition, the back of the room was dotted with the proud parents of "unsuspecting" honorees, waiting with their phones poised to get the best shot of their child flashing one of the highly coveted certificates. I tried to look nonchalant, offering whispered congratulations to the other parents as the recipients made their way up to the front of the class.

Mrs. Grimm had given me the heads up over a week ago. By now my excitement should have quelled, but still I was anxious. She began, "This award goes to a student who works really hard every day. I have seen him put so much effort into everything he does… Jack Winking, the 'Most Improved' Award goes to you, come on up." This was no surprise, but when he hustled up to the front of the room and was handed the certificate and asked to freeze for a photo-op with the teacher, was I proud? You bet your sweet cardstock paper I was! Pete had to work, but I was there, camera in hand, documenting every sweet moment. Until I exited the front doors, my face was plastered with a smile that could not be erased.

It was not until much later, at night, that I allowed my mind to drift toward the negative. Had Jack really earned this award or was this a gratuitous hand-out, a manufactured achievement so that the "different" kid would not be sidelined? My thoughts raced back to when the teacher announced his name. I wondered, among the 50-some kids assembled, was Jack really the "most improved"? I fought the tendency toward cynical speculation. *Quit complaining,* I told the skeptic in me, what better award for Jack than one that acknowledges effort and perseverance. Here is an award that promotes the precise dispositions that are necessary for growth. I was the one waging the holy war for Jack to get messages that encouraged him to keep practicing, keep working harder. I knew all these things; I just wanted to make sure that this was not a token. I wanted to believe that my kid was not caught up in the mascot mentality that often surrounds the amiable "special kid." I did not want him to be the kid who intercepts lots of gratuitous high fives in the hallways but has no real friends.

Those elementary school years were a haze of class parties and school-sponsored events like Medieval Day, Roman Day, Pioneer Day, Dissect-a-Fetal-Pig Day (not my favorite), History Day, and May Fair. Between themed days and field trips it was astounding that teachers re-captured enough old-school, sit-in-your-desk-and-learn days. But these teachers were wizards of time management, multi-tasking, and creative appropriation, making all things possible each year.

Through it all reading remained a big thing for Jack. Where movement failed him, reading redeemed him. Jack was an avid reader and a big fan of Dav Pilkey's *Captain Underpants*. With titles like *The Attack of the Talking Toilets* and *The Wrath of the Wicked*

Wedgie Woman, Pilkey's superhero stories grabbed kids, especially elementary school boys, right where they lived—in the toilet.

Jack loved to follow the adventures of George and Harold, two lovable elementary school bad boys. However, he found his alter ego in the unassuming, uninspiring Principal Krupp, who transforms into a superhero and rights wrongs throughout the school. The best part of every book being when Krupp inevitably sheds his trousers and repurposes them around his neck, superman style, as the indomitable caped crusader, "Captain Underpants." Captain Underpants was the champion of all kids who were getting bullied on the playground or mocked by mean menopausal lunch ladies. Jack identified with the unsung hero of these books so thoroughly that whether it be in the middle of the living room, a park, or a birthday party, he could be seen unceremoniously shedding his jeans or cargo shorts and tying them around his neck announcing with a flourish, "This is a job for Captain Underpants!" This bit never failed to get laughs from parents, snickers from boys, and shrieks from little girls. Some kids decided it was not cool to laugh, and his attempt at humor did not alter Jack's nerd quotient in their minds. Some kids may have made fun, but I knew that Jack's sense of humor and earnest desire to make other people smile would serve him well in life, so only in rare cases did I attempt to curb his Captain Underpants impulse.

Elementary school was a collage of joyful, absurd, unexpectedly tender, challenging and mundane moments. But a theme through it all was that too often Jack was left out, passed over, ignored. He had taken to talking to himself on the playground. I recall the 5th grade holiday party at school. Kids were spent after a particularly zany game where they stuffed balloons into each team's "Santa" aka a kid (typically a popular one) wearing a red union suit. The winning team was the one that created the fattest Santa by lodging the most balloons into the red suit by the time the timer went off. Flushed and exhilarated from the game, all the kids pulled up chairs for the piece de resistance of elementary school parties: the gift exchange.

One particular girl, Rachel, finding herself in the unlucky position of being seated next to Jack, got up and made a big show lifting only two legs of her heavy chair and noisily dragging it across the linoleum, weaving among the chairs as she passed directly in front of Jack. She did not have to say a word, the way her eyes rolled back and her lip curled slightly on one side said it all: *Not only do you have the gall to exist, but that same existence has created for me the inconvenient circumstance of having to relocate.* This public show of disgust continued with the rest of the class watching, aware of her plight, until she repositioned her chair at the opposite end of the semi-circle of students, leaving a conspicuous gap next to Jack's chair: a no-man's land separating him and his lone chair from the group. If the other kids were bothered by her cruel behavior, they did not show it. I did not see any of them protest or call her out for this bald-faced unkindness. I don't know if it was because, like pre-teens the world over, they were all caught up in their own personal dramas and insecurities, or if this treatment of Jack had become ubiquitous by virtue of its frequency.

Doling out cookies, fruit, and punch on a serving table strewn with candy canes, I was in full room-mom persona, expecting a diverting day pleasantly immersed in kid pursuits. Instead, I was witnessing this indignity directed toward my kid. Dying inside, I still tried to put on a brave face, not letting my anguish show in front of the other cookie-serving moms, who presumably had also signed up for an afternoon of holiday merriment. But, as I watched, like a rubbernecker who cannot turn away from the scene of a grisly accident, I saw something even more disturbing. Jack appeared unsurprised, like he expected it. Not only was he accepting this display of cruelty, he was sitting there with a blank look on his face. I saw in his vacant stare not even the sliver of denial that would indicate that what I was witnessing was an intentional coping mechanism on his part, but rather a lack of expression that signaled this treatment as just "business as usual." I did not want this to be true: that in order to sit "in privilege" among typical kids, Jack had to endure such indignities, as if that was the price of being included. I worried that his resignation meant that Jack thought that he was getting what he deserved.

In that moment, I wanted to transform into the hero of his books (minus the underpants part) and anonymously swoop in and right this elementary school injustice. I did not have the benefit of disguise, but I could bear it no more. Once the girl was seated, brown tresses framing her face, and the class focus had shifted to the next excitement of the day, I approached her from the side, and told her she had been unkind. Unfazed is my clearest recollection of her reaction to being called out.

This was not new, I had seen it many times before, kids giving Jack a sideways look, pretending he was not there, picking him last (or not at all) for teams.

So, what was it about the chair-dragging girl that pushed me over the edge? In fact, it wasn't her behavior that caused me to act, it was Jack's reaction to the situation that enraged me. It was the way he took it, as naturally as if she was casually passing out papers to the class and he was getting "his." I wondered how many times similar exchanges had transpired. How often had he experienced other subtle, Machiavellian cruelties at the hands of classmates for the one on this day to register as normal?

I did not want to let myself dwell there, but slowly, like a bad dream coming into focus I saw it. My efforts to raise Jack as if he was not saddled with a syndrome had prevailed. But now I was seeing the price. I did not want to raise a child who was tolerated or who was numb to ill treatment. I did not want to believe that all my strategic parenting may have just exchanged one unsettling outcome for another. But I found myself staring down the barrel of that possibility and it did not feel good.

Chapter 23

THE FINAL FRONTIER

*I would rather walk with a friend in the
dark than alone in the light.*

—Helen Keller

"**MOM!** Jack was walking around on the playground talking to himself," announced one of my younger kids in a sing-song tone during carpool. *What was this supposed to be? A public service announcement?* I privately rode out the gut punch. No space to react, my job in the moment was to get a carful of energetic kids home safely after a long day of learning. After all, moms on active duty do not have the luxury of breaking down. Dying on the inside, I responded casually, underplaying the comment "Ok honey, we will talk about it later."

At home, I approached Jack about finding friends on the playground. Wanting to please his always loving, but part-time hair-on-fire mom, he would nod yes, indicating that he would find a friend. But I needed to see for myself.

The next day I took to my car, cruising the street behind the building, which afforded an unobstructed view of the school playground. As a regular volunteer, I was a familiar fixture around school. I needed camouflage; I felt like I should be sporting dark glasses, hat, and a rubber nose. It was as ridiculous as it was painful. Here I was conducting my own reconnaissance mission to check out the kids' claims of Jack talking to himself on the playground. Perhaps they were just embellishing, as brothers and sisters are prone to do, particularly if a sibling's perceived "uncoolness" threatens to upset their place in the social pecking order. (What can I say? kids are cruel, even our own).

Unfortunately, seeing is believing, and as much as I wanted to debunk them, their reports were not exaggerated. I witnessed Jack pacing the perimeter of the chain-link fence line that bordered the school, alone, with his mouth moving. Again, with the daggers to my mother's heart. Where were all the "friends" with whose moms I had strategically cultivated play dates? Where were the teachers? Could they not see? Was it not within their purview to swoop in and assemble small groups of organized play so that my kid was included? My initial reflex was to be angry with the adults. Could they not see that my kid was in pain? Where was their compassion, would they let their own child aimlessly wander the hinterlands of an indifferent playground all alone? It felt good to indulge my internal rant, too good. I shook myself back to a state of reason.

What did I really want for my son? Above all, I wanted Jack to have friends. Not even "friends" plural, just one true friend. It broke my heart to see him excluded. Why was this so hard?

The cold, hard truth of it was that so much of what I had orchestrated when I made that promise to raise Jack with high expectations was procedural. I say "procedural" in that I was working with Jack on specific developmental skills. These were skills that lent themselves to a step-by-step process which, if followed over time, would lead to a desired result, or at least to progress. Skills like head lifting, torso strengthening, writing with a pencil, keeping hands in pockets, making speech sounds, and turning in assignments on time. In each of these areas, "I" identified the desired skills, whether academic, behavioral, speech, or motor. "I" determined how to best teach them, whether as they naturally occurred during the day or through planned repetitions or opportunities. Then, "I" determined who the best person was to teach the skill, whether it be a teacher, therapist, or a family member. Finally, "I" put the plan into action. Once a skill was mastered or, if not mastered, at least improved, "I" would lather, rinse, and repeat with the next skill. The truth was that the common denominator in helping Jack acquire a wide range of skills was *who was in charge*. In all these cases, me or another caring adult was in control.

Progress for kids with challenges can be fitful and slow, but generally effort produces some level of improvement that enhances everyday life for the child and that is satisfying for the adult. When I say satisfaction, I mean the "I-did-something-for-my-kid-and-it-mattered" kind of sweet satisfaction that allows parents to sleep soundly at night. After all, parents worldwide are nourished by the mere possibility that we can make a difference for our children, and on those occasions when that possibility actually bears out and something good happens, we are supremely gratified.

This feeling is exemplified in Steve Martin's portrayal of an attentive dad in the classic movie *Parenthood*. It illustrates with comedic precision how an adult's happiness can be wrapped up in the simple successes of a child. Despite losing his job and marital discord, the main character's emotionally disturbed son catching a pop fly during a little league game sends him into spasms of glee and a tribal-like happy dance that fills the screen. Earlier scenes show the dad engaged in hours of painstaking catching practice with his son, which result in the successful moment on the field. Hollywood ties every story into a pretty bow, but art does imitate life and we, too, join in Martin's happy dance whenever we put in the hours, search out effective therapies or programs, or identify just the right doctor resulting in a win for our child.

While there are a range of skill deficits that can be whittled away by a particularly committed parent, usually with the help of professionals, there is a limit to what we parents can do for our children. Sure, I had found a formula of sorts for addressing some skills, but this formula landed with a resounding thud when applied to the challenge of social competence. Here I had met my match.

There is no way for an adult, no matter how "caring" they may be, to control the process of relationship building. There is not a formula that I know of for fostering social skills and friendships. The mosaic of social cues and personal preferences that signal the attraction of one kid to another defies mapping. The quantity and quality of connections that lead to a single friendship is beyond complex. Add to that the unique sensibilities, securities, and insecurities of every individual child and adolescent, and you have a brew so mysterious that it transcends teachable formulas and procedures.

To be sure, we can teach our children to care for themselves in ways that "up" their friendship desirability quotient. Making efforts in the areas of personal hygiene and stylish clothes (or at least apparel choices that don't mark the child as different) can create the conditions under which one might expect friendships to blossom. We did all that. However, there was no combination of training, reinforcement, setting conditions, and communicating high expectations that could guarantee Jack a friend.

It took a couple of particularly tough years at the school of hard knocks to teach this take-charge mom that friendships were utterly out of my control. The preschool and early elementary years were navigable because friends and play dates were the sole province of parents. If extraversion were a crime, I'd be charged with a life sentence. Working half-time and living in a newly constructed neighborhood of stucco homes largely comprised of young couples and families, I had lots of friends. And, bonus, my friends had kids! Between neighbors, church ladies, and women I met at the twin's club, there were plenty of play dates. Sure, we ran across the occasional parent who avoided associating, as if Jack had something nasty their child could contract, but fearful folk were easy to dismiss because there were plenty of good natured, beleaguered moms eager to pass the time together in one of our backyards.

Preschool kids may not have been choosing Jack, but then again preschool kids were not choosing anyone; their parents were doing all the choosing. These were days of endless excursion to parks, jumping castles, and pools where all manner of children were thrown together by virtue of parental affinity. If I enjoyed the company of another mom and she enjoyed mine, we made plans to spend time together. Our kids were "friends" by default, because we adults were friends and that was it, case closed. The kids bought into this logic, too; they had no say in the matter. That was just the way friends happened in that simpler time.

In retrospect, back then things were good. A neighborhood friend sent from heaven with two boys of her own took Jack under her wing. Voila, Jack had not one but two boys to sled, trick or treat, and have sleep overs with. Our families went camping together. I watched her kids when she and her husband left town for the weekend and they watched mine. They even used their highly prized Bronco's seats to treat Jack to a pro football game. These were tranquil days, where if I squinted and eyed the situation from just the right angle, I could lull myself into believing that Jack had friends.

The difficulty arose as Jack moved through elementary school and the adults were no longer in control. That is when the play dates began to dwindle.

Thus, I found myself cruising the streets bordering the playground actively puzzling over how to help my child, all the while knowing somewhere deep inside that "creating friendships" was this super mom's heartbreaking kryptonite. There was not much I could do.

That day I spoke to him, Jack had assured me saying he would "get a friend," but the dynamics on the playground did not change. I wanted the problem to go away overnight. However, looking back, I see that Jack was outmatched by a morass of social rules—some subtle, others not so subtle. This was not like practicing making eye contact with a target when throwing a bean bag or remembering to adjust your grip on the pencil to correctly form the tail on your Y's. The playground was a lawless wasteland that, unlike the standard PE class, boasted no adult mediators to structure games, make sure that each kid was picked for a team, or direct traffic so that all got a turn. On our elementary school playground, adults were stationed at strategic points to make sure that no blood was drawn, but beyond that it was a state of anarchy where the strongest survived and the weak, at best, were sheltered by the mercy of a few benevolent kids.

From the start, I had not wanted Jack singled out as different, treated as if he was "special needs." Being treated as typical meant that there were no special programs that "engineered" recess time so that it was more inviting, and certainly it meant that there were no specialized personnel assigned to entertain my kid. Of course, the big world that lay before Jack was impervious to his needs. People who were not changing their behavior to meet his social maturity level were not being purposefully cruel or callous, they were just being people "doing" their day. No, Jack would have to alter his behavior to meet them.

Even knowing all of this, I did say something to a teacher who was also a friend. We had confided in each other in the past and I felt she was safe. Sheepishly, I unburdened my concerns (as if she could not see my kid traversing the edges of the playground). Not wanting to sound too desperate, I told her that I would appreciate "anything" she could do to encourage Jack to join in with other students. I knew at the time that people acting as external monitors was not the long-term solution, but I was grasping at straws. I just wanted my pain at what I perceived to be my kid's pain to end as quickly as possible. I mourned that I could not just "fix it" for him by putting a "structured program" in place that manufactured a friend for him as I had been able to do to remedy balance, strength, speech, and writing. I found myself defeated, outmatched by the Darwin-esque arena of the elementary school playground. As maddening as it was, I had to look at the situation dispassionately. I resigned myself to the fact that this matter of friends would ultimately be Jack's work, not a task that could be outsourced to a compassionate teacher, even if she also happened to be his mama's friend.

Grimly resolute that I could not do it for him, I thought that I might at least be able to set up conditions so that he could be more successful at recess. I stopped focusing on my own pain and began looking at what was actually occurring on the playground.

Among the pursuits I witnessed were an organized soccer game, small groups of kids who acted out fantasy games by capturing kids on opposing teams and sentencing them to the "dungeon," trysts of (usually) girls who shared secrets, and kids who deftly crossed the monkey bars or sat perched upon them looking down on the masses. There were also lively four-square games with a queue of kids waiting to join, as well as kids shooting baskets. Lastly, there was the jewel of the playground, the swings, which were lorded over by the recess-one-percenters who were fortunate enough to claim them first. Considering and discarding several options, I settled on the basketball hoops.

Shooting hoops was a respectable recess pastime that Jack could engage in alone or with friends. I knew Jack did not have the social prowess to join a game in progress, so we devised a strategy where he would bring a basketball to school every day—a perfect age-appropriate prop for a 10-year-old boy. The plan was that he would take the basketball out to the playground at recess and after lunch. He would start shooting baskets, which could lead to the long-term goal of striking up a conversation—asking bystanders if they wanted to shoot with him. Because, as with many public elementary schools, there was a perennial shortage of playground equipment, this plan sweetened the pot by offering another fully inflated "community" ball.

This plan in no way "fixed" Jack's social issues, but it did supply a universally accepted, even marginally "cool" replacement for his solitary pacing. I so preferred the image of Jack shooting baskets (even if alone) to him aimlessly roaming the edges of the playground, that I checked every morning to make sure that he had his basketball before leaving the house. The plan offered real-time practice in shooting and palming the basketball, which had the side benefit of working on balance, eye-hand coordination, and hand muscle strengthening. For a time, this was a winning solution. Until it wasn't.

Social conditions are as fluid and unpredictable on the elementary playground as they are anywhere in the world. All of this underscored the truth that we parents can foster conditions where friends can be found, but we cannot solve "friendship problems" for our kids.

Herein lies the unsettling conundrum of social skills acquisition: the best way to acquire social skills is through real-time social situations, but too often the kids who need them the most are overlooked or excluded from those very situations. If social skills are sharpened through repeated practice, and yet kids are excluded from those social opportunities by virtue of their deficits, where is a parent to turn?

Not willing to give up, we summoned the experts. We located and enrolled Jack in a social skills group run by the Colorado State University Psychology Department. This group of dedicated assistant professors and aspiring psychology clinicians worked on specific communication skills with children displaying behaviors across the autism spectrum. These kids had atypical communication and social skills, including: repetitive speech patterns (sometimes called echolalia), lack of eye contact, topic perseveration, as well as garden variety friendship issues. Since all the kids in the group experienced communication and social difficulties, the graduate student leaders served as the role models for the group, mirroring appropriate interactions. Group leaders offered conversation prompts, modeled appropriate ways of communicating, and reinforced kids for adding to the conversation and showing positive social behaviors. After a few sessions, I found the context to be contrived and determined that the time investment in getting Jack to and from the group was not offset by the gains made. But never wanting to pass up new ideas for helping my kid, I hung around just outside the door and listened during the sessions, taking note of specific prompts used to encourage socialization. I committed to adding to my repertoire the strategies that I judged helpful. But, for Jack, it felt like progress could be better found in the act of "doing life." So, while the strategies taught were valid, and I was grateful to the clinicians for their efforts, Jack completed the prescribed seven-week course and exited the program.

Doctors and psychologists have determined what they call "therapeutic levels" for the drugs they prescribe. I am no medical doctor, but by my read, "therapeutic" is the point at which the drug protocol or regimen reaches a level where it positively impacts the patient's symptoms. Coming from an educational model, the science is not as exact. It is difficult to say how and when the interaction of various teaching strategies, interventions, and therapies reach the tipping point where they actually change a child's behavior. It has been my experience that regularly scheduled therapy, whether it be speech, occupational, physical, or sensory, provide critical tools to improve skills and daily functioning. They did so for Jack. But scheduled therapy sessions alone do not provide the level of intensity, repetition, or authenticity necessary to create lasting change. If one chooses therapy, it needs to be supplemented with lots of outside, in-context practice. For my money, real-life situations provide the most fertile ground for meaningful, repeated practice that produces results. The same is true for social skills.

Jack needed lots of real-time practice in social interaction. In my estimation the best way to get that practice was by being in the world, immersed in as many social opportunities as imaginable. We did cub scouts, youth groups, basketball, and track teams, and any other after school activity that promised to put Jack in impromptu, real-life social situations with other kids. If it is true that communication and social interaction improve with practice, then the question is how much deliberate practice is needed to create that tipping point. If that amount can be quantified, then ultimately the devil is in the details. I was playing a numbers game. How could I locate and take advantage of the number of quality opportunities needed in authentic social situations to help my kid find friends?

Chapter 24

BULLIES

Never allow yourself to be made a victim.
Accept no one's definition of your life,
but define yourself.

—Harvey Fierstein

FRIENDS WERE THE HOLY GRAIL of my imagining; the thing
that would make everything right. I worried that talking to himself
was too often becoming the company Jack kept, instead of associating with other kids. In seeking out the one thing I wanted most, I
underestimated its dark underbelly: Bullies.

Sure, all kinds of kids are bullied. Even typical kids report being
targeted, but no group in school is bullied more than students with
identifiable differences. Kids with specific learning disabilities,
autism spectrum disorder, emotional and behavior disorders, health
problems, and speech or language impairments report greater rates
of victimization than their peers. The only group that is bullied at
higher rates are students who identify as LGBTQ.

Difference put Jack in the bullies' crosshairs. I avoided thinking about it because I was the voice always encouraging, entreating, and cajoling him to go outside his comfort zone academically, physically, and socially. Getting involved with peers in school, sports, and extra-curricular activities offered exciting opportunities for learning, growth, and friendship, but to the extent that Jack performed "differently," each of these also made him a potential target.

To be sure, if there was trouble in the halls of our small school, Kyle Kozlov was most assuredly at the center of it. Kyle Kozlov was one of those kids who was cursed with being consistently referred to by both his first and last name as if they were a single unit. It was always "Kyle Kozlov" this and "Kyle Kozlov" that. Kyle Kozlov was also a natural athlete and gregarious trickster with problems of his own who seemed to thrive on setting up situations that would get him a laugh at another kid's expense. Jack was one of those kids. Perhaps Kyle instinctively knew that Jack was susceptible to his gags because it meant acceptance, even if just for the duration of the joke. *That* they had in common; while Kyle Kozlov entered the group by serving as the jokester, Jack's entre came by being the butt of the joke.

One afternoon the other kids walked in the door going on about how Kyle "made" Jack swallow a tablespoonful of wasabi at lunch as the other boys cracked up. Jack did not tell me, my other kids did. I tortured myself imagining what other juvenile atrocities Kyle Kozlov had masterminded. However, I was equally afraid of Jack identifying as a victim. I knew that someone in Jack's situation could easily come to see himself as "that kid that others are always *out to get.*" Or even worse, he could begin to believe that he somehow deserved the treatment that was served up by Kyle and his comrades.

Being on the school board, I knew well a few parents who had crippled their child by feeding the idea that he was a victim. I avoided giving oxygen to these notions. So, while I knew that Kyle Kozlov's conduct was, in fact, bullying, I refused to use the word "bully" with Jack. Instead, over and over again, I told him to get back out there and "show Kyle Kozlov who Jack Winking is." I reassured him that he was better off not shying away but showing Kyle his sense of humor and what a good guy he was. My calculation was that over time Kyle Kozlov would tire of bothering Jack if it did not prompt the typical reaction that bullies crave. So, I sent my son to school, day after day, directly into Kyle Kozlov's path.

But I did one more thing that Jack did not know about. While standing outside the middle school gym one day awaiting a basketball game where I knew Kyle would be, I seized an opportunity to talk to him. As luck would have it, I found him sitting on a bench all alone. There on that bench, I told Kyle Kozlov that he had opportunity to a leader of the 7th grade class because of his athletic ability, popularity, and sense of humor. After building him up, I also let him know that I would be watching him to see how he was leading and building up Jack and the other kids. Even as I gazed upon this boy who was targeting my kid, and whom I imagined had been systematically making him feel anxious, I softened my message. First because, although I wanted him to stop, I wanted to stop short of him hating me. I secretly held on to the hope that he and Jack could, if not be friends, at least get along. After all, they both had something that kept them from feeling at ease in the world around them. Could they not find common ground in this uncertain space? Besides, wasn't making friends the goal? Jack did not have a surplus, and he definitely did not need enemies. As I looked down at Kyle

Kozlov on that peeling wooden bench, I felt sorry for him, like one feels sorry for all bullies. I knew his mom, and I also knew that his dad was not in the picture.

Regardless of the fact that I turned out not to be the take-no-prisoners vigilante for justice that I imagined myself, Kyle Kozlov got the message. I gently "outed" him for picking on Jack. Now Kyle knew that I knew what was going on, and that going forward he would be subject to round- the-clock mom's-eye surveillance. A terrifying prospect for any middle schooler.

In the end, neither this encounter between Kyle and myself, nor my repeated directives to Jack to get out there and show the world "who he was" was the magic bullet that solved Jack's bullying problem. But over time, as predicted, Kyle Kozlov lost steam and became harmless. I even saw him smile and say, "Hi Jack," when they happened to enter the gym or the school at the same time.

I was so concerned that Jack did not think of himself as a victim that I refused to acknowledge that he was being bullied. By not intervening in a public way, it was possible that Jack's exposure to Kyle's antics was prolonged. On the other hand, if I came out full Rambo-Mom, guns a blazin' and fought this battle for Jack, it is likely that he would see this as yet one more area in which he was not capable.

While I claim no expertise in the area of bullying, it seemed like the right thing to do in this particular situation with my particular kid. Although the wages of verbal bullying are no less devastating than the physical variety, upon reflection, I imagine that if Jack was getting punched, I would not have taken this tact. So, while I don't offer this story as anything approaching a patented bullying solution, I do know that Kyle stopped his attacks and that to this day Jack does not harbor any ill-feelings toward the boy. I had not made a scene that embarrassed my kid (although I no doubt mortified him in any number of other ways over the years) nor had I contributed to a victim mentality.

While not saying mine was right, I contrast this approach with that of another parent of a child at the school. When I was on the board, this parent of a 5th grade boy stormed into the principal's office demanding that the bully be punished and kept separate from her kid while on school grounds. Coincidentally, or maybe not, the transgressor again was none other than Kyle Kozlov. The parent went on to seek a restraining order from the local police so that Kyle could not be within a legally specified distance of his child. One could not mistake the anger and vitriol in this parent's voice as he enumerated, in front of his son, the details of how he was being bullied. Of course, none of this was news to his child, who was perfectly aware that Kyle was treating him badly, since he was the one who had experienced the treatment.

I do not fault this dad for wanting to protect his child, it is a primal instinct imprinted upon us when we are handed the role of parent. However, I could not help but wonder about the impact of this dad barreling in and drawing public attention to his son in this way. It appeared to me that the parent (by definition the most influential person in the boy's life) was sending him the message that he was a victim…someone in need of protection, who did not have the capacity to work out his own problems. I have no idea if this is what the boy felt; one would have to ask him to know. But he *behaved* as one offended, hurt, and wronged.

This is the age of "safe to tell," "If you see something, say something," and "Me too." I am squarely behind these long overdue movements designed to empower victims and send zero-tolerance messages to the bullies and intimidators of this world. But, ever vigilant of the messages I was sending to my kid, I did not want to engage in any behavior that would inadvertently place the mantel of "victim" upon my child, and this goal suppressed my maternal need to protect at all costs.

Chapter 25

BREAKING THROUGH THE DOWN-CUSHIONED CEILING

*Every day I wrestle with the voices that keep telling
me I'm not right, but that's alright.*

—MercyMe, *Greater*

AS JACK PROGRESSED THROUGH THE GRADES, I remained committed to reducing the special services that he received, no matter how well intentioned or immediately helpful they appeared. As I saw it, the very presence of specialized services maintained an altered set of expectations for him. I imagined that every day that he was pulled out for special education intervention, speech, or occupational therapy, his view of himself and his place in society was being shaped. I could not know what was going on in this sweet, compliant, and often frustrated boy's brain, but I feared that feelings

231

of inadequacy, fear, reliance on external supports, and modified expectations were calcifying over time. I had developed a close relationship with Jack's special education case manager where we were able to sit down and bare our souls, ex-teacher to teacher.

We dissected each service, accommodation, and support that was written into the Individualized Educational Plan (IEP) that had followed Jack from his previous school district. We analyzed line by line the intent of each academic, occupational, or speech objective. Together we asked these questions: 1) To what extent did each objective support improved functioning? and 2) What could be the unintended dependencies or deficits created by each?

We continued this process of reductionist analysis and over time the meat of Jack's IEP went from multiple pages down to a precious few. In the year and a half that spanned the beginning of fourth grade through the second semester of fifth, he decreased from twice weekly OT pull-out sessions, to "consultation only." This required intensifying our own OT exercise at home, and at the same time, Jack had already created some work arounds and so needed less support. The special education teacher also began tapering off academic intervention services that pulled Jack out of the classroom and separated him from his peers.

As we analyzed the utility of each special service, we found that speech and language intervention was another animal altogether. It was not that Jack's need for these services had lessened, it was the type of service that was the issue. The particular kind of therapy that he was most in need of was not offered by the school district. While Jack still struggled with speech articulation and use problems (also called pragmatics in the speech therapy world), he had also developed a classic stutter that persisted. The school therapists, while excellent, did not have expertise in stuttering therapy and so were focusing solely on articulation and usage. This approach, by definition, did not meet Jack's most pressing need, so we jettisoned the school- provided speech/language therapy in favor of articulation exercises we did at home. In addition, we supplemented with after-school therapy that was geared directly on stuttering.

Now within reach was the pearl of great price: complete and total exit from special education. I indulged myself, daring to imagine Jack living a life of no special services, no modifications, and most of all, no label. As enticing as these thoughts were, there were still cold hard realities to be dealt with—long standing crutches that needed to be shed.

By now, Jack's special education case manager was firmly on "Team Exit" with me. We talked about developing "maintenance programs" for any supports he was still receiving. Special education jargon is not helpful to laymen (or laywomen, for that matter) and so I have done my best to keep it on the down low. The terms vary regionally but "self-determination," "maintenance," or "generalization" IEP goals, objectives and programs are just what they imply: Objectives, goals, and programs that are written to decrease external support ideally until the child is *maintaining* his own behavior in the desired area. For example, for all the occupational and handwriting therapy he received, Jack's printing and writing had stalled at less than legible. The special education teacher supported Jack by reviewing his written work and flagging letters, numbers, and words that were illegible and providing him with time dedicated to do the necessary corrections under her supervision.

Another accommodation in his IEP allowed Jack to dictate his ideas, which the teacher then captured in writing. This accommodation is designed to help students express their ideas in academic areas like social studies and English without being encumbered by the mechanics of writing or keyboarding. Both supports allowed Jack to turn in handwritten worksheets and papers that could be deciphered by his classroom teachers. They resulted in his assignments being graded along with the rest of the class, but they did little to make Jack personally responsible for ensuring that worksheets were readable or that essays were typed with complete thoughts. To move Jack toward independence, she developed a maintenance goal where Jack was increasingly responsible for checking and correcting his own work and for typing his own essays. Addressing this goal was time consuming. It required creating space within the school day and at home for Jack to take on oversight and correction of his own handwritten and typed work.

Possibly fatigued by the physical demands of printing and handwriting, Jack used the tactic of "hiding" worksheets he did not want to complete in a "black hole" that was the bottom of his backpack. To address this "out of sight, out of mind" attitude, the special education teacher provided Jack with time management and pacing support. She checked his work for completion before it had to be turned in to his classroom teacher and made sure that Jack submitted all of his assignments on time. This support insulated Jack from receiving the "incompletes" or zeros that other students were subject to, and kept him tracking along with the class, but it did nothing to make Jack responsible for his own deadlines.

Since complete independence was the goal, the special education teacher developed a maintenance program that earned Jack tokens that could be exchanged for edible rewards for assignments he managed and turned in on time, on his own. This support was effective. What kid, "specialness" aside, doesn't love candy and treats? Any of my other three children would have loved getting a piece of candy or sticker for independently turning in their work and would have stepped up their efforts for the promise of such a reward. But not being "special education," they were not entitled to this external perk, and so neither would Jack if he were to shed his label. The special education teacher gradually reduced these external rewards as she taught Jack to use his planner to meet timelines.

The very existence of these supports and accommodations caused me to consider the toll that such special considerations may have already had on Jack. Had these altered expectations already been etched in his psyche?

I was clear that exiting special education meant that "special treatment" along with its external motivators would disappear. One could not have it both ways. The customized and "special" of special education could not exist without altered expectations and a potentially crippling label. They were mutually exclusive. Exiting special education, I was convinced, was what Jack needed to participate, compete, and be given the dignity to seek his fortunes in the real world, whatever they may be. But it also meant saying goodbye forever to individualized time with compassionate professionals, who gave my kid their dedicated attention and unconditional support. These were professionals who genuinely cared about and reveled in each of his accomplishments, no matter how small. They fretted over challenges, brainstormed solutions, and created workarounds that helped Jack write, speak, move, or manage academic expectations just that much better.

It is not only students who come to rely on extra supports. They can be as seductive to parents. It is gratifying to have someone to talk with and confide in, someone who "gets" your child's trials and struggles, someone who is designated by law to follow your child's progress. What parent does not appreciate another adult whose job it is to "talk up" their kid, even if it is only on a quarterly basis at IEP reporting time?

Exiting special education promised a new reality. Shedding the label that had followed Jack for ten plus years hinted at blissful ordinariness, but it would also leave a vacuum. I wondered what would remain when "special" was left behind? I worried that letting go would usher in feelings of invisibility and mediocrity. Now I considered, maybe for the first time, the prospect of Jack's new reality. Yes, he would be free from the prejudicial specter of categorization, but would he be left with the sense of never quite "measuring up"? Without the cover of "special education," would he be left clawing to hang on to the bottom rung of whatever was "normal"? It was true, being "special" had its perks.

While I grappled with various scenarios that lay just beyond the label for Jack, one basic truth was clear—any perks of being considered "special" were fabricated during childhood and did not exist in the grown-up world. Measuring up on a modified scale and earning rewards for doing what was expected of others as a matter of course, would not serve Jack well in the real world. Accepting manufactured awards might feel good to Jack (and me) in the moment but would not hold up to the scrutiny of day-to-day expectations. Kids who offered cheery greetings in the hallways and tried to help the "special" kid were not real friends. In short, being a token was just that: something of lesser value, a stand in, not the real thing.

I wanted more for my son and I knew "more" came with no external supports. I was crystal clear on that point and wanted to make sure that Jack was clear as well. After all, it was his life, and here I was preaching my vision of the one true path. He had experienced specialized supports of various stripes since before he could remember. Getting help was the air he breathed. By age 12, it was his "normal."

So, I sat Jack down and told him that leaving special education meant there would be no one checking his work and no one making sure that he turned assignments in on time. There would be no go-between with his math or English teachers adjusting the quantity or difficulty of assignments. There would be no one transcribing his answers or writing essays as he dictated his thoughts. There would be no one offering to take over when it appeared his hands were getting tired. There would be no one excusing illegible words, numbers, or sentences. Occupational and speech therapy would end at school. He would have to commit to practicing speech exercises at home. We would find ways to do the small muscle work prescribed by the occupational therapist through a combination of contrived tasks and intentional daily practice, tasks like garlic crushing, can opening, rubber band stretching, and grip squeezing.

Jack had more than just one particularly motivated special education teacher in his corner. There were definitely those folks who lowered expectations and who questioned whether he could do the things that other kids could. But they were eclipsed by other awe-inspiring teachers who did not let Jack off the hook, allow him to opt out, get away with doing less, or lower the bar. I loved these dedicated professionals because I did not detect qualification, excuses, or dare I say, pity in their voices. They were the antithesis of the "I don't know if Jack can…" types.

I felt this was particularly true with one English teacher, and I know Jack felt it too. She called me in to school around the time that

Jack had adopted an "I don't care" attitude toward everything academic and was resolutely choosing not to try for fear of failure. Instead of tallying all of Jack's deficits, writing him off academically, and off-loading him as a problem for the special education staff, she hauled us into her classroom. During that meeting Jack learned in no uncertain terms that Mrs. Samuels "wasn't having" any bad attitude in her class, and he also learned that she expected him to do *all* the assigned work. She offered support, without any "woe to you, poor kid" hint of compromise in her voice. Kids can tell whether their teachers believe in them and they respond in kind to those expectations.

Jack had *his* own quirky rating system for all the middle school teachers. On Mrs. Samuels, he bestowed the grandiose title of "Best 6th Grade English Teacher Who Is a 'Girl.'" He had a male math teacher that he really liked, so he did not want to exhaust this category, should a guy English teacher ever materialize at school. It was not lost on Mrs. Samuels (or any of us) that she was the *only* 6th grade English teacher, male or female. Never mind that it was a somewhat dubious distinction, she considered it an honor, and was known to remind Jack of it, typically after assigning a particularly onerous assignment.

'What is the problem, Jack?" she would say. "Need I remind you I have been awarded the honor of 'Best English Teacher Who is a Girl'"? As large as Mrs. Samuels loomed in my mind, when I asked her later about her contribution to Jack's success, she offered no grand strategy or highbrow theory of expectations. She seemed somewhat perplexed by my question. Mrs. Samuels simply operated from what I would call a "success default." She flat out believed the best of all her students and challenged each of them to try and try again, before modifying or lowering expectations.

As for my special education exit strategy, I don't know that at the time Jack wanted out so much. He was just a compliant kid doing his life the way he knew it. He did not ask for much. Perhaps he trusted me, or more likely, it was just easier to go along with the force of nature that was his willful mom.

So it was, a couple months into Jack's 6th grade year, I found myself again sitting in a meeting flanked by the special education teacher, occupational therapist, the principal, and a school district representative. I was seeking to extract my kid from special education. But this time it felt different; we were not unnaturally folded into tiny chairs around a kidney-shaped elementary school table. We were seated in regular-sized chairs arranged around a regular-sized table with Jack gathered among the most influential adults in his life. The special education teacher described Jack's progress, making the case that Jack no longer required an IEP. But this was all "educational theater," meant to honor the federally mandated process. Her presentation may have contained new bits of information for school district representative, but everyone else there knew Jack and me. They were intimately aware of my long-running peaceful campaign to move Jack out of special education. There was no question that Jack would exit, but it was important for Jack to hear and understand what was happening to him. He had so often been assigned the role of passive recipient of whatever life served up, be it diagnoses, labels, prescribed therapies, or special services.

The outcome of the meeting may have been a foregone conclusion, but it was one in which I needed Jack to be an active player. From his middle school perspective the meeting that day may have been a convenient excuse to avoid dressing out for PE, but idealistically I hoped that he would recognize this day as the first in a new future. I wanted Jack to get the message that things did not "just happen" to him, but that *he* creates results for himself. People make choices and this was a choice that he was making. I wanted him to see that making choices, taking chances, and accepting the consequences of your decisions is what fully being a person means.

Chapter 26

OUT.

*You have brains in your head. You have feet in
your shoes... And you know what you know. And
YOU are the one who'll decide where to go...*

—Dr. Seuss, Oh, the Places You'll Go!

WE ARE SO MUCH BETTER *at getting them "in" than getting them
"out,"* I remember thinking after reading in a national education
journal of the razor-thin margin of special education students who
manage to move out of special education into general education each
year. It is true the percentage of kids that exit special education for
general education is less than four tenths of 1 percent per year. (That
is, if you do not count kids whose sole label is a speech deficit). It is
also true that US schools have fared well with respect to one of the
primary obligations of federal special education legislation, which
is to "search and serve" students in need. It is just that we have been
much less adept at exiting students from special education. The result
is that many students enter special education, but few ever get out.

But *my* kid would not be a "lifer." He was out. I had followed my theory to its logical end. I had tried my best to treat my son as if his delays made no difference. I had ensured that he was exposed to and participated in every opportunity or activity that was offered as a matter of course to his brother and sisters. I had treated him as if he did not have special needs, and to the best of my ability, I intervened to ensure that others did the same. In terms of the educational system I had supported, advocated, intervened, pushed, and cajoled Jack *out* of special education.

Why don't more kids get out? There are lots of reasons for the low exodus rates including the fact that students are benefiting from special education and that many parents want ongoing services for their child. In short, the market is satisfied and there is not a sense of urgency to get out.

Don't get me wrong, kids in special education do fare better but that doesn't translate to getting out. The rise of early identification and intervention for students with delays has resulted in improved reading performance, higher graduation rates, better physical health, and has even reduced criminal activity, but all under the sheltering umbrella of a special education label. Paradoxically, all these successes have not translated to the reintegration of special education students into the general education population.

I was part of that system. As a special educator I have always felt that as a profession we have been acutely focused on the quality and continuity of services to children. That is, making sure that each child was getting a suite of services, accommodations, and therapies that would best help them make academic, social and/or emotional progress. At the same time, I have long felt that we are much less attuned toward deliberately and systemically phasing out supports over time, so as to reduce the need for special education overall.

Here I was, euphoric with the realization that my son would move through life without a label. He would be accepted with a wide embrace into that enviable category of "typical" that I had been grasping for him since preschool.

Jack was "out," but out to what? I learned quickly that the world that existed just outside the bounds of special education was no Disneyland. Shedding the label did not come with a "fast pass" where you were ushered to the front of the "typical" line. It did not change Jack's relationship to his classmates. Kids may have known who in their class was "special education," but the teachers at Abigail Franklin were pros who were stealth-like in keeping the identity of those "pulled-out" for special services on the down low. There was no ticker tape parade for those who exit. Or, to bring the discussion into the current century, no one changes their Instagram or Snapchat story to tell the world they have exited special education. There was no outwardly tangible reason for kids to think of Jack differently because of the meeting that was held on that fateful Monday afternoon.

Practically, not being labeled meant that Jack now had to fend for himself without the protective cloak of special education. As a teacher, I had witnessed the cover that being recognizably different often gave my students over the cruel judgment of their peers. Be different enough and you engender empathy within the student body. You might even get asked to do special things like serve as honorary soccer team manager or help with lighting at the school musical. Good-hearted kids will take an interest in you and want to help. Be "special" and you get hellos and high fives in middle and high school hallways the world over. Difference confers a perverse sense of status.

Removing the label and services had also stripped Jack of any trappings that might come with them, like sympathy, patience, and insulation from unkindness. Now he was just an awkward kid who was different but in a way that people couldn't exactly put their finger on. They couldn't neatly categorize him as special education or disabled. He had no protections. He was now just a kid competing on the same level, who had learned a lot of work-arounds, and was hanging in there, susceptible at any turn to be found to be wanting. In this new reality at worst you are bullied, and at best you are ignored, forgotten, or passed over.

Yes, Jack was not getting coddled, pitied, treated as the mascot, an oddity, or the special kid in need of help. He had fully joined the ranks of regular kids, swimming alongside his peers in the general education mainstream. But how was it affecting him? I had already witnessed how he had accepted being conspicuously ignored, and how he appeared immune to unkindness. I had seen how he was left out and often passed over. He had taken to talking to himself.

I did not want to think about it, but slowly, like a bad dream coming into focus, it emerged. My efforts to have Jack "pass" as typical had prevailed. There were no "visible" supports, accommodations, or modifications that would mark my son as different. This was precisely what I believed had to happen in order for him to have a future where he could choose his destiny instead of having it chosen for him.

But ironically, the same supports I despised and tried to hide or explain away, offered a buffer against the vagaries of a harsh world; indifferent and competitive. I mourned this fact and questioned my choices. Was this austere program of "normalization" worth it? Jack was "out" of special education but trapped in some "not quite"

existence. Was exiting special education a version of the Eagles'
"Hotel California" where you could check out any time you liked,
but you could never leave?

Chapter 27

THE
TALLY

Success is not a random act. It arises out of a predictable and powerful set of circumstances and opportunities.

—Malcolm Gladwell, *Outliers*

FOR ME, THE OLD ADAGE, "success breeds success," was not just an upbeat greeting card sentiment, it was absolutely necessary for the image of "capable" that I wanted for my son. Most of us would like to propagate a universe with more shape and texture than a simple tally sheet of winners and losers; a black and white world where a rigid definition of aptitude funnels us all into dichotomous categories of winners and losers. We seek a world where sincere effort creates ability. This is the coin of the realm for mindset researchers. The rest of us just call it sweat equity.

As appealing as it is for us to craft this world for our children, real life too often telegraphs subtle messages that get stacked up in "plus" and "minus" columns in our psyches. Mindset research gives us a framework for digesting those messages: Struggle is to be expected; it is the necessary fuel for future successes. But how are those messages mediated within young minds? From what I saw with my own kid, the internal columns assigned to wins and losses were tilted way too far toward the negative.

Jack always had struggled with self-esteem and I believe this internal tally sheet was in large part responsible for anger issues that I saw incubating. When you speak and the kid next to you predictably rolls her eyes because she doesn't like how you look: loss. When kids talk over you as if you are not there because there are too many "uhms" in your delivery: loss. When kids walk away as you are telling a story because it is just plain taking too long for you to get it out: loss. When you run out of steam during PE: loss. When you whiff the ball and kick the air during the kickball game as everyone watches: loss. When the point you make repeats what another kid has just said because of the extra time it takes you to process your thoughts: loss. When the classmate reading your paper says she can't read it because your handwriting is too "babyish": loss. When you shoot 500 free throws in your driveway only to sit on the bench the entire game as your teammates fly down the court oblivious to your presence: loss. When kids are talking about the party that everyone is invited to but you: loss. When kids are egging you on to drink hot sauce because they know you don't have the confidence or social capital to say no: loss. Even as I proselytized about the virtue of hanging in there and preached the gospel of effort creates aptitude, I saw that Jack was sinking under the weight of this invisible tally sheet.

I had always skated the fine line between high expectations and expecting too much. I was afraid to let go of what I had latched onto as normal school benchmarks and experiences. My credo had become, "Jack will do everything that "typical kids" do, and, by definition, he will become typical." That is how I judged each experience or opportunity as it came along. So, when the orange-colored flyer came home in Jack and Livie's backpacks enticing kids to apply for a NASA-supported space camp, I said, Jack can do this! I recalled helping him, probably too much, with the application.

I had decided that Jack needed this NASA Camp scholarship and, unlike social interactions or impromptu contests of strength or agility, this was an area where I was not helpless. I could help even if it meant putting a thumb on the scale a tiny bit. On the line where the application asked about "special circumstances," I directed Jack to mention that he had exited special education that year, thinking that this measure of overcoming adversity would be looked upon as laudable, or at least be seen as introducing some diversity into the ranks of the chosen scholars.

Proud is too tepid a word to express how we felt when Jack received the email saying he was selected for the NASA camp. Finally, I thought, this will be the big fat checkmark in the "wins" column that my kid needed. Empirically, this was a success. Other smaller wins were scored when the principal announced the NASA Camp scholarship winners on the school news broadcast for the entire student body to hear and when teachers talked up the camp in their classes. While I assume at some level it registered with Jack that it was his mother who had pushed him to apply and helped him with the application, I used the fact of his acceptance to add to the narrative that he was capable. At home, we celebrated him. I mentioned to friends, extended family (and virtually anyone who did not know), that he got the scholarship all in service of building a positive narrative.

How much weight a kid gives to getting accepted to a camp devised by grown-ups is an unknown quantity. I also did not know how this particular "win" would stack up against other 'losses' attributed to falling short in the eyes of his peers. But to me, each and every positive mattered in the story that was being forged.

We packed up all the kids and headed up to the University of Wyoming to see Jack off on this momentous 10-day science camp adventure. All six of us and Jack's duffle bag caravanned into the dormitory, crowded into an elevator, and tromped follow-the-leader style down the narrow hallways to the room Jack had been assigned. His roommate had not yet arrived. So, "Bonus!" His dad told Jack he could choose either bunk. Still bursting with pride, we headed to the auditorium where we listened to program leaders ceremoniously present an overview of camp activities. There would be experiments undertaken, rockets launched, planetariums visited, and even an overnight campout. The icing on the cake: an ex-astronaut was recruited to bless the proceedings and encourage the kids.

After all this science frivolity, Jack split off with the other campers as we hung around for the family reception, hoping to get a glimpse of any interaction that would confirm that Jack was blending in. I was preoccupied, but my peripheral vision told me that Livie, Rosie, and Will were stalking the refreshment table scoring more free food than would be considered polite. So, we exited triumphant, but I still worried, knowing I would not be there to bridge awkward exchanges or smooth any edges that might signal an unacceptable level of difference. I reminded myself that infinitely more important than my mediation of every potentially painful and uncomfortable moment was the positive message Jack was getting from us sending him on this adventure alone: "The people who know me best think

I've got this. They wouldn't expect me to do this thing if I couldn't."

Part way into the week, they let the campers contact home. Part way into the call we learned from Jack that his dorm-mate had moved out; and he was to spend the balance of the camp without a roommate. Already my mind was screaming: loss. I knew that Jack registered this as a rejection, but he offered no more information than that. A quick exchange with a not unkind but shockingly matter-of-fact graduate student leader offered something of an explanation. He said that Jack's roommate said Jack smelled and that he wanted out of the room. That was it, no further insight was provided.

Having spent ample time in middle schools and raising four preteens of my own, I knew intimately that there are an astonishing range of odors that kids of a certain age excrete. These odors are further intensified by the degree to which the individual has prioritized video games, fidget spinners, slime, or other tween obsessions over basic hygiene. It is possible that the roommate's reaction was purely olfactory; Jack was not great at changing his socks. Or it could have been how this kid dealt with what he perceived as difference. If this wasn't my own kid, this would have been just another opportunity to marvel, on a purely academic level, at how people relate to that which they don't understand, and log it among the range of reactions from curiosity to fear to outright rejection. But this was not an academic study, this was my flesh and blood, and regardless of the ex-roommate's motivation, the outcome had been the same. Jack was on his own when all the other campers had roomies. I only hoped that this reaction from a kid he barely knew did not fuel further negative self-perception.

We truly never learned the whole story behind the roommate jettisoning Jack. Possibly it did not matter. It appeared that Jack had logged the entire adventure at NASA Camp squarely in the "wins" column regardless of the roommate snafu. For my part, I saw it as an early alert, a canary in the coal mine. It reminded me that part of denying the syndrome and holding typical expectations for my kid meant no one was going to be around to intervene, accommodate, or provide extra support. That included no mama swooping in to spin the situation or to make it "all better".

Chapter 28

THE UNBEARABLE WEIGHT
OF BEING "NORMAL"

Via does not see me as ordinary. She says she does,
but if I were ordinary, she wouldn't feel like
she needs to protect me as much.

—R.J. Palacio, *Wonder*

IT WAS HOURS AFTER THE BUS RETURNED to school following an away game, back home in the privacy of his bedroom, that Jack broke down. He had warmed the bench for the length of an entire middle school basketball game, watching 6th and 7th graders sprinting down the court as he, the tallest eighth grader by nearly a head sat on the sidelines. This was typical, but his reaction to it was not. My son cried real tears as I slid down to his level onto the bedroom floor, using the railing of his bunk bed to support me each agonizing inch of the way down. He said between sobs, "Why does everything come so easy to Sam?" As with every parent who witnesses their child hurting, I felt daggers piercing me. I wanted to cry too. Looking back, I should have joined him in a raging tear fest.

My strong suit has never been acknowledging the bad. However, I knew I was supposed to take the time to hear my son out and empathize before I moved into my all-too-familiar cheerleader routine. In that moment, I silently raged on behalf of my son, "You are not strong, you are not coordinated, you move awkwardly, you are slow, prone to slurred stuttering speech, you have a hard time getting a thought out, and you still can't hold a pencil properly. You are right, it does suck." Audibly I refused to go there. There was no room to indulge pity or admit weakness, if we were going to do "typical." To sit with Jack and bemoan his lot would be to sidle up dangerously close to acceptance that something was wrong, possibly irretrievably wrong. Indulgence would lead to excuse making and give way to a belief in absolute limitations. I could not risk opening that door, entertaining with words the idea that his challenges were static, unchangeable.

Come to think of it, I don't think I even offered an "I'm sorry" or empathized, a fact I now regret. On the fly, I launched into my patented strengths and weaknesses pep talk. This was a version of the improv I used on all of my kids when they were feeling sorry for themselves. It involved a shell game tactic where I accentuated an area in which the affected offspring excelled. All those years when moving was slow and labored, from the early days when Jack had trouble holding his head up to later, when walking was unsteady, and running was impossible, stories had been a retreat. He listened to books voraciously until he could read the stories himself.

"Everyone has strengths and weaknesses, Honey." I'd said. "Sam may be good at basketball, but there are plenty of kids who can't read, who are afraid to pick up any book, far less big thick ones like you read. There are kids who can't learn from what they read." Either my words began to soak in acting like a salve, or Jack was attempting, even immersed in his own pain, to make *me* feel better. He visibly calmed. That was how I remember getting through any moments of despair that arose; talking about strengths, the merits of persevering, and avoiding a victim mentality at all costs.

It has been said that no one makes it out of childhood unscathed. As Jack got older, he got angrier. There is a special kind of frustration that accompanies never quite measuring up. He never gave up, but it made him mad. There was a sullen look etched into his thin face. He did everything that was asked of him, but often he completed it with hostile resignation. We would trudge through what should have been pleasant recreational activities, as if we were on the Bataan death march. I recall too many years of family hikes, museum trips, and even theme parks where Jack would separate himself, moving alone through the exhibit or attraction. Finally, we would discover him sitting cheerlessly on the bench under the exit sign, as if he were being forced to take some bitter medicine and was holding his nose to get through it. Jack did not refuse or complain; he pushed forward, constantly checking his watch or his phone as if counting the moments until he could go home. He always seemed a little tortured, as if he could not wait to get back to the comfort of his room, his desk chair, his computer, and his books. I could not be sure if this anger and stubborn unwillingness to enjoy life was a by-product of my parenting choices or just an expression of garden variety tweenage angst.

Regardless, I was not above blaming myself. I indulged those sharp pangs of guilt reserved just for us moms, the remorse we nurse for everything we did, or didn't do, did too much of or not enough of.

I let myself go down the rabbit hole of "if only we had taken the other path" to see where it would lead. If we would have simply embraced Jack's diagnosis, label, special services and all that comes with it, he may not have been so angry. He would have been peacefully insulated from competition with peers, feeling secure and loved in his own unique place in the world, instead of working his tail off without recognition, trying his best, and always falling short. He would have been the recipient of clique high fives and waves in the hallways from the "good" girls. Other kids would be assigned to help him.

Whenever I engaged in this anguished exercise, I invariably came out the other side at least, if not vindicated, resolute in my decision. I consoled myself: It was true, his perseverance had not affirmed him yet, but it still could at any time. Jack was in there fully participating in the game of life, without accommodation. This meant his fortunes could change, no doors had been closed to him, no one had told him he couldn't. No one had taken away his choice.

Chapter 29

HEARTBREAKS
PART 2

Pain is certain, suffering is optional.

—Buddha

WE PARENTS GET OUR HEARTS BROKEN on behalf of our kids all the time. It's part of the deal; we have the singular joy of being entrusted with this precious being who is a part of us, but at the same time, it hurts like hell. And that is just the standard pain that comes with the job. However, I have found that there is a special kind of heartbreak that is reserved for judgments arising from how our children "look."

There was the math teacher at back-to-school night who voiced her concerns about Jack in front of 22 middle school parents crowded among the art room stools and tables. She mused out loud, "I don't know if we can expect Jack to open his locker." That was a shot over the bow; typically, people are talking to me one-on-one when they minimize my child. My first thought was, "Next time you want to make prejudicial statements about my kid because of how he looks or moves, I'll thank you very much to do it in private."

We were all first-time middle school parents, whose kids had aged out of the relative safety of the upper elementary grades where kids spend most of their day in a single classroom with one teacher who knows them well. Now we found ourselves with 6th graders. We were staring down the barrel at a stunning array of new freedoms and responsibilities our kids would be afforded, not the least of which were locker partners, computer generated class schedules, passing periods, student council, and hall passes. We were a captive audience in this back-to-school night information session.

I knew this teacher well, which made her statement even more shocking. Despite what amounted to atrocious "desk-side manner," I am sure she thought she was just dispensing with one more classroom practicality, in a world where not dealing with practicalities can sink a teacher. Even so, there was so much wrong with her comment that I did not know where to start.

My mind immediately went to the teacher's mindset. I worried that Jack would be subjected to a teacher for an entire school year who thought less of him and who did not even have the sense to hide her prejudice. *Please don't let her be an over-helper*, I silently pled. Next, I considered the people who were in the room when Mrs. Kramer spoke. By making this statement in front of an audience of parents she was passing along her toxic low expectations and prejudicial notions to them. It is true that most of these folks likely had already formed their opinions about Jack. He had attended two years of elementary school with their children and most had met or seen him at school functions. But it did not help to have the teacher, the authority figure in the room, inciting or legitimizing prejudicial beliefs.

No time to dwell on this unnecessary blunder now. It is amazing what can go through the human mind in a few seconds. I remember a movie that was shown in my own middle school days where a convicted union soldier's entire life flashed before his eyes in the time it took for the stool to be kicked out from under him and the hanging rope to cut off his circulation.

In the space between Mrs. Kramer's unfortunate words and my response, I visualized the task of operating a middle school locker. Opening a combination lock required a series of coordinated fine motor movements and dexterity. It called for strength in all the small muscles located in the center of the palm that contract and work in concert directing the fingers to spin the dial right 67, full twist, left 42, and finally, right 13.

By the evening of this ill-fated parent meeting, Jack and Livie were already two days into their first week of middle school. I was sure that Jack was challenged by his combination lock. I was also pretty sure that teachers or other students had seen him struggling and had helped him. What to do? These lockers had spin combination locks built in so there was no work-around where the spin lock could be replaced with an old school key-activated padlock. Even though Jack could not do it yet, I knew he would have to, it was what middle schoolers did. This all ran through my consciousness in the moment of awkward silence that followed Mrs. Kramer's public announcement about my kid.

Hiding my humiliation, I countered her firmly, yet respectfully, "Do you expect the other kids to open their lockers?"

"Yes" she offered, demurely now.

"Then, Jack will open his locker."

We returned to school later in the evening and practiced. Before long, Jack was opening his locker. Honestly, what choice did he have?

That summer our church youth group made the trek to Faith Day at Elitch Gardens, a Six Flags-esque amusement park teeming with gravity-defying roller coasters, soaking wet water rides, and kids of all ages. I served as a chaperone for Jack and Livie's middle school group. As a chaperone I was allowed to bring my younger kids, creating the extra enticement that I sought, an activity where no one was left out and where I was the hero successfully delivering a fun day to all my kids in one fell swoop. Drop the mic.

So, with a group of middle schoolers and Rosie and Will in tow I set out for Denver, mom-van bursting at the seams. As you'd expect on a summer day, the rides were crowded, the lines endless. I was waiting with a gang of seven or eight kids to repeat the log flume, because, why not? Everyone got soaked the first time around and many of us had donned sweatshirts to take off the chill as we waited in the snaking line. As I was taking pictures of Livie and some of her girlfriends at the front of the line, it tangentially registered with me that Jack was playing peek a boo with a little boy a few rows behind us. Good, he is occupied, I thought. After an extended wait we strapped into our rubber rafts made to look like cut timbers for one more thrill ride. As Colorado weather would have it, rain started coming down just as we splashed down. Our group piled out of the boats and rushed to the warmth of the frontier themed ranch restaurant. As we were reminding the unruly entourage of how much money each kid had to spend for lunch, I was shocked to see that not one, but two policemen had pulled a kid out of the concession line. Upon closer inspection I recognized that kid was Jack. There must be some mistake. The blue uniforms with Jack at their side approached our group just as I was struggling to extract myself from the line to get to them. One officer asked, "Is he with your group?" It was so surreal, and the incident transpired so quickly, that I did not have time to fear…it just struck me as so bizarre, my son being brought to me by two police officers.

"Yes, he is, and he also is my son."

The officer said that they had followed and intercepted Jack because a parent had reported that "a strange guy" had approached their little boy at the log ride.

"Officers, he is a seventh grader." I was revving up to go fully indignant on these two unsuspecting public servants, but I dialed it down when I noticed that they were softening. One of them spoke up and said that they had to follow up because the woman had made a complaint, but they realized as they talked to Jack that he was just a kid too. A little embarrassed, they explained that they were just maintaining protocol as they apologetically returned Jack to the safety of the line.

An innocent case of mistaken identity by an overprotective mother? Maybe, but I knew what had gone down: a soaked Jack, oversized for his age, with his hoodie up engaging her child looked menacing to this mother. My son, someone to be feared because he looked "different." I longed to track down this parent and correct her. What she had really encountered was not a predator, but a sweet boy, no more than a kid himself, who wanted nothing other than to entertain her little boy to pass the time as they waited in line. Interesting how quickly an innocent, unconscious act like sensing difference can translate into a conscious judgement, a threat assessment.

⁓

Among my proudest moments was when Jack was part of a basketball team. Even after years of practice, he remained the slowest, and least coordinated on the team, but he was out there among his peers. On this particular day, we were sitting in the bleachers praying someone would feed Jack the ball. One thing he had was height, if only someone would pass him the ball, he might get an opportunity to sink a basket. Ever hopeful, Pete and I rarely missed a game. This particular day we were sitting within ear shot of a small group of parents, who whispered to one another as they watched the action on the court: "Honestly, I don't even know if he is safe out there."

I was devastated. When Jack joined the team, I had fooled myself into believing all was resolved. In fact, endless drills had improved Jack's coordination, but when players are out on the court, there are not organized drills, players instinctively act. It was the speed, intuitive processing and the unpredictability of the game that continued to foil him. I had been fooling myself and perhaps putting my son in exasperating situations. Jack wasn't passing, he did not fit in. Their comment transported me back to that day at the shore when Pete wondered out loud if Jack wouldn't be more comfortable, better off, SAFER if he was left at home.

There it was again; someone was making presumptions about my kid's safety and where he belonged. Of course, this was 8th grade and life had become infinitely more complex. This was not family, these were other people, adults motivated by the raw electricity of competition. Who knows what aspirations these parents had for their kids, what challenges they faced? One thing was clear: they wanted to win. Couching their comments in terms of safety on the court provided cover for the crux of the issue. They wanted victory for their kids, and, at the moment, Jack was getting in the way of that goal.

As with many teenage boys, it was an act of God to get Jack to attend to his appearance. He hated, I mean hated, to get his hair cut. Jack was not a fashion plate and he wanted nothing to do with sitting in a salon chair staring at himself while some lady fussed with his hair. But the time had come, he needed a cut. Would he have been more comfortable in a barber chair with a middle-aged man holding the clippers? Maybe so. But with four kids to be shuttled, time was a premium and the local Great Clips was infinitely more convenient. So, having errands to do, I had no qualms about dropping him off with a twenty-dollar bill. I told him to tell the stylist that he wanted the same cut he always got.

As I drove away to make a grocery store run, I reminded him to give the change to the stylist as a tip. I motored off to do my shopping, promising that I would be back before he was out of the chair. I picked up the milk, eggs, and other essentials that our hungry family of six was forever low on and quickly circled back to the salon. I was shocked to see my kid sitting on the edge of the curb, head down and legs splayed out on the pavement in front of him. Why didn't that darn kid go in, I thought, already irked. I did not have time to wait around. I pulled up and parked and got out ready to escort Jack inside.

"Why didn't you go in?" I interrogated.

"I did, Mom, they told me they would not cut my hair because I had lice."

My inconvenience now forgotten, I felt awful for Jack as I saw how dejected he was, the look on his face saying it all: "This is just another thing I got wrong."

Well-practiced, I immediately jumped into self-esteem triage mode. "This is not your fault, Jack, lice can happen to anybody." I wanted Jack to feel better, but was secretly worried about exposure, I did not relish a house full of the critters spreading across kids.

I called Pete, who was already out, telling him to get all the lice abatement supplies, the special shampoo and the nit comb. Once home, I stripped Jack's bed and started going through his hair looking for the pesky little vermin ready to vanquish them with the strong-smelling soapy solution. I continued parting one section after another of Jack's thick hair, but the confounding thing was that, as long as I searched, I didn't find a single piece of lice, not even an egg. Convinced that I was the problem, I had Pete go through his hair. Then it dawned on me, the random stylist who got assigned to Jack just did not want to cut his hair. Whether it was his labored speech or how he carried himself, she had decided he was undesirable, and either imagined or fabricated the lice story to get Jack out of the salon.

I was thrilled that my son would not have to endure days of lice treatment, but I also longed to return to the salon and vindicate Jack. But the moment for that had passed. I never told Jack what I suspected had happened. He was happy just to have my meddling hands out of his hair. Still, I silently mourned for my son, who was so often summarily and harshly judged by those who did not take the time to get to know him, enjoy his humor, or see his kindness in action.

No doubt these experiences made me want to indulge my protective instincts, but I was intentional in willing myself to not submit to fear but to encourage Jack to continue putting himself out there. To retreat would be to admit limitations and I could not risk Jack thinking there were situations, experiences, or people he needed to fear or avoid. The next week I sent him back to Great Clips, but this time I sat silently in the waiting area leafing through an outdated hair magazine.

Chapter 30

THE LAST WORD ON COMMUNICATION

Hoonie was not a nimble talker and some made the mistake of thinking that because he could not speak quickly, there was something wrong with his mind, but that was not true.

—Min Jin Lee, *Pachinko*

IT IS ENCRYPTED IN OUR DNA to think our kids are great. On top of that hard wiring, I witnessed daily how hard Jack worked just to get a single thought out. Sometimes his face would contort as if trying to consciously push the words out. Other times his enthusiasm to share an idea out-paced his brain-to-voice box processing ability and left him with only a series of "umms" that were ultimately rendered useless because somewhere along the line his listener had moved on. In my estimation, that measure of sincerity and effort should earn a little appreciation, if not a few friends. But none were forthcoming. As painful as it was, I had to take a steely-eyed inventory of exactly how Jack's style of communication got in the way socially, just as I would later have to do with his academic delays. I began by listening to my other kids. They were my eyes and ears in classrooms and school hallways, on school buses and in carpools. All of these were critical social settings to which I was not privy.

With a ruthlessness that lives in the honesty of youth, my youngest daughter would always give me the unvarnished truth. "Sam rolls his eyes because Jack repeats what other kids in the car have just said." I had always assumed this kid was Jack's friend by virtue of the fact that I had a relationship with his mom. Apparently, there is no gentlemen's (or gentlewoman's) agreement that just because you have regular lunch dates with someone's mom, her offspring had to like your kid. It did not work that way in middle school.

There is no doubt that easy communication greases the wheels of friendship. Early on children adopt communication styles and paying attention to these styles has a role in maintaining their place in the social strata. By first grade, Jack had begun to develop a stutter that experts said had no connection to Sotos syndrome. By the end of third grade, Jack had strengthened the muscles in his mouth, tongue, and throat that govern speech, making his words more understandable, even when he was tired. This was no small feat and a success that deserved celebration. Unfortunately, I don't remember too many pats on the back, because on the heels of this success emerged a classic stutter, which threatened his communication in other ways.

Like Oliver Twist, the hero of the Dickens classic, I was always eager to accept another heaping dose of mama guilt, "May, I have some more please, sir?" I secretly fretted that Jack's stutter developed because of stress derived from expectations I had placed on him. Thankfully, experts in the neurology of stuttering published studies that reminded me that I am not that important. While it was comforting to learn that parents are not responsible for a child's stutter, it was at the same time extremely frustrating that stuttering was yet another circumstance in my son's life that I was powerless to fix. Prevailing research confirms that although brain science and genetics are always evolving, the root cause of stuttering remains unknown. The best explanations involve differences in coordination within the internal mechanisms that govern speech. Although we parents don't cause stuttering, there are definitely things families and those close to people who stutter (PWS) do that can exacerbate it. If life in our house were a sitcom, the sketch would be called "The Loud Family." Too often our default was to talk over one another, interrupt, and to increase the decibel level to be heard. For Jack, this every-man-for-himself approach to conversation did not provide the best medicine for minimizing stuttering.

The speech therapy Jack had received over the years focused on articulation (making sounds), fluency (stringing sounds and words together), and pragmatics (the social rules of communication). While he had abandoned the pull-out speech therapy the school offered, we sought additional support for stuttering. The school system offered speech therapy, but not professionals who focused on this riddle of a condition. Consistent with the goal of avoiding stigma, we searched until we found a private therapist whose specialty was stuttering.

One unfortunate consequence of stuttering for Jack was that it caused other kids to count him out. Because kids are easily distracted and not particularly patient, they would move on, or walk away while Jack was still working on getting his answer out. On many occasions, kids physically turned their backs on Jack, literally moving on to their next thought or adventure while he was still mid-sentence. People who stutter are very articulate about the stress and feelings of inadequacy that these responses cause. It was heartbreaking for me and surely sent Jack debilitating messages about his place among peers. I witnessed instances where he continued to try to get out his thoughts even as the other child had rendered his response irrelevant by moving on to the next topic or person. I also observed times where Jack declined to respond at all, likely anticipating the unsatisfying sequence of events that would follow.

Throughout middle school and into high school stuttering confounded many a potential friendship. I remember being so proud of my two "big" kids. On Christmas their 8th grade year we gave Jack and Livie high school hoodies featuring the ferocious saber cat who would be their high school mascot for the next four years. Then, before you knew it, we found ourselves in the high school the week prior to the first day of freshman year. Parents could be seen trailing behind their kids through the hallways, helplessly waiting to pay fees as their kids ran the gauntlet of orientation stations: receiving class schedule printouts and being requisitioned standard issue textbooks, laptops, photo IDs, and locker combinations. Curious to see where their lockers would be for the year, Pete and I followed Jack and Livie through the wide hallways, zigzagging in and out of the maze of metal cabinets until the kids finally came upon their lockers. The 6th grade teacher who had chosen to publically "out" Jack for his locker-opening difficulties was burned into my subconscious. Even though he had mastered the coordination necessary to manipulate the lock while simultaneously sliding the latch up to open the middle school lockers, I silently wondered what the mechanics of high school lockers involved. Not wanting to be that mom, the one who hovers over her 14-year-old, I respectfully loitered around the corner pretending to be heading (very slowly) toward some other important business within the school, perhaps a meeting with a teacher or counselor.

As I lingered, I was relieved when I heard the melodious sound of Jack's locker latch disengaging from its metal housing. Confident that Jack had won that battle, I was just about to make my exit and head down to a distant cluster of lockers where Livie was presumably going through the identical process of depositing books in her locker (only with the additional step of adding blingy locker decor, a ritual usually reserved for freshmen girls.) As I turned to go, I heard voices coming from Jack's direction and one of them was feminine. A girl was talking to Jack! (High school was going to be great!) In my surprise I missed the first part, but gathered that she was asking for help opening her locker, which Jack did with ease. Score! (High school was going to be really great!) Then I heard the girl offer, "My name is Allie." Jack started to respond but was confounded by pronouncing his name on demand. 'I'm.... long pause, Jjjjjjjjjjjjjjj..... long pause, Jjjjjjjjjjjjjjjjjjjjjjjj, then nothing. I could not stand it any longer, I violated the sacred promise I had made to myself to remain unseen. I craned my neck around the corner into the locker bay just in time to see Jack pull out his freshly minted high school ID card and wordlessly hold it up in front of her. Confused and taken aback, Allie did the only thing she could do in the moment, she read it aloud, "Jack."

Her "Oh, hi, Jack" was followed by an abrupt, "see you around," and as quickly as Allie had appeared, she disappeared, absorbed into a sea of yoga-pants-wearing, ponytailed adolescent girls. How many times can a mother's heart break and still function? In the moment saying his own name under pressure was so daunting that the most expeditious workaround he could find was flashing his ID card, as if he had no speech. Jack had overcome much, only to be stymied by stuttering, a riddle of a condition, the origins of which remain uncertain.

When I examined Jack's communication patterns, I noted that he used many of the coping mechanisms people who stutter rely on. These are reasonable strategies that any of us would turn to if we were rendered speechless. For example, if Jack was speaking fluidly, he would continue in a kind of monologue without stopping. While this behavior helps the person who stutters avoid the unpredictable stops and starts in conversation that can prompt a stutter, it does not allow for turn taking. He also avoided using certain words and people's names for fear of initiating a stutter. I noticed him calling his twin sister "what's her name" regularly as in, 'I am going to the library with "what's her name."

In my ignorance, I thought he was exhibiting typical brotherly rudeness until I realized he was consistently avoiding her name because of disfluencies that emerged with the "L" sound. He resorted to speaking with a British or Irish accent because, for unknown reasons, like singing, use of accents diminishes disfluency. While initially entertaining, a Cockney accent can become really annoying to people, particularly when they know you are from Colorado and not Liverpool. He avoided making eye contact with the person he was speaking to because eye contact can increase stress, which increases stuttering. Jack's penchant for not making eye contact caused more than one concerned citizen to ask if he was autistic. Off and on throughout elementary and high school, Jack continued working with a stuttering specialist, an amazing man who lived with a stutter himself. He told Jack a story about a boy with a hippo who could choose to carry the hippo on his back like a burden or engage the hippo as a friend, walking by his side. The obvious moral was that even though the stutter, like the hippo, would always be with its owner, it could be tamed.

Jack had developed other speech habits that, while not associated with stuttering, also got in the way in social situations. He would perseverate on a topic not always recognizing that the listener did not have the background to understand or join the conversation. He also overused particular phrases in ways that rang as odd to listeners, euphemisms like "said" person had "said" meal etc. All of these taken together did not ease his path into new friendships.

I took note of and mimicked the techniques I saw speech therapists using. Things like putting my fist into my cupped hand; the cupped hand signaling that there was a hole in my understanding, and the fist signaling that he needed to supply information to fill the hole. His dad and I talked to him about asking questions of other people; first because people love to talk about themselves and second, because asking questions took the pressure off him to continue talking.

Admittedly, I did a lot wrong. In my zeal to promote friendships, I interrupted too much and did more than my share of indiscrete prompting: "Jack, do you want to ask George if he is into Star Wars?" This was not helping, proving again that a caring adult, even a particularly perky one, cannot plaster over social issues. It pained me to overhear counterproductive communication behaviors. Not surprisingly, Jack did not like me micromanaging his conversations. He invariably became defensive. No matter how positively I couched it, "…you are doing great, and these are some other things to remember," to him it must have seemed like just another reminder of just another shortfall.

As he got older, I created a communication cheat sheet that fit on a half-page of paper. It included specific communication do's and don'ts and an example of how to use them in a conversation. I imagined (unrealistically) that he would neatly fold it up and tuck it into a pocket or school folder as a handy reference. He took the sheet begrudgingly. I knew he was beyond done with me for offering what must have seemed like endless unsolicited feedback on how he communicated. However, I walked into his room one day and found the cheat sheet purposefully laid out on his desk in a way that made me think he had been using it.

Chapter 31

THE PATH NOT TAKEN

I shall be telling this with a sigh
Somewhere ages and ages hence
Two roads diverged in a wood, and I—
I took the one less traveled by,
and that has made all the difference.

—Robert Frost

IN THIS HUMAN EXISTENCE, once a path is chosen and followed to its conclusion, one can never truly know what would have happened if the other route were taken. Somewhere around ninth grade I recognized that I didn't have any particular affinity for math, but before I hung up my calculator and mechanical pencil proclaiming that numbers were not my thing, I remember learning about the null set. The null set: two curly brackets holding an empty space. The path not taken reminds me of that null set, a reality not experienced, for which there is no information, only an empty space. We can't know how we might have been shaped by that which did not occur; what contours our lives might have assumed if we had experienced more of this or less of that. That which would never be, simply because we took another route.

However, the God I believe in sometimes throws hardworking mortals a bone, giving us the slightest glimpse onto that other path. I believe that these flashes of what might have been are often revealed, if to do nothing more than just keep us chugging along. This day, I believe, was as close as I would get to coming face to face with what might have been for Jack, had I gone another way.

Allow me to preface this story by saying that I don't presume that my expectations of a life well-lived are shared by all. Further, I am not judging anyone else's choices, but only sharing how one day in May I happened upon a rare window into what might have been.

It was the twins' 9th grade year. Livie had signed up to be an athlete mentor for the regional Special Olympics. Our high school hosted the event for schools across the entire district and students who volunteered to mentor were excused from classes for the entire day. Certainly, reason enough for any self-respecting high school student to sign on the dotted line. But a "get out of jail free" card was not why Livie had signed up. She confided in me that she was uncomfortable around people with disabilities in general and, in particular, the special education kids she saw every day walking the high school halls with their teachers. Somewhere inside it made her feel bad. Livie was an introspective 15-year-old who was hard on herself. She was still coming into her own like we all were at that age, beginning to take shape but not yet having emerged into a uniquely formed self. She suffered from all the insecurities reserved just for teens, but above all, she was a tender, creative, empathetic soul. I could not hide my pride when she told me that she wanted to overcome her fear by volunteering for a whole day as a companion for one special Olympian. Brave as she was, she remained a little uneasy about going alone. Being that I was a teacher before becoming a mother, and now out of the classroom for years, I loved any excuse to be around kids. I wasted no time telling her that I would be happy to volunteer with her. I could not attend the entire day because of work, but I would join the event in progress and pitch in for as long as I could.

When the day came, true to form, I showed up late missing the opening ceremonies. By the time I got to the field, Livie had already been paired up with her athlete, James. She was getting him psyched up for his first event by pacing the outdoor track. I tagged along, taking pictures of her and James as they prepped for the 50-meter dash. We had just rounded the corner of the oval when I saw Mitchell Michaelson, his long legs barely covered by track shorts. As my eyes focused, sharpening the image, it registered with me that he was not a volunteer like Livie and her friends because I could now make out the official paper number attached to his midsection. That number signaled that Mitch was not there to cheer on the athletes as I had assumed. He was, in fact, a special Olympian. I knew this boy, he was the same Mitchell Michaelson who had shared park dates with Jack when they were little guys. Mitch had Sotos, too.

Characteristic of the syndrome, both Jack and Mitch were extremely tall and lanky; they shared the same low muscle tone and awkward gait. Both had broad foreheads, wide-set eyes, and thin faces that converged into a pointed chin. The only characteristic that would have distinguished these otherwise physically identical twins were the wire-framed glasses that Mitchell wore.

Seeing Mitch on the track participating in the events caused me to imagine how life might have been different for Jack had I taken a different parenting route, that illusive glimpse of a path not taken. Mitchell's dad and I had not talked much, but I knew that for all the striking similarities between our boys, we had made different choices all along the way. I did not know much, but I knew he had been enrolled in special education throughout his public school career. I also knew his dad had told him early on that he had Sotos syndrome. The football team at Grand, his high school, had chosen him as an honorary team manager, and he could be frequently seen carrying a bag of equipment out to the football field or taking pictures of the players at practice. I knew that he was not taking driver's training along with kids his own age. A year older than Jack in school, Mitch identified as a kid with special needs. On that day at the athletic fields, I was left to reconcile the few things I knew with the image of Mitch competing in the Special Olympics.

The scene took me back to those park days a lifetime ago. Jack and he had a few play dates when they were little guys. Mitch had a younger sister, who was Rosie's age. We did not live close, but his dad and I had talked and begun to set up play dates so that the kids could play together semi-regularly. However, it was not long before I retreated. It was too painful seeing Jack with this carbon copy of himself. It reminded me of how some misguided folks erroneously think all kids with Down Syndrome look alike. I had always assumed that I was the problem, but maybe Mitch's dad felt the same way I did; just a little uncomfortable seeing the boys together.

This was about the same time that I had become preoccupied with my theory of expectations. I simply did not want this reminder that Jack had a syndrome. For Jack to pass as "typical" I could not risk people lumping these two unique boys together—the pair of "special needs kids." Jack did not have many friends; in fact, all his play dates had been orchestrated between myself and another equally enthusiastic parent. I desperately wanted Jack to have his own friends.

Admittedly there were a lot of plusses to these two kids coming together. Here, finally, was a friend who would not lap him in races, would not have an unfair advantage in games, and would not challenge him because they were the same. It may have been cruel of me, but I could not let Jack stay in this comfortable place with his genetic twin. (And for all I know, Mitchell's dad felt the same).

So, with unstated mutual consent, our families drifted apart, but not before Mitch's dad asked me if I wanted to go to a conference with him. In an ironic turn of events, even as I tried desperately to escape it, this year Sotos followed me home. It turned out this year the National Sotos syndrome conference was to be held in Denver. I did not even know that such a thing existed, I had assumed that the condition was too rare to have national gatherings. I was wrong again.

I politely declined the invitation and privately wished he hadn't alerted me to its existence. I had been part of many educational events, always eager to learn something new, but I did not want to go anywhere in the vicinity of this one. For me to attend, as the parent of an affected child, was nothing short of surrender. It would mean raising the white flag and accepting the label, the community, and all that was wrapped up in it. I ran the other way.

After that, even though they were at different schools, we would occasionally see Mitchell and his dad at community functions. We would each wave enthusiastically to the other, offer pleasantries, and promise to get the boys together soon, never once doing so. One time, Livie, always my quietly astute observer of human behavior, said, "Jack looks like Mitchell. Does Jack have what Mitchell has?" At the time, I denied it, shrugging off the subject and it was never brought up again. Fast forward to this moment, where I am watching Jack's genetic twin, a proud special Olympian, likely one of the fastest, most capable athletes out there, rounding the track.

Cynics may chalk this whole experience up to healthy rationalization, a tidy way of comforting myself that I was right all along. Me, with my militant and sometimes risky parenting choices; this was a way to avoid having to make peace with the decisions I had made. But the feeling that overwhelmed me that day on the high school track, already sticky under a cloudless Colorado sky, was not even close to a rationalization. It was palpable and it screamed, "What you are doing is worth it!" For that moment, the years of causing my son discomfort, being the bad-guy mom, embarrassing exchanges, and awkward situations, all dissolved. Mine was the path to what I wanted for Jack.

But what trade-offs had I made to travel this road? Jack seemed to be angry more often than not and struggled with self-esteem. I recognize that "angry" and "esteem-challenged" could be the tagline under the vast majority of teenage boys' yearbook photos. However, in Jack's case, I wondered more than once if my choices had contributed to the situation. To the extent that my refusal to acknowledge the limitations pronounced by his diagnosis was to blame for his demeanor, I was sorry. But I also knew for a fact that Jack did not view himself as having "special needs" and he would not, even for a moment, have considered himself as eligible to compete in the Special Olympics.

It is important to note that I do not presume to know how Mitch is faring today. It is possible that following high school, Mitch found other ways to overcome his genetically determined challenges. Today, he may be successful and confident, while having avoided the frustration that Jack encountered by being cast as "typical." Regardless, this was the reality I experienced on the athletic fields that fateful day in May. While my path did not avoid "potholes" of doubt, difficulty, and discomfort, it was the way I had chosen for my son and I was not wavering, turning back, or considering any short cuts. In that moment, still frozen in time in my consciousness, I had been affirmed.

I believe that every one of us who is blessed to be a parent moves forward governed by our better angels, determined to do what we think is right for our kids. My resolve to raise Jack as if he had no limitations was firmly rooted within me. The decision I made long ago at the Jersey shore required that Jack not know his diagnosis. I did not want him to identify with a label. I enjoyed imagining the descriptors the boy I was raising would identify with—tall, sports fan, Star Wars geek, environmental crusader, and rabidly uninterested in anything that resembled fashion or getting a haircut. There was no room on that list for "special needs" or "Sotos syndrome." Contrary to the start he got in life, comments from teachers or neighbors, or sideways looks from kids at school, I wanted to scrub from his identity any association with disability.

I didn't have any weighty scientific insights to prop me up at the time, but my dad's words "don't borrow trouble" kept ringing in my ears. This oft used phrase was Dad's way of warning "us kids" not to become hobbled by the thought of something possibly happening. Using this logic, I decided it could not be good for Jack to ruminate on all the possible vagaries his diagnosis predicted. This would just be borrowing trouble. He was better off not knowing. Well, who knew? It turns out that if you live long enough, science will catch up with your elders' wisest sayings.

A few years ago, researchers conducted a study revealing that merely knowing ones' risk for a genetic malady can cause a range of ill effects from negative feelings to impaired performance and even changed body physiology.[14] It seems that the human mind is trying to predict what is going to happen because of the new risk information and the body responds by actually taking on some of the characteristics associated with the genetic condition. In this study, knowing ones' genetic risk created a negative mindset about ability, impacted subjects' efficiency in converting oxygen, increased their perceived exertion around tasks, decreased their running endurance, and made them actually produce more of a certain hormone associated with the condition they feared. This official "don't borrow trouble study" underscores a truly mind-blowing mind-body connection that my Dad knew all along and bolstered my decision not to tell Jack about Sotos.

Days turned into months and years and Jack still had no idea that something called Sotos syndrome existed. As he grew, I explained away the obvious by saying, "You were born with a muscle weakness." It was a useful explanation because in it lay a prescription for hard work and practice. Not only was it a sufficiently innocuous explanation, it was also a handy motivator. A weakness can be improved. A weakness is a temporary condition that can be overcome with hard work. I would say, "you have to practice this or that because you were born with a muscle weakness." "If you are going to watch TV, you have to do it on your stomach with your head propped up in your hands because it will help build your muscles." In this way, I avoided the stain of a label. We replaced the insinuation of an irrevocable disability with a "temporary" condition that promised relief through effort, perseverance, and ingenuity.

As a teacher seeing my parents and students interact over the years, I had always assumed that the beliefs and actions of influential adults impact kids' performances. Now I had proof from my own life that parental beliefs shape what children come to think about themselves. Based on experience I was even more determined that my beliefs about and behavior toward Jack should signal in no uncertain terms that he was *capable*. My idea or "vision" of capable for my son included exiting special education and the system that was setting lowered expectations for him. This was my path, the route to realizing high expectations for my own child. This was the path to capable for my child. I believe that every parent should set a path to capable for their own child, understanding that the path may be laden with obstacles and detours.

Chapter 32

NOT MAKING
THE CUT

Try your hardest, make the effort, do your best.

—John Wooden, College Basketball Coach

JACK WAS UNDONE WHEN HE DID NOT MAKE the high school basketball team; at least that is what I wanted to believe. I was working out of town when I remember getting his call. He said sheepishly, "I did all I could, Mom, I could not do anymore." What quality did I detect in his voice? Was what I initially pegged as devastation, actually resignation, or possibly relief? Perhaps more precisely he was devastated that I might be devastated.

"Your best is all you can do, 'I am so proud of you, and I love you" was all I could get out before I hung up. I vacillated between anger and sadness. As I look back now, I think as much as Jack did not want to let me down, he was just as happy to find the exit ramp off one more competition highway.

In the weeks leading up to tryouts, Jack never missed a practice. Our large public high school held a special "camp week" before tryouts that the "in kids" and "in parents" knew about. Jack was not "in," so we did not know about the camp. Still, he showed up every night for the four nights of tryouts that followed. Except it turned out not to be four nights as he was cut by the end of the third night. He did not make the team; not the A, B, C or even the D team.

It hurt to see all the kids he practiced with get a spot on one team or another. I was angry at God and the universe for not bending the tenets of competition and school politics, the two pillars of high school sport, for a boy who was not strictly deserving of a spot on the team, but who would so benefit from one.

The powers that be that evening, including the coach and all the various assistant coaches, did not care how much Jack had practiced, how many free throws he had shot on the driveway, how he had worked with a private coach to summon better coordination through endless clapping drills timed to a metronome-like computer prompt. Nor did they care a fig about my idea that raising a child as if he were able could make it so. They did not know that everything hinged on building "positives" in Jack's experience ledger. They may have been familiar with the spirit behind "effort creates aptitude," which I had taken as my religion, but for them, on that day, Jack just plain wasn't good enough.

I had tried to build a world around Jack where encouragement was designed to increase effort and where effort in turn would create ability. And so it did. Jack was a better basketball player than he would have been minus those endless free throws, practices, and clapping drills. But there were still plenty of players who were much faster, more accurate, more coordinated, and much more confident than Jack.

Beyond my anger at an indifferent world that was impervious to all I had tried to create, I was sad. I cried for this boy who was keenly aware of letting his mama down, and I cried too because I feared this was another time when Jack put himself out there and fell short.

Simultaneously, I felt convicted. Did Jack put himself out there, or did I put him out there? I knew that it was not Jack's will or competitive drive that landed him on that basketball court that September. It was the culmination of years of encouragement, endless basketball camp sign ups, and sessions with a private coach. Jack found himself on the court as the result of a lopsided calculus on my part.

Why *did* I do this? I reminded myself of the route that had gotten us here. Jack needed an unlimited number of repetitions of slack muscles to improve the compromised tone that was a signature characteristic of Sotos, infinitely more than could be provided by thirty-minute therapy sessions. Determined to not give in to labels and the stigma attached meant that this practice had to happen through real-life activity and not through a cavalcade of special services. Typical kids strengthen muscles, gain coordination, decrease processing time, and increase confidence and self-esteem through sports. Lack of grip strength and eye-hand coordination ruled out sports involving small balls. Jack's height was an asset and led us ultimately to basketball. Was there a point where I or his Dad should have said, Jack you don't have what it takes to play competitive basketball? Maybe. In these moments I was and still am left to ponder the wisdom of my calculus. However flawed, it was fueled by love and the theory that Jack would be raised without yielding to the limits of labels and diagnoses.

I exhausted myself weighing the pain of this loss with the benefits that basketball offered over the years. All told, Jack had learned the game of basketball, all that clapping to the rhythmic metronome had improved his eye-hand coordination and hopefully created new neural pathways, and even if the balance of game time was spent on the bench, countless basketball drills and working out with the team had stretched his endurance and improved his speed. Perhaps most importantly, Jack had been ON the team and that meant he spent time with boys his age, interacting and socializing. I knew that equivalent opportunities which offer "typical" peer-to-peer interaction virtually disappear for kids with labels, especially as they move beyond elementary school. Without heterogeneous mingling of kids with and without special needs, skill gaps and social differences become more pronounced over time. All told, I was thankful for the opportunities basketball had afforded and would not have wanted to trade them to avoid this moment of "failure."

Even so, as much as I wanted to swear, complain, and cry out at an unfeeling, unsympathetic world, I knew the cost of airing my emotions in front of my kid. I feared that showing overt anger or sadness would translate as expecting differential treatment. Not that parents of "typical" kids do not stomp their feet and have tantrums when their child does not make first string. But Jack knew where he stood in the pecking order for selection on the high school team. If I displayed anger or acted like he was being "ripped off," he might interpret it as his mom thinking he should be given a pass, or that the bar for making the team should be lowered because of his "special" circumstances. That would send Jack a message that he was less than and should be held to a lower standard…and that would never do.

I am certain that in the moment my emotions would have betrayed me. But thankfully I was in a hotel room in another state, so I did what many a working mother has done, I alternately railed, cried, and complained to a co-worker, a successful, practical and kind man who listened patiently. With the benefit of time, and a particularly cathartic venting session complete with colorful expletives, I arrived home from the airport the next evening having resolved grievances toward this universe that did not seem to be on my side at all.

We let a few days go by before his dad and I posed the question, "So what sport would you like to do?" We threw out the question as if the fact that he would participate in a sport was already decided. 'You have to do something that gives you exercise and connects you to your school. Livie does soccer, Rosie is in theater and track, and Will swims."

The words "Livie does soccer" resonated as I spoke them. I was transported back to the cozy Jersey shore house covered with greying weathered shakes. A frail boy lay in a navy polka dot canvas Pack'N Play. His arms lay splayed at his sides and his legs lay slack from his torso, unlike his sister next to him, who was scaling our enormous beach bag, pulling herself up, fixing to take on the world. On that day in a show of defiance, I proclaimed that my son would do everything his twin did. I wasn't about to let go of that commitment just because a high school basketball team did not work out. Naturally, Jack was going to find something else to do.

Not unlike that day at the shore, I got no protest from Jack. He knew he would have to find an activity. Maybe it was because we had established a pattern so long ago that there was no thought of opting out, or if there was, he never voiced it. Through the years, expectations had been bolstered by the advent of other siblings, first Rosie, barely 21 months after the twins, and then 3-year-old Will when Jack and Livie were not quite six. For as long as Jack could remember, there were three living, breathing examples of "typical expectations" growing up around him.

For me, too, the other kids served as benchmarks of typical expectations. I am reminded of Jodi Picoult's book, *My Sisters Keeper*, which tells about a sibling who is brought into the world to help the other frail child survive. In this fictional story, one child was used as the instrument for the other's survival. I would not say I "used" my kids. I love them all fiercely and singularly. I could write a book about my wonderment at each of their unique gifts and struggles. However, they *were* instrumental in Jack's success in that they served as constant visceral reminders of regular developmental and cognitive benchmarks. My years in special education had made me all too aware of how norms can be skewed when one does not have examples of "typical" for comparison. Rosie blowing out birthday candles with ease, Will holding a pencil with a tripod grasp, and Livie writing complex essays were all nagging reminders that Jack needed to get on with the business of mastering these things as well. A blessing, afforded by the chaotic course of doing life with four kids, was that Jack and I were regularly confronted with developmental realities.

With years of basketball in the rearview mirror, no one in the family questioned whether Jack would find a new sport. But which one? Middle school with its "ya'll come," inclusive approach to school sports was a distant memory. High school was full of athletes who had been in the process of mastering their sport since before elementary school. Football, soccer, baseball, lacrosse, and swimming—all of these were out of reach, but what about track and field? Basketball drills *ad nauseum* had increased Jack's endurance, so we thought of track because it was an individual sport where athletes could participate competitively or non-competitively. Of course, only students who were fast enough were eligible to participate in the meets, but track itself was a non-cut sport. I don't know that any of us (including Jack) gave much consideration to whether or not he loved running. The simple fact was it checked all the required boxes—developmental, physical, and social. It was a sport, it would help him continue building coordination, strength, and endurance, and it would make him part of a team.

I had hoped that finding another sport would change the narrative from "you failed at basketball" to "you *weren't* beaten by basketball; you persevered and found something else." It was settled. Jack signed up, brought home the uniform and participated in track. He hung in there all season, but it was clear he did not enjoy it. A non-cut sport, he avoided the stress over "making the team," but ultimately, we learned that track is a sport that exists in flashes of glory. The names of the events tell the whole story. You had your fifty-yard dash, hundred-yard dash, even the 800 Meter was named for the distance it took to finish. This athletic pursuit rewarded quick bursts of energy, and that was not what Jack was about. He gravitated to the long-distance team where endurance was as important as speed. He practiced with the team, but he was never invited to a meet his entire freshman year. I feared that Jack would add track to the failure column and would hang up his size 13½ running shoes for good.

But taking chances has its rewards. Exposure, even when painful, can crack open doors just wide enough to usher in sweet possibility. As it turned out, even struggling to be one of the last finishers on the track team afforded opportunity. A coach, seeing Jack's misalignment among the spritely runners, and maybe seeing his heart, suggested that he join the cross-country team. I knew nothing about the sport, not even that it was a sport. I soon deduced that speed remained important but was not the only factor in cross-country. Here was a sport that truly valued perseverance, drive, and maintaining consistency. Fast was ideal, but you did not have to go fast, you just had to go long, and that was just fine with Jack. While there were super competitive athletes out there, the cross- country model also offered a space for runners who were non-competitive. Best of all it afforded a community.

The four-to-seven-mile practice runs were punishing, but Jack was no stranger to difficulty. Throughout his life, generalized muscle weakness through his body ensured that most things were difficult. Self-care activities like shoe tying, academic building blocks like writing with a pencil, processing thoughts and producing a verbal response, and even actions that most dismiss as effortless, like blowing out birthday candles, required effort and practice. Here was a boy who *expected* life to be hard. So perhaps Jack took it as a matter of course that runs would be long and grueling, and that he would stop at intervals and even walk as other runners whizzed by, and that he might be one of the last athletes to cross the finish line. All of these became realities of Jack's participation on the high school cross-country team, yet he returned to practice every day.

Even the scoring rules of cross-country worked in Jack's favor. Each team's top seven runners' times were calculated to determine where the school places in a meet. Beyond those top seven runners (and a few more who were vying to get into that top tier) most athletes are running to beat their personal records or PR. Anyone who has taken on a 5K run will attest to the power of the running community and the spirit of positivity and encouragement that pervades race days. It is the same with cross-country races...early finishers flank the course with enthusiastic cheers that spur the remaining runners to the finish line.

Now cross-country presented itself, a natural way for Jack to continue to push, challenge his limits, and gain endurance. Furthermore, wonder of wonders, being part of the cross-country team included an optional weightlifting "class" with one of the football coaches. So, Jack was able to engage in strength training three days a week with teammates while being supervised by the football coach. I knew nothing about high school football, but I mused, "who knew more about getting strong than a football coach?" I had no idea what transpired during these weightlifting sessions, but I surmised that they could not hurt. What was the worst thing that could happen? Jack would lift too much weight and pull a muscle? Would he get made fun of or ignored by other athletes?

Raising a child without fear requires a good deal of faith and trust in the universe and a belief that he or she is going to make it. One must take on the conviction that if things go wrong, the amount of learning that is bound to occur in the mistakes and muddling through is infinitely more valuable than what he or she would gain in a protected environment where there was no opportunity to try.

Children thrive with a balance of challenge and support. The message a child gets loud and clear when you let go and deliberately throw him or her into challenging situations is that you (the most influential person in his life) believe he is capable. I don't know what happened in those weightlifting sessions, nor do I know if other athletes doubted Jack's ability; what was important to me was that Jack saw that his parents thought he could. And so he did. A kid or two may have made a derogatory remark behind his back. As heartbreaking as it was to think about, I knew that Jack would sustain significantly more long-lasting damage if we, his parents, gave voice to sentiments like, "I don't know about weightlifting for you," or "You can't run that far," or "It's hard being last, you don't have to go to practice today."

Spring and summer of freshman year marked the beginning of three uninterrupted years on the high school cross-country team. I do not have the records to back this up, but I believe it is a fact that Jack never missed a practice. Although we would have allowed him to opt out occasionally, Jack did not want to. He felt he was part of something. On race days, Pete or I, or both of us, would plant ourselves at the beginning of the course, and cheer like crazy; then we'd take a short cut to the middle of the course, wait for Jack to come by and cheer again; and finally, we would wait at the finish line and cheer like crazy one last time.

Teammates clapped and high-fived each other as they arrived at the team tent following each race. It did not matter that Jack finished near last. He was logging much bigger wins. These included seeing himself as a member of the high school athletic team, as a person who competes without accommodation, and as a person who finishes what he starts. All these significant life victories were accomplished at the same time that he was strengthening muscles and building coordination and stamina. Perhaps an aggressive physical therapy regimen would have targeted some of these areas but, for my money, tackling deficit areas in the course of being on a team provided immeasurable social and psychological benefits. Further, none of these would have happened if Jack had adopted a victim mentality and thrown in the towel when basketball did not pan out.

To be sure, there were moments of extreme pride mixed with awkwardness and discomfort. During his three years on the team there were 5-foot 4-inch freshmen runners easily passing this nearly 6-foot-4 senior. I own my moments of cowardice when I gave coaches a wide berth at meets, as if by avoidance I could ward off comments I did not want to hear like, "He (Jack)walks when he tires," or "perhaps cross is not right for him."

Ripples of discomfort were dwarfed by waves of elation that washed over me when coaches offered positive comments. One cross country coach, who also served as Rosie's biology teacher, Ms. Tabor, cornered me one evening at parent-teacher conferences, not to praise Rosie as I had thought (teachers were always praising Rosie), but to go into detail about how Jack was such an affirming team member, how he was always the first to encourage other runners, and how she thought he had the qualities to be a great teacher someday.

It was one of those moments where I simultaneously thought "This can't get any better" and "Lord, take me now!" I did not want to risk her continuing to elaborate for fear she might qualify these angel-breathed words in a way that would unravel the glorious moment that was now mine with an after-the-fact clause like, "… for a kid with his challenges" or "…as a 'special' kid." But, in the moment, Ms. Tabor paused, her mouth ceased moving, waiting for my response. That was it; all she had to say. There would be no gut punch. In these instances, I was convinced that a benevolent God had again tossed me a bone, saying, "It ain't over yet, not by a long shot, but hang in there, you are doing the right thing."

At the end of the season, senior year, we assembled for the Cross-Country banquet and awards ceremony. Pete and I sat in stadium-style seats among the proud parents, with Jack seated a few rows in front of us among some team members. We listened patiently as the head coach called up each senior and in turn gave them a gift, sometimes sincere, sometimes a gag gift, but each was accompanied by a brief story about what made that athlete a unique or valued member of the team. My mind wandered, imagining the words of affirmation the coach would offer Jack when his name was called. We waited expectantly, shifting in our seats as they moved from Berns to Drummond. Maybe they were not going in alpha order? We sat as they called Stiles, Turner, and Zolfo. Maybe they were reserving Jack for some character-based honor, like "perfect attendance," I thought, or (hoping against hope) "most valuable teammate"? Optimism sustained me.

We waited until the very act of waiting became futile. It was over. The coaches had finished honoring seniors and still Jack's name had not been called. Some parents sitting next to us realized that Jack had been omitted and were shifting awkwardly in their seats as well, likely feeling our pain. My gaze landed on the back of Jack's razor cut blond head a few rows down, knowing that he too realized that not only had his name not been called, it was not going to be, the moment had passed. My heart plunged; this was basketball tryouts all over again, except worse. Hadn't Jack endured enough? He, who went to every practice, who never complained about extra workouts, who despite his excellent attendance, struggled to come in among the proud final few at each meet, was he also to experience the humiliation of being overlooked, forgotten, erased as a team member his senior year?

Mercifully, another student called out Jack's name, presumably to alert the coaches who had moved on with the presentation. An assistant coach caught the utterance and hastily called Jack up. Jack hustled up to the stage, letting everyone involved off the hook by not registering the slightest disappointment regarding the obvious slight. I thought now certainly the coaches would offer a story or a few encouraging words that would atone for their dereliction of duty. But the speaker made a generic passing comment, shook Jack's hand and motioned him to join the line. This coach was so thrown off balance by being alerted to the error that he committed the further offense of awkwardly and summarily shuffling Jack to the lineup of seniors who had received their planned remarks. Another knife to my heart; again I silently railed against this cruel world that was indifferent, once more, to my kid. In the end, although it was not easy, I had to shrug off the evening, after all, Jack was still part of the team.

But it hurt. There was no positive spin left even in this perennial optimist. Jack had given cross- country his all. Coincidence maybe, but it was one he did not need. Why couldn't Turner or Stiles or Drummand have been overlooked? Another kid left out, so that the audience would assume that it was just a random error and not an oversight made because this kid meant so little to the team. Processing later I found the lesson: In the "real world" sometimes things suck. People make mistakes and are callous about making them. Making other people feel valued is not at the top of everyone's list. Finally, when you swim in the deep water among all the fishes, sometimes you get lost in the unforgiving current. That is the cold, hard truth of real life, as painful as it was. I recognized that it would be hypocritical to preach the dignity inherent in risk and then to only accept it when things go well. These hard knocks were a part of life and insulating Jack from them would be to rob him of dignity.

Chapter 33

MOMENTS OF TRUTH AND OTHER OCCASIONS THAT CALL FOR A BLIZZARD

"The truth." Dumbledore sighed. "It is a beautiful and terrible thing, and should, therefore be treated with great caution."

— J.K. Rowling, *Harry Potter and the Sorcerer's Stone*

IT WAS THE SUMMER BEFORE JUNIOR YEAR when we decided it was time to tell him. I intervened, supported, advocated, and swooped in to protect as necessary. But now Jack was getting too big to coerce. As he grew, I was around less and less to protect and temper the looks, comments, and unkindnesses perpetrated against him. I was no longer present to offer a ready model for how others should behave. I was no longer the buffer between him and the world. I was not aware if kids were making fun of him at school, if the PE teacher was allowing him to sit on the sidelines, if the math teacher was letting him off the hook when he did not offer an immediate answer, or if fellow students in study groups were relegating him to lesser parts in their group presentations. Until now, I was afraid that if Jack knew he had been born with a syndrome, he would cloak himself in this knowledge, use it as a crutch; an excuse to opt out of activities that were uncomfortable or to justify expecting less of himself.

Looking up at my nearly sixteen-year-old who towered over me, I could see the advantage to him knowing. By now he had overcome so much and achieved much more than skeptics or textbooks claimed possible. He might take this information as a triumph, a badge of honor. It was the way to pass the torch of responsibility from us to him. He needed to be in charge of his life.

But how to tell him? With four teenagers, our house was zoo-like on most days. Each one of them in turn acting out their emotional highs and lows as the spirit moved them. We did not dare risk Jack's brothers and sisters interrupting or overhearing. Livie had only once asked about Jack. Perhaps it is the twin bond they share that gives her a special respect for him, or that rarified air of empathy that she possesses. However, as Rosie and Will got older, they would return from school feeling embarrassed, likely experiencing the fallout of some indignity that Jack had suffered at school. They would ask, "Is Jack autistic?" or "Why is Jack so weird?" because that was the only "language" they had to describe kids who were different. My protective instinct was to become indignant and correct them, relying on the now firmly enshrined explanation of a "muscle weakness condition."

Not knowing how Jack was going to react, Pete and I lured him to a neutral location that he could not resist, Dairy Queen. I say lured, but it was actually an unbelievably easy task because, as a teenager, above all, he loved food—especially fast food. I chose this particular

Dairy Queen because regular customers overwhelmingly opted for the air-conditioned indoor seating area, leaving the outside benches vacant; the perfect solitary spot for confidential discussions. Ice cream to get his attention and privacy to insulate us from eavesdropping siblings were the trappings I required to reveal this long-held secret.

And so, it was there at a picnic table under an ancient oak tree, with the comfort of a large cookie dough Blizzard, that we proceeded to tell Jack that he was born with a syndrome. I began awkwardly, as best I could, by offering the story of my own difference… "You know how Mom was born with organs on the outside of my body and I had to be in a cast for a long time? I still have some problems with that today. They told me I could never have kids, but I was blessed with four. I have learned that being born 'different' is a part of my story, but it does not define me."

Jack looked at me truly confused and more than slightly repulsed. Why was his mom talking to him this way about gross stuff like bodies, organs, and childbirth? And why was she doing it while he was eating? Did she want him to hurl? Clearly, in his mind, I had once again crossed over that fine line by offering too much information. My kids often accused me of violating this basic parent-teen tenet of peaceful co-existence.

"Mom… TMI," they would warn me, Too Much Information. No doubt he likely also thought, "And why *now*, with Dad here next to me on this bench, and with none of the other kids around?" And most mysterious in our way of: always-keep-all-the-kids-even household, "why am I getting ice cream, when no one else is?" I suppose the entire situation was altogether incomprehensible to him.

So, having put behind me what I now see as a way-too-circuitous lead-in, I finally got to the point. "You see that circumstances don't have to define people, Jack. We thought it was important not to tell you, in fact, we thought telling you might hold you back, limit what you thought you could do."

"Tell me what?" Jack's face beseeched me to make sense.

"Like I said, we did not want it to define you, but you were born with a syndrome. It is called Sotos syndrome. It causes overgrowth, muscle weakness, tumors, developmental delays, and learning problems. We did not tell you because we did not want it to hold you back. You have come so far and have overcome so much. Dad and I won't be with you all the time now that you are getting bigger and we can no longer push you into therapies and activities. Now you need to do what is right for you, make choices that will continue to challenge you and help you improve."

I went on, "We have taken you this far, now you have to decide what you want to do with this information. You can use it to feel sorry for yourself or you can use it as a motivator. Think about what you have achieved—through speech therapy, occupational therapy and physical therapy. You have gotten out of special education, into regular classes and went on to STEM (Science Technology, Engineering, and Mathematics) in high school..."

I went on searching Jack's face for a sign of recognition to replace the confusion that was still plastered there. Like most kids, the only word that Jack had heard paired with syndrome was "Down...

"Like Down Syndrome, Mom?" he questioned.

"No, it is not Down Syndrome. That is another syndrome," I offered.

Understanding was starting to take shape on Jack's face. I saw him trying on this new revelation with the events, impressions, reactions and feelings he had experienced in his short life.

"You see," I floundered, "whenever you had trouble doing something and it required an explanation, I called it "a muscle weakness condition," because I felt that would satisfy you, explain the need for therapy, and help you understand why you had to practice things so much harder and longer than other kids."

I went on to explain that I wanted "muscle weakness" to stand for something that could get better with effort. "People generally associate "syndrome" with an absolute, a permanent condition, something that cannot change, and something that maybe even gets worse over time. Dad and I could not allow you to believe that about yourself. We were also afraid that other people might treat you differently, that they might saddle you with that label, if we told them what it was. We could have talked about Sotos a lot when you were little, and we could have left you in special education where accommodations would always be made for you, but we were afraid that it might limit the person you could become."

Now, with it all out there, I allowed myself to take a breath.

The spoon now abandoned in the cup, Jack had lost interest in the Blizzard and was instead digesting this new knowledge. I wanted to fill the silence, say something. But then mercifully, a look spread over his face that took the form of relief.

"Ryan, at school, called me socially awkward, that must have been what he meant," Jack said.

Now I was crying. I had replayed this moment in my head like a movie so many times in the past couple of years knowing that there would be a day of reckoning, only hoping it would be billed as a poignant coming of age story and not a tragedy.

In my imaginings there was an overriding concern that swallowed up all other possibilities. My concern was that, among all I had revealed, Jack would fixate on the label that I had so painstakingly tried to inoculate him against all these years. He needed to know the word, to hear it. But I did not want him to internalize it or wear it like a second skin. I did not want this information to become him. Words have such power. I feared that this would give him permission to use the word "Sotos" and the diagnosis behind it as "a pass" for not trying harder, doing more, for believing he was disabled. I did not want Sotos to be the ready excuse for everything he struggled with in life.

So immense was my fear that he would be hurt or devastated by the news that I had not considered that this moment of truth could evoke another wholly different emotion: relief. But that was the emotion that I read on his face, and his words confirmed it: "Maybe that is why he called me awkward."

In his teenage understanding of the world, this had been as far as he went outwardly processing his feelings, but now that he had put it out there, I could begin to see things from his vantage point. This new word "Sotos" gave him a reason for why kids had ignored him, people had looked at him askance, and why the mean kids called him retarded and other derogatory words when he moved awkwardly, spoke haltingly, or completed a task differently using one of his practiced work-arounds.

Relief was a positive emotion. It was not what I had expected, and not one that I wanted to be replaced with self-pity, excuse-making, or settling. His initial reaction was followed with a few of the more obvious questions, which I had expected, "Does it last forever?" "Does it make me retarded?"

We reminded him again, "It doesn't mean anything; you know what you can do. Look at what you have already done; you are succeeding in high school."

Then I shared with Jack one of the practical reasons I thought he needed to know. It was now time for him to take this information and use it to keep working to defy the diagnosis.

"One of your old therapists in California, when you were just a little guy, said something that I thought was very important and I have never forgotten it. The therapist said, 'Jack is a kid who is likely to plateau in his skills unless he continually pushes and challenges himself.' I want you to remember this, in light of what you have already achieved. I want you to always challenge yourself. You can use this new knowledge as a source of pride for all that you have overcome."

I closed with: "You have the power, you can use it to motivate yourself, to do anything you want to do with your life, now finish your Blizzard."

Of course, like any Gen Z-er, when we returned home, he turned to the Internet to learn what he could about Sotos. I found him in his room poring over websites. I asked, "Why do you care? You know what you can do."

He said, "Mom, I need to know." At that, the old fear of mine resurfaced. Would he latch on to the syndrome, use it for comfort or protection? I hoped not. Luckily, this behavior did not last. After a few days, I heard no more about it. When I entered his room, I was relieved to see him playing one of the time-sucking video games that I had previously cursed. Now it meant he was no longer hunched over the computer typing in key words "genetic," "syndrome," or "Sotos."

Chapter 34

THE WAY THE BALL BOUNCES

As it turns out, the applause is not as fulfilling as the work.

—Jen Hatmaker, *Of Mess and Moxie*

BY ALL INDICATIONS, high school basketball ended for Jack before it even got started that summer heading into 9th grade. I was frustrated that high school also signaled the end of opportunities for recreational basketball. It did not seem fair and I did not want Jack to feel like he had been defeated by the tryout experience. I wanted to believe that the high school team was not the only place where a kid could go to dribble a basketball. Apparently, I was wrong. The kids who were talented enough to make their high school teams continued to be invited to play on various travel and competitive teams, but there were precious few opportunities for 9th, 10th, and 11th graders who did not make that initial cut. Jack had gained from basketball, and I did not want the skill building to end for him.

I contacted the park district leagues, but even here, teams were pre-formed by groups of boys who were friends. Jack had no such network. We tried to add him to existing teams that needed another player, but this became awkward when potential teammates prejudged Jack's skills.

I was ready to cry uncle and admit that I was beat; high school ball, it seemed, had become too competitive. However, that day, as fate would have it, I was at school to drop off food for the cast of the high school musical when I happened by the gym. Basketball season was over, but the gym was virtually bursting to the seams with spectators, cheerleaders, and band members fringing the sidelines. A double take through propped-open doors confirmed that there was, in fact, a game in progress where two teams of particularly determined athletes were going head-to- head. Because of all the fanfare in the stands and overflow spectators flanking the court, one had to really inspect the scene to detect that the players had disabilities. Stopping a minute to watch this match-up that had all the intensity of a varsity game, I made a few inquiries among the teachers on the sidelines and returned home ruminating on an idea. I learned that this league, the Unified League, was looking for what were known as peer coaches. Peer coaches were volunteers without special needs, who helped the students with special needs in a variety of ways. They were responsible for assisting the students with the mechanics of the game, feeding the ball to players so they had shooting opportunities, teaching the rules of the game, and modeling sportsmanship.

It hit me that this was a way for Jack to play basketball, as well as to give back to his school community. Jack liked the idea but did not have the confidence to contact Mrs. Emmett, a special education teacher who doubled as the basketball coach, so I reached out to her.

Apparently, most of the Unified team's peer coaches were current players on the girls and boys Junior Varsity and Varsity teams. I explained that Jack was not on the high school team, but he had experience. She was pleased to hear of Jack's interest, and no more explanation was required. Jack filled out the paperwork and was added to the team as a peer coach.

For a parent approaching the world with an eye toward every endeavor creating an opportunity for her child to gain strength, build coordination, endurance, and confidence, a chance for one more "rep," if you will; this was a dream come true. As a peer coach on the Unified team Jack would also actually get to play the game of basketball, instead of what it had become for him, an exercise in bench warming, punctuated by a few minutes of court time, when a benevolent coach calculated that the score was such that he could afford to be generous. Given the skills gap I had briefly witnessed between the peer coaches and the players, I knew this was a team where Jack could contribute. He would be able to run drills, feed other kids' shots, model good sportsmanship, and demonstrate ball handling techniques.

Through the Unified League, my kid would be in a position to LEAD. Being on the outside, trailing others trying to keep up, always coming up short, "looking in" at the cool kids, getting picked last, and just plain being left on the sidelines; these circumstances and the feelings associated with them were familiar to Jack. They were so familiar in fact that I believed he was coming to accept them as his lot in life. He had known leaders; his elementary school friend was a leader, his sister was a leader, but he himself had never viewed the world from that enviable vantage point. This would be another chance for Jack to build a richer narrative for himself, not as the kid who struggled to get through, did his time (because his mom made him), and invariably finished last. But instead, he could be the kid who taught, showed others the way, and whose name the coach shouted out first to get onto the court.

While this was a rare, not-to-be-missed opportunity for Jack, basketball was not the only thing at play here. I had to make peace with some conflicting emotions. Since that day at the beach so long ago, it had been my quest to make sure that my child was not identified as disabled. There was more than a little bit of irony in the fact that part of this odyssey was now dependent on the help of the disability community. Perversely, one way in which the whole world (or anyone wondering) was going to see that my kid was not "special needs" was by having him help peers with special needs.

I did not quite know how to feel about this. Would I be, in effect, using other peoples' kids to show that my kid was not one of them, not even close? If I thought about it for too long in that light, it did not feel good. But the fact was, Jack had practiced basketball for many years and he knew the game. The Unified team needed peer coaches, and he certainly had time to spare since he would not be playing for the regular high school team. Among the students on the team who identified as having special needs there was a vast range of abilities: kids who moved agilely down the court but who could not communicate verbally; kids who had to be physically placed under the basket and helped to toss the ball into the air; and still others whose skills fell somewhere in between.

We have established that humans are creatures who want to sort and categorize. We seek to create order and decrease ambiguity, and the act of labeling helps to organize information in our brains. I considered that there may be times during the season where parents, staff, or casual observers would not be quite able to place Jack, and that they would want to assign him a label to decrease their ambiguity. Was he peer coach or a special needs player? Did he have a disability or not? I admit I had that fear, but I had to dismiss it for two reasons. First, this was good news for Jack and I was not about to put my own uneasiness in front of that; and second, because I had to come to terms with the fact that he was going to run into people who wanted to judge him throughout his life. Steering Jack clear of any association with classmates, potential friends, or fellow players who identified as having a special need was not going to insulate him from prejudice, presumptions, or wonderings.

Jack and I were just going to have to push through that ambiguity. He would have to show those people that he was capable and that their first impression was wrong. He would have to do that over and over again, so I surmised; and he might as well get started now. I wouldn't think to keep Livie, Rosie, or Will from associating with friends who happened to have special needs because of assumptions about what that association said about them, so I could not do that to Jack either. I had to believe in my kid, and in the end, if certain people walked away pegging Jack as this or that, it did not matter. His dignity required that he have the freedom to pursue his interests on his own terms without an eye to what others might think.

I reminded myself that none of us are immune to assumption-making. Most parents have done time in a pediatrician's waiting room with toys strewn around the floor to entertain toddlers and pre-schoolers. When we see a 10-year-old "typical" kid moving around the little figures in the plastic doll house or playing with the My Little Ponies, we take for granted that they are just checking the toys out, that they think they are kind of cute. But if another

10-year-old kid with an identifiable special need, let's say Down syndrome, is doing the same thing, we assume that it is a sign of delayed development, retardation. Naturally, we all seek information that confirms our biases. The behavior of a "typical" older child playing with a dollhouse is dismissed as endearing or as an expression of a passing interest; yet, in a child who looks "different" it is a sure indicator that something is wrong. These thoughts made me feel more charitable toward those who might judge my kid because, in truth, I have been them at least a time or two in my own life.

As it turned out, Jack thrived as a peer coach on the Unified Team. He never missed a practice or game. As an "integrated team," during the games, all the students were considered as players, whether they had a disability or not. The peer coaches simply served the added role of modeling and ensuring that the play on the court moved forward with points being scored at a similar pace across both teams. The rules held that there would be no more than two peer coaches per team on the court at any time. These two peer coaches, combined with three unified players, created a full team.

Pete and I were in the bleachers for as many games as we could attend. Just as I was confused about what I was seeing that first day I happened upon the scene, so were all the uninitiated who ventured into the gym on Unified Team game nights. The stands were bursting with parents and spectators from both sides shouting and holding up signs supporting their respective teams. Cheerleaders led the crowd in spirited chants and bounded onto the court periodically to stack themselves into precarious formations. If not the entire band, there were band squads on the sidelines belting out tunes. During the opening ceremony, the name of each player was announced as they, one by one, assembled at center court. Some ran, some walked, and some had to be led; all receiving enthusiastic high fives.

We could have been watching the NBA for all the reverence in the stands. Each game began with silence; a kinetic crackle of expectation built as both teams ascended onto the gleaming waxed hardwood for the opening tip-off. Jack was among the first out, a starter, ready to lead his team to victory. Beautiful is the only word I can find to describe the sight of this diverse collection of players who varied widely in their skill and knowledge of the game, but who all played to win and entertain enthusiastic spectators. Jack knew that his job as a peer model was to feed the ball to players who needed help and to take shots only when necessary to keep the score competitive. However, more than a few times, he fell prey to the roar of the crowd and his love of the game. I could see him forgetting himself, as he dribbled the ball down the court, sinking one basket and then another, playing with all his heart. At these moments, my heart skipped a beat, "Remember, you are on the team as a helper… this is not about you," I mouthed wordlessly. But then, as if coming to his senses, he would slip back into his coach role and pass the ball to a teammate who needed to stand under the basket and take two or three tosses in a row to sink one. This lapse of judgment was not too out of norm for a peer coach and could be easily explained away by a mix of the excitement for the game and the bravado of a teenage boy showing off. Besides, such moves got cheers and made the games all the more thrilling.

The Unified season included only seven or eight home games and not all peer coaches were allowed to go on the bus trips to away games. Regardless of the short season, for Jack it was pure enjoyment. Sweaty, smelly, and smiling as we left the gym one night, he remarked, "I always wanted to play for my own school, in my own high school gymnasium, and as it turned out I got to."

I could not hide my pride. Reflecting on times when I'd pouted over the smallest of trivialities not going my way, I stood humbled by this amazing kid who took whatever life gave him and called it good.

Jack peer-coached on the Unified Team for two years, even getting to play an "exhibition game" under the bright lights at the Pepsi Center before a Denver Nuggets game; a feather in the cap of any 16-year-old. He also got to learn what it felt like to lead, serve, and mentor while playing a game that he loved. It built confidence into Jack's narrative. While recreational teams for 16- and 17-year-olds remained in short supply, this experience opened the door to other avenues for Jack to play basketball. We learned that there were also basketball camps for young elementary school students that appreciated teenage volunteers, and Jack added those to his growing "resume" of positive experiences and community involvement.

Chapter 35

BOOK LEARNIN'

The skill I was learning was a crucial one,
the patience to read things I could
not yet understand.

—Tara Westover, *Educated*

"I DON'T CARE" was the stock retort we heard reverberating through the slammed door. Jack was explosive when asked about his grades. He was hyper defensive and could not handle inquiries about upcoming assignments or tests. Like many kids who are failing, Jack was angry with himself and deflected all questions about schoolwork by feigning disinterest. His dad and I knew that as the work got harder, this attitude would create ever greater gaps between him and his peers. Jack had successfully exited from special education halfway through 6th grade, but if this academic chasm continued to widen, he would not be able to tackle the exponentially increasing difficulty of high school material and would be on the road back to special education; destined to stagnate there.

Like most kids, by the time Jack reached high school, much of what he thought of himself as a student had calcified. He approached studying in ways that did not challenge him. It became clear that academics was another area where he would have to leave his comfort zone and stretch his limits.

When it came to academics, I found myself staring up at another mountain that caused me, yet again, to question the veracity of my high expectations credo. I believed that raising Jack to believe he was able would shape his behavior and that over time he would come to perform within the typical range. The bulleted listing of Sotos syndrome characteristics: "developmental delays," "learning disabilities," "cognitive processing deficits," and even "intellectual impairment" loomed large in my mind. What if I was wrong? What if performance differences in kids with Sotos could not be explained by the cumulative effect of low expectations, protective parenting, and "less than" messages delivered over a lifetime? What if intellectual limitations were physiologically inherent in the syndrome? Could it be that pervasive low muscle tone somehow affected cognitive processing speed in ways that were not fully understood? There were no studies I knew of that definitively confirmed that the delays observed in children with Sotos were a foregone conclusion. Since there was no way for me to know for sure if delays were due to physiology, experience, or both, I doubled down on my theory of high expectations and barreled ahead.

Even so, I could not deny that Jack's inability to lift his head and move like other babies and toddlers had likely impacted Jack's formative years. He moved slower and took more time finding words, processing information, and forming responses, but I comforted myself that these were temporary circumstances. When I lobbied a trusted physical therapist with my wishful theory that there was nothing intrinsic to the syndrome that would cause Jack to have any lasting cognitive delays, she did not reassure me. All she said say was that "Jack had missed some important developmental building blocks."

While we did our best to raise Jack the same way we had all our kids, I cannot estimate or quantify all the ways in which the reality of having Sotos syndrome changed his life experience. To what extent did his not being able to lift his head alter his early view of the world? How did compromised balance affect how he experienced his body in space? How did difficulty getting his slack muscles to move affect his participation in critical early learning activities? Did compromised auditory processing speed impact the number and quality of learning opportunities that came his way? How did being ignored or receiving negative feedback from peers affect his motivation to try? Learning is a result of synergy of three things: the child's specific mental dispositions, his attention and motivation, and the rigor of the instruction provided. There were just plain differences in the chips Jack brought to the table due to early experiences and physiology.

There was also the question of rigor in the instruction he had received over the years. In my job, I have been interested in how conscious or unconscious bias effects the expectations teachers have for their students. Studies have shown that teachers of every ethnicity let the mistakes made by their black and brown students slide more often than they do the mistakes of white children. In addition, teachers give children of color less specific feedback on how to improve their work. While unintended, this bias alters the school experience for these children in ways that are not helpful to their future success. The result is that these students receive less rigorous instruction over the course of their school careers. I expect the same is true of students that teachers presume to have special needs. So, while I was vigilant that everyone in Jack's immediate orbit held him to the same standards they held other kids, I could not control the unconscious bias held by the array of teachers, coaches, and other authority figures who cycled through Jack's school life.

I could not say for sure whether Jack's present learning difficulties were the scourge of the syndrome itself, how the syndrome's characteristics restricted his early learning opportunities, or how his behavior was shaped by the subliminal biases of the teachers and other adults he encountered throughout his life. Likely the problem was some gnarly combination of all three. Regardless, the effect was that Jack was struggling academically in high school. His middle school performance was not stellar, but he had passed. By freshman year, Jack was getting low grades particularly in math and science, and if this pattern continued, he was at risk for failure. His attitude toward schoolwork did not help. Jack would not acknowledge what he was doing wrong. He became explosive when asked about his grades. He was hyper defensive and could not handle inquiries about upcoming tests or assignments. Like many kids who are failing at school, Jack was angry with himself and he deflected questions about his performance with feigned disinterest. His stock retort was, "I don't care." His dad and I knew that as the work got harder these counterproductive habits would create ever greater gaps between him and his peers. Jack had successfully exited from special education in 6th grade, but if this academic chasm continued to widen, he would not be able to tackle the exponentially increasing difficulty of high school material and would be on the road back to special education, destined to stagnate there.

Sure, the initial diagnosis, and later the educational labels provided useful information for identifying interventions and were our ticket to accessing services; however, they were not the final word on my kid's ability, not even close. This was true in part because no one can fully understand the relationship between the proclamation of a clinical diagnosis and how a child is subsequently viewed and treated by everyone in his orbit. The water is muddied, making it difficult to tease out what is real and what is the result of years of interplay between expectations, how the child is treated, and the extent to which opportunities are seized upon or denied. This includes the beliefs and actions of those around the child.

I wanted to be vigilant against the tendency to attribute every skill deficit or aberrant behavior to my kid's label or diagnosis. I feared it would lead to the blanket acceptance of a characteristic or behavior by the mere virtue of the fact that it is known to be associated with Sotos syndrome. I knew that wholesale acceptance of a symptom or indication is usually too simplistic. Because, while it provides a tidy explanation for inattention, failure to attend to the teacher, lack of social skills, or substandard academic performance, it also leads to a sense of complacency. For example, Jack's poor performance on an essay or a math quiz did not mean he had the substandard intelligence predicted by the Sotos diagnosis. I definitely did not subscribe to the attitude that "this is just how things are going to be for this, Jack, see it says so right on the label." But it is a tempting trap to use what you see and experience to confirm what has been predicted by expert sources whether they be tests, diagnoses, or educational labels. But what happens then, inevitably, is that the behavior gets more aberrant, social skills regress further, or gaps in school performance widen because we expected them to do so.

We take cover behind the characteristic or symptom as if failure or poor performance is a foregone conclusion. Rosario has autism so we expect her to be uninterested in other people; Jamal has ADHD so we expect him not to attend; Johnnie is a person who stutters so we expect that he does not want to respond in class, and so on.

The listing of characteristics associated with a clinical diagnosis are also sometimes called "indications" of a diagnosis. In the case of an educational label, they are called characteristics. Instead of buying into that list of indications or characteristics lock, stock, and barrel, I tried to pay attention to my kid and how he was behaving, acting, moving, and communicating. I trusted what I saw in Jack over what the label or diagnosis proclaimed he was capable of. I wanted to be a steely-eyed realist about specific issues, and weaknesses, but I also wanted to give at least equal effort to identifying Jack's idiosyncratic assets, motivations, and interests. I found that they are not to be ignored because they may give your kid an edge in overcoming challenges. For example, although the Sotos anomaly visited generalized low muscle tone, poor balance, reduced cognitive processing speed, and lack of coordination on Jack, it also gave him height which opened the door to basketball.

Attending to the academic struggles that threatened to sink Jack meant having to peel back labels and demystify nebulous terminology like "developmental delay," "learning disability," "intellectual impairment," and "cognitive processing speed." To do this we had to get real about his strengths and weaknesses. This involved identifying exactly what Jack did well; the specific assets he brought to schoolwork. I looked for whatever positives I could "mine," no matter how meager or undeveloped. This was akin to a technique called "shaping" that I practiced in a past life as a special educator.

Behaviorists pioneered shaping, which involves calling out and rewarding the approximation of a desired behavior, no matter if it is only a primitive version of what you ultimately want to see. The idea is to reinforce these beginning steps or partial attempts (regardless of how much help is required) until the behavior starts to look like what you want to see, thereby "shaping" the desired behavior over time. Early in my career, I remember teaching a student with severely impaired movement to turn his head to the side, hitting a switch that activated a lever that brought a damp washcloth across his face. The motivator for this child was the sound of my voice. There was nothing special about the tenor of my voice, it could have been anyone's. This sweet boy had little functional use of his arms or his legs, though sometimes they kicked and spasmed without his permission. He lay much of the day positioned sometimes on his back and sometimes on his stomach. So monotonous this existence must have been that he delighted at the sound of fellow humans.

I would say, "Wash your face, Chris," and he would move his head ever so slightly, but not nearly enough to trip the switch. I would then move his head for him enough so that the switch was tripped, and the cool cloth passed across his face. "Good job, Chris, you washed your face." We repeated this exchange over and over, day after day, until he finally actively willed his brain to tell the muscles in his neck to turn his head just enough for his forehead to make contact with the switch, which in turn caused the cloth to brush against his face. Voila, behavior shaped! Chris met the goal and gained a bit of control over his life, learning to use his own volition to make something happen, in this case giving the sensation of the cool cloth brushing his face.

Not many kids experience anything even remotely close to the severe challenges that faced my old student. Still the principle of shaping holds for all kinds of skills, academic and otherwise. For Jack, reading was the strength to be leveraged. He loved books. When he was little, we all noticed that Jack was somewhat of a "story crasher." He would gravitate to any random adults who were reading to their children in a bookstore or library and join the party. If a television show caught his attention, he was drawn into it, even if it was the type of show that was not normally his taste, so enigmatic was the power of "story" for him. He often wrote stories. His stories were not short page-length tales; they were long stories marked with chapters. Though the writing wasn't legible, the stories convoluted, and the sentences meandered seemingly aimlessly without the benefit of punctuation, he continued to write. He also enjoyed history, possibly because it, too, is based in "story."

To be sure, these were assets that we reinforced and leveraged to achieve other academic goals, but perhaps the most helpful of all was Jack's tolerance of discomfort. He had a knack for resigning himself to situations that he did not like. Although this quality included shades of perseverance, it was not solely that. Perseverance is defined as steady persistence on a course of action, toward a purpose or a state, particularly, in spite of difficulties, obstacles, or discouragement. At first Jack's sticking with things looked more like resignation to his circumstances rather than perseverance motivated by a specific purpose or goal. His attitude seemed to be: "This is what I've been given and I am just trudging through it to get done." We leveraged this quality to shape Jack's response to academic tasks over time.

His struggles may sound familiar as they tend to be universally shared by teens at risk of school failure. In addition to being defensive whenever he was asked about his grades, he had a fear of examining misconceptions in his thinking and identifying what he did not know. He suffered from what educators call a lack of "meta-cognition." He did not have a good grasp of what he did and did not know and was afraid to explore it. When asked how he thought he performed on a test he just finished, he would reply "Good." This behavior could not just be chalked up to that chronic condition infecting teens the world over, that is, dismissing adults around them, a condition immortalized by Pete Davidson's character Chad on Saturday Night Live, who responds with a vacant eyed "K" to everything his elders say.

We knew Jack lacked metacognition because, even when we did not ask him how he did, he would offer that he had done well, only to learn later that he had failed or nearly failed the test. He contented himself with skimming his notes over and over instead of studying with purpose. He did not have the discipline or desire to quiz himself, ask related questions, or create new problems to solve. Nor did he have the social connections to seek out study groups, so he was rarely in the position of having to defend his thinking. He did not identify and analyze errors, but instead would console himself by reading over the material that he had gotten correct. All of these behaviors were further complicated by his specific difficulties with math concepts and handwriting.

It was not fun or easy to isolate the specific behaviors that contributed to Jack's low academic performance. Living within the vague generalities of "developmental delay" and "learning disability" was less ominous than acknowledging the laundry list of real issues. While disconcerting, the act of seeking to understand his specific strengths and weaknesses supplied powerful knowledge. It pointed to potential interventions, solutions, and possibilities. Some of the behaviors boiled down to fixed mindsets based in fear. Among the mindsets that had to be surfaced included, "Looking at what I got wrong makes me feel like a failure." Some were habits that we could work on at home, like analyzing errors or making up new problems and solving them. Still others required outside expertise, like filling in the holes in specific math content.

Pete and I became a tag team going after these issues. I sat with Jack in the evening and made him talk through and explain his science. Initially, he would complain, then, realizing that all protest was futile, he got down to it. I think over time he actually came to enjoy explaining and defending the concepts. Talking through ideas, rather than just filling in answers, required Jack to activate more than one thought process. Talking and writing about the material ensured that he would better retain it. Pete, exponentially my better half (pun intended) when it came to math, would create a range of problems substituting numbers to give Jack repeated practice. Even with this we knew that Jack needed more than we had to give. To address math deficits and lingering misunderstandings, we made sure that Jack took advantage of all available teacher office hours. When that was still not enough, we enrolled him in Mathnasium, a for-profit tutoring franchise ran by a family friend. Jack became a regular there after school for a couple of hours, twice a week. There, tutors calmly talked him through sine and cosine, supplementary and complementary angles, exponents, and two variable polynomials. These easy-going young guys who looked as though they moonlighted in the summer as whitewater rafting guides offered a welcome contrast to his haggard, middle-aged parents.

Chapter 36

COLLEGE BOUND

*Education is the one thing they
can't take away from you.*

—Jeanette Winking, My Mom

THERE WAS ANOTHER BARRIER between Jack and school success. He had a hard time passing tests. When I quizzed him at home on science or history, I would swear that he had a solid grasp on the concepts, but when the test rolled around, he would predictably miss questions covering the same material. His teachers reported that Jack "aced" study guides and practice material only to go on to fail nearly identically worded tests. It was confounding. He consistently earned B's and C's, with an occasional A thrown in, on homework, but performed in the D and F range on tests. Perhaps all those years of struggling to keep up in so many areas had made him fearful of tests, the ultimate competitive exercise; creating anxiety around falling short, which caused him to choke on material that he knew. Whatever the explanation, the fact was that tests were not a reliable indicator of what Jack knew.

For a long time, he was not able to articulate the problem, it was like he just accepted that there was no relationship between what he knew and the grade that was ultimately plastered on the test paper. After a lot of probing and coaxing, Jack began describing being nervous when he saw other kids finishing ahead of him. With prompting, he verbalized that he became distracted by the actions of other kids when they put their pencils down, logged off the testing terminal, or closed their laptops and left the room. Each student finishing made him feel like "there goes another kid beating me, I'm behind again." How could anyone maintain his focus on test content or bubbling in a Scantron sheet with this mindset? My kid had extreme test anxiety.

An obvious hurdle was the granddaddy of all timed tests: the ACT. Jack had classes where teachers taught all manner of test-taking skills, but test anxiety is not a procedural problem that can be remediated with a patented strategy like "underline the important information in word problems," or "eliminate obviously wrong answers." I was convinced that a severe lack of confidence was wrapped up in his performance anxiety and, sadly, confidence is not a skill that can be taught, but rather it is a disposition that is acquired over time. Confidence is fueled by feelings of competence and success, and Jack did not have a surplus of either.

Ironically, while I had spent most of Jack's life untangling and extracting him from special services and supports, I now began searching for them. In the case of testing, I felt the answer lay in changing the game, rather than asking Jack to change—at least in the short run. We knew that time pressure and perceived competition fueled Jack's test anxiety. After all, he did well enough on homework when there were no arbitrary time constraints or contrived rivalries with other students. I believed that if the act of testing could occur without the distraction of peers and/or ticking clocks, he had a chance to succeed. The only way to alter the test environment was to prove that Jack needed accommodations, and so, junior year, we worked with the high school counselor to qualify Jack for a 504 plan. A 504 plan is a non-funded national mandate that provides eligible students with accommodations such as additional time or testing in a quiet room. Thankfully 504 plans do not require a label or diagnosis, only evidence of need. To provide this evidence, the student has to complete a round of psychological testing. We knew the drill. The irony was not lost on us that Jack had to go through another battery of cognitive and behavioral tests to get the accommodation he needed on tests, because he has test anxiety. What? Yes, really that is a thing.

Gradually, between the end of sophomore and senior year, Jack bent his academic trajectory from barely passing to respectable. Something else was also operating in the background: he was maturing. I cannot parse the impact that natural maturation processes had in the evolution of the 15-year-old Jack to the 17-year-old version of himself. But through it all; painstakingly hard work, at-home help, and hours of paid tutoring, he received one consistent message— you are college bound. He saw his twin sister visiting colleges and he visited many himself. The twins attended all the informational sessions that the school district offered on navigating the college application process. Pete and I talked (read preached) about the need for them *both* to save money for college. While Jack was doing the hard work of filling in gaps, learning new content, adopting productive study habits, and becoming acutely aware of his role in his own learning, he was consistently exposed to experiences that sent the message that he was capable, and that we believed that, naturally, he would be heading off to college when his sister did.

I am sensitive to readers who might presume a note of arrogance in the narrow framing of the message "you are college bound." No doubt there are any number of post-high school paths that promise their faithful followers prosperity and purpose. Some are drawn to the military, some to the world of work and entrepreneurship, and still others to vocational programs that short circuit the academic meanderings of four-year institutions and deftly turn technical skills into careers. Any of these would have been admirable goals for my kid. Setting the bar at college was a deliberate decision borne out of knowing our kid, recognizing his assets, and seeking to minimize the impact of lingering challenges.

We knew young men and women in Jack and Livie's graduating class who could sell ice cubes to Eskimos. A few were modern day Eddie Haskells, who ran a good con game…but the vast majority were just confident, articulate kids who had the innate self-assurance, precision of purpose, and silver tongues to promote themselves at job interviews or to pitch a new product. These kids had the makings of budding entrepreneurs, venture capitalists, and salesmen.

These were not qualities that Jack possessed. But he was a master at persevering, sticking with tasks that did not offer immediate reward, following rules, and reading informational text. In addition, new assets were emerging as his study habits improved. All of these supported a college path. Jack's pronounced stutter, tendency to talk around the point, and unsure posture did not lend themselves to post-secondary paths that required unabashed self-promotion. All this led us to believe that he would benefit from a diploma and credentials that a specific college degree would bestow. An engineer is an engineer, a scientist is a scientist, and an accountant is an accountant. The bearers of these degrees can rely, to some extent, on the course of study that produced them as vouching for their competence. We contrasted this with the English, communications, or liberal arts major who pounds the pavement to convince a consulting firm or advertising agency that he or she has what it takes for the job. It was this reasoning, and not disdain for non-academic paths, that led us to encourage Jack to pursue a college degree program that would amplify his strengths.

Chapter 37

TAKING
CHANCES

*Most people see the world as a threatening place, and
because they do, it is a threatening place for them.*

—Paulo Coelho, *The Alchemist*

SOPHOMORE YEAR was the year that Hurricane Sandy wreaked
havoc on the northeast coast. Even though his brother and sisters
could not attend the youth group mission trip to rebuild damaged
houses, I sent Jack. We were told that the days would be long and
the work would be hard. Good, all the better, in my mind. This trip
would increase Jack's endurance, while exposing him to new friends
and experiences and show any parent or kid who had questioned his
ability that Jack was as able as any of them. What no one had counted
on that summer was the unprecedented ferocious heat wave that hit
New Jersey. With the heat index, temperatures reached 107 degrees
as our kids were nailing on sweltering roofs, repainting exterior

walls, and repairing sagging porches. It was on the return trip at Denver International Airport while we were loading the car full of aromatic teens and their equally aromatic gear, when the youth leader informed us that Jack had passed out due to heat stroke on day three and had to be placed on an ice-packed air mattress in the gym until he recovered. We were no strangers to the toll that humidity took on Jack. We experienced it every summer when we returned to the Midwest to visit my family. It was true that extreme humidity exacerbated Jack's low tone and he seemed to move through the thick air in slow motion. While there were a host of reasons to love the home we had made in Colorado, I numbered close to the top the fact that the near non-existence of humidity was a plus for Jack.

I felt bad that Jack had literally fallen prostrate to the heat, but it was just as important to me to know that the incident had not benched him for the remainder of the trip. The youth leader must have looked at me confused when my first question was not how was my son doing, but whether he was allowed to return to work the next day? While I can only imagine how uncomfortable it must have been, if I had a crystal ball and could have predicted this extreme heat wave, it would not have changed my decision to send him. Although it may sound insensitive, I had long ago bought into the idea that privileging comfort and safety over risk and challenge would not help Jack over the long haul. These experiences, even the calamitous ones, were all part of what typical kids encountered and they were exactly what I wanted Jack to feel.

The summer after his junior year Jack had no luck finding employment. First, his timing was not great; he began applying for jobs just as the initial wave of high school and college kids descended upon the grocery and fast-food establishments in our small town.

Second, he was also fighting his stutter, which likely caused some employers to make erroneous assumptions about his ability to meet their standards of superior customer service. But everyone worked in our family, and Jack knew he needed a job. He was no stranger to hard labor, even when he was younger and strength and endurance were a major challenge. At age 10, he was cutting the grass with a push mower. In the winter he shoveled snow. Although he was painfully slow at the task, we maintained the expectation that he could do it, without commenting on the pace. Over time, neighbors saw him toiling in the driveway and began asking for his help, including a retired couple up the street who became his regular clients. So, there was no doubt this time, Jack would get a job.

At his dad's urging, Jack finally applied on-line and landed a landscaping gig where he spent his days shoveling gravel and digging holes that would serve as the resting place for trees and shrubs of all varieties. The work was back-breaking, but we were not going to tell Jack that it would be too hard, that his muscles were not up to the task, that according to his diagnosis he was not supposed to have the endurance for such a job. Not only was he an unlikely physical match for the job, he was also the youngest on the crew by far. Jack was a tall, lanky 17-year-old working on a crew with grown men, most in their mid to late twenties. It was grueling and he quit a couple weeks before school started, exhausted. But during the entire summer he never heard from his Dad or me that the job was too hard or unsuitable for him.

After a week or two of landscaping, Jack, who never had the luxury of being selective about friends, began to relate to us stories of his coworkers. Potential friends, I thought, promising. At the very least, this would be a chance for Jack to hone his social skills. My sunny prediction quickly faded as Jack offered more on the crews' antics as he guzzled water and slumped in a kitchen chair at the end of each sun-drenched day. The information came out in dribs and drabs, brief installments that sounded increasingly disturbing. His stories included "the guys" smoking cigarettes and marijuana on breaks and bounding out of cars proclaiming, 'White power!', among other more offensive racial slurs that they uttered in the presence of the few black and brown guys on the crew. Clearly this was not an elite crowd. If they were targeting people for their color, we began to wonder how long it would be before Jack was targeted. Jack had heard his Grandpa disparage people of other races and he definitely knew a racist comment when he heard one. As he continued to share tales of his crew members' exploits, we told him that while we wanted him to stick up for what was right, it was not worth getting beaten up.

I could not have been prouder when Jack came home one day, hot, tired, and smelling of sod. We listened as he related that on this particular day, his ruckus co-workers had made some comment about white people being superior within ear shot of the crew chief, an older black man, who according to Jack's telling was a good guy who kept his distance from this morally questionable contingent. Jack said, "Mom, I told them, 'We drove out the red man and enslaved the black man. You guys are white supremacists."

I have to say I was proud, but more than a little worried that these miscreants would retaliate against Jack for calling it as his teenage-self saw it, devoid of any measure of restraint or fear that those of us with more experience would have exercised. However, the next day at work Jack found that they had not taken his rebuff as an insult or a challenge as we feared they would. When the crew arrived at the first job site of the day, instead of yelling the now familiar "White

Power" battle cry as they piled out of the truck bed, they proclaimed, "White Supremacy!" Apparently, while we thought Jack had taken them to school for their prejudicial beliefs, he had not shamed them; he had merely increased their vocabulary!

Chapter 38

FINDING
HIS VOICE

If a man does not master his circumstances,
his circumstances will master him.

—Amor Towles, *A Gentleman from Moscow*

IT WAS NOW ALMOST TWO YEARS to the day after the oak tree
revelation outside Dairy Queen when we'd told Jack of his diagnosis.
The pace of life had notched up to a fevered pitch as all four kids were
going through their teen years. Our youth group had just announced
tryouts for its annual variety show. Rosie, a talented musician, song-
writer, and actress, had always been the natural performer in the
family. However, Jack enjoyed the fellowship of youth group and
so wanted to participate too. It was when they announced that they
were seeking a couple of kids to offer monologues, personal testi-
monies of their teenage experience, that I took notice. I suggested
to Jack that he tell his story. He was 18, well into his senior year and

discovering that with effort and intent he could impact his grades.

"Did you want to tell the story of your challenges and successes?" I asked. I imagined that it might be cathartic. He had always enjoyed writing, even if the legibility was questionable. At the same time, I recognized that his stutter made a mockery of the mere suggestion that he deliver a five-minute monologue to a packed auditorium. What was I asking my kid to do? Was this yet another instance of me over-zealously pushing him into the deep end?

This time I sensed not. As difficult as it was for him, I knew he liked talking. How often had Jack experienced kids growing tired of listening and walking away because of his halting speech. On a stage, he would have a captive audience. I imagined that in this space he would finally have the satisfaction of being listened to without interruption. It would be a chance for him to speak without having others finish his sentences to help him out or, less nobly, because they had grown impatient waiting for him to spit it out.

"You have a real story of adversity and perseverance," I offered.

"Yes," Jack said, he would like to try. Could it be that he felt the same way I did? Interested parties were to submit a half page monologue summary to the director within the week and she would then select two or three from among the submissions. With some editing help from me, Jack turned in a half page. For him it may have gotten lost among the daily demands of high school, but for me it had not. Time passed without a word from the director. If what they were looking for was fortitude in the midst of teenage trials, I thought Jack had it sewn up. Not to create hierarchies of teen angst, but his was not a tepid tale of an isolated trauma like missing the prom, finding oneself on the outs with friends, or being overlooked by the coach. In fact, it was all those things, as well as a story of perseverance, faith, and dogged grit in the face of relentless difficulty.

But then I kicked myself and conceded to the fact that there is no hierarchy among pain, no bragging rights among the wounded. Each pain is uniquely excruciating to its bearer and each man's challenge is their own personal Everest. Who was I to think Jack's brief life story was any more deserving than another's struggle with depression, surviving a broken home, or loss of a beloved grandparent. I revised my prediction. Maybe his monologue would not be selected. Now my thoughts drifted selfishly to my own guilt around encouraging him to enter one more "competition," only to be rejected again.

At church one Sunday I ran into the show's director. Somewhat timidly I inquired about Jack's submission, afraid of her response. She offered almost as an afterthought that, of course, she was going to select Jack's story. *What?* She went on to say that it had brought her to tears and she had meant to tell Jack but was literally buried under the work of the production; there were group numbers to be choreographed, skits to be written, and props to be built, and by the way, would I be willing to coordinate the set painting?" "Uhh, yes," she had me at "of course Jack was selected." At that moment I would have signed up to give a kidney if she needed it. Caught up in my euphoria I had to pause to appreciate yet another reminder that the world does not run on my timeline and that one person's everything is another's inconsequential detail.

We made a big deal about Jack's submission getting selected. His pride at being chosen was unmistakable, but selection was just the beginning. Next commenced the work of creating a tight monologue in which Jack would tell his own life story including the role faith played along the way. Jack got to work writing but became frustrated as he tried to make the monologue descriptive but still brief enough to be digestible. Because I was the closest one to him, I felt the brunt of his anger. He did not like my early cuts, but he had to pare it down to 4 1/2 minutes.

In frustration, I yelled at his slammed door, "Just forget it if it's too hard, you don't have to do this!"

Later that same night he came to me and said, "No Mom, this is a story that has to be told."

It was hard for him to talk about the bullying, loneliness, and difficulties doing simple things, and it was hard for me to hear him read it in his own words. I thought that I had felt the extent of the pain, had swallowed it all, and survived. A few nights into his writing process, he read for me the final version he intended to present. It was then that I finally heard him voice it, a discordant scratch, fingers on a chalkboard. There it was, laid out in the first line of the monologue. Our exchange went something like this:

Jack: "So I was born with Sotos syndrome…it is a condition that causes…?"

Mom: "Whoa, whoa, Jack are you sure you want to say that?"

Jack: "Why not, Mom?"

Mom: "Well… all the kids and parents who know you from youth group will be there, Sam and his family will probably come, other people outside church who you know…"

Jack: "Yeah, so?"

Mom: "Do you want them to know you have a syndrome?"

Jack: [Confused look]

Mom: What if it causes them to think differently of you?

Jack: "Mom, if they were going to think differently of me, I think they already have."

Again, with the youthful wisdom. What had I done to deserve

this amazing person? Sideswiped, I had not seen it coming, my kid had gotten out ahead of me. I felt the floor collapse beneath me. I had thought Jack had a story of triumph over adversity that was unique and worth telling. He had experienced feelings of inadequacy, being left out, overlooked, and bullied. In Jack's case, what would have otherwise been labeled as garden variety teen trials were exacerbated by that peculiar roll of the genetic dice that assigned him Sotos syndrome at birth. I had imagined that he would recount the endless work of overcoming muscle weakness, exiting special education, school struggles, and feeling like he never quite measured up. The mental model of expectations that I had embraced so long ago required that I dismiss labels and diagnoses, whether they came from the medical community or the school system. I had fought them so hard that it never occurred to me that my son would lead off with those two words: "Sotos syndrome." Of course, he was right, these were people who knew Jack, stuttering, social awkwardness and all. Stand down, Mama.

It was so simple and yet so profound at the same time. I had spent all of Jack's life fighting the diagnosis, attempting to cheat it and prove it wrong; working with him voraciously to overcome it, trying everything I could to get him to "pass" as a child without special needs, and yet here he was, planning to get up in front of 500 people and lay it on them. My son was not afraid, but I was.

This was his story to tell, I would not intervene or try to override him, but I was still worried. I conjured images of discrimination and prejudice. As best we could, we had raised Jack in a world without labels. I thought of my coworkers who told stories of their children who did not know they were black until, at some point in elementary school, another child used a slur. They went on to recount how life for them was forever changed after. I would never suggest that the effects of labeling around disability are equal to the effects of racism. I have spent years trying to understand the experience of racism as utterly incompletely as a white person can. This is a wholly different type of discrimination. One is rooted in a despicable tradition of slavery and oppression, while the other is undertaken ostensibly to help those who cannot do for themselves. However, both shared the outcome of discrimination and viewing another human as "less than." Would Jack's decision to lead his monologue with a label help or hurt him over time?

Jack had lived, moved, and worshipped among most of these people for years. He had hung out in the church gym with them, sung praise songs at youth group, and worked alongside them on mission trips; what difference could two little words possibly make? They had heard him stutter and seen him come across as less than adept in social situations. Still, I was afraid of what the word "syndrome" would invoke. Knowing our human affinity for sorting, I knew all too well how we use labels to help explain and put fences around that which scares us. Would people use the word to pigeonhole Jack: "I always knew there was something wrong with him." And what about all the kids, would this give them further license to treat him differently, to avoid him, to leave him out?

I thought I had taught my son a lot over the years but, in the end, it was he who took me to school. "Mom, if they were going to think different of me, I think they already have." The monologue would contain his words, not mine. While he still faced long nights of paring down the word count, reciting the text, exchanging words to avoid disfluency, and employing strategies to overcome stutters, he persevered. Ultimately it was his courage that landed him on a stage in front of hundreds of people over the course of two nights telling HIS story.

On the first night, as the lights went down, Jack came out in jeans and a red flannel shirt untucked over a white tee. He was out of breath from the previous all-boy rendition of the Beatles *Help!* He wiped his nose with the back of his hand (Relax, I told myself, you can't rehearse everything) and began.

I am Jack Winking...

... and I was born with a neurological condition called Sotos syndrome. It causes a number of setbacks and can really mess a kid up. My muscles did not work as they should. As a little kid I found I had to put in so much effort just to do what other kids would do with ease. Simple things like lifting myself out of a swimming pool, throwing and catching a ball, blowing out candles. Even getting out certain words was a challenge. And still is.

What I did not have in skill and coordination I tried to make up in humor. My mom tells a story of how when I was a kid, I fell through a screen door and onto the floor. I was dazed but not hurt as I looked up and said, "I just dropped in to say hi." But I digress.

No matter how hard I worked, I would always fall short of the other kids. This made me want to give up, but I worked and worked to overcome these challenges. I had to endure countless therapy sessions working on my speech, motor skills, and other things. I stuck to it and I finally achieved some portion of success. When I was in sixth grade, I made the middle school basketball team, but just barely. I was on the lowest team possible, throughout the season I always felt that I had to work harder than the other kids in every area of the game. This made me extremely sad, I remember sitting on the floor in my room with my mom. I was crying and I was saying to my mom, "Why does everything always comes so easy for my friends? It's not fair." It makes me think of John 16:33, "I have told you these things so that you may have peace. In this world you will have trouble but take heart for I have overcome the world."

So middle school went by and I enjoyed minor successes in basketball and all was good in that regard. However, I still had some other problems to take care of. Years of struggling as a kid and doing things differently to compensate made me a victim of bullying, which worsened my mood and led to sadness and anxiety. Things began to change when, one summer, a friend of mine and I went to Six Flags Elitch Gardens in Denver. In the late afternoon we accidentally stumbled into a Skillet concert. The words of one of their songs called "Hero" says, "I need a hero to save me now! I need a hero to save my life. A hero will save me." It really spoke to me. In fact, to be honest it was on that night that I really started to believe...let me explain.

Before I came to Trinity, I went to a Catholic Church and it didn't help (I don't want to "diss" the Catholic church, it may work for some people, but it did not work for me.) All the rituals didn't bring me closer to Jesus, I questioned a lot about my faith during that time. I was in the dark. But John 12:46 says, 'I have come into this world as a light so that no one who believes in me should stay in darkness.' My coming to Trinity made me realize that church is not about following rules but about following Jesus' example of loving. Also, that it's not about your denomination but about what gets you closer to Jesus and faith in him.

So, when I was in ninth grade, I thought that I finally hit the big time. I was going to play basketball in high school and I thought that I would finally "fit" in. Unfortunately, I didn't make the team despite my best efforts. This hit me hard. All I knew was basketball. I wasn't sure what to do. All those feelings of failure were back again. I truly wondered where God was and what he had planned for me. Then I found Cross Country. I ran hard and I kept on running and I am still on the team today. And in running I realized that God wants me to be in it for a marathon, not just a sprint. He wants me to be in it for the long haul regardless of the situation.

As for basketball, God found another way for me to use that passion. This past year I responded to an opportunity to be a coach for the Unified Basketball team at high school. This is a basketball team that allows special needs kids to play basketball and play a full and legit season. So now, here I am, a guy who once struggled, getting to help other kids who continue to struggle. I get to coach them and teach them about the beautiful game of basketball. We even played a game at the Pepsi Center in Denver in March. We went on to win the league tournament and we beat all of the high school teams in town—but I digress. My point is that we can't know God's plan. Maybe this was the plan for me all along. At the time, all I could see was the despair of not making the basketball team my freshman year. Now I see that God was saying that he has something bigger in store for me.

All I have been through to stand in front of you today has made me aware of how much American society, and particularly teens, are concerned with outward appearance in high school and fitting in. And really, that being "normal" is considered a virtue. Well, I wasn't born normal in the least, so why should I live just a normal life? In fact, I challenge you all to step out and not be normal. The world is colorful so let's all not be gray. Don't be afraid to be a circle in a room full of squares. I mean, after all, we only have one life here on Earth to leave a legacy that gives glory to God. So why not start now? All I know is that the future is big and bright for me; and only God knows the plans he has for me.

—Jack Contino March 2017 monologue presented at *Greater Than*.

Jack finished to a room silent, but kinetic with a particular type of electricity. It was one of the few times I remember a cliché holding true: you *could* hear a pin drop. That was until every person in the audience, from gray-haired church ladies, to phone-clutching teens, rose to their feet in a deafening standing ovation. I faintly remember the pastor yelling out, "Amen, brother!" from the audience.

As the lights went up and the people filed out of the rows, I felt an undeniable sense of lightness. I had warned about leading with a label and I had worried that people might view Jack differently. Underneath it all, I still feared that what I tried to hide for so many years would be laid bare. But that night, I will tell you, it felt good. I watched as Jack received countless 'atta boy' pats on the back, and "fantastic jobs." I basked in that positive attention for him. Chalk up a big one in the positive column. I imagined he would internalize the fact that he, a stutterer, had braved a crowd of 100's to tell his story and that these two nights would figure large in a growing positive narrative. The standing ovation, and each word of encouragement, would be forever recorded on the plus side of that internal ledger.

These were good nights. Jack was surrounded by admiration for his honesty, grit, his willingness to be vulnerable, and most of all, for his courage. If anyone was put off by the Sotos revelation, it did not matter. Jack owned those two nights.

In the weeks following the youth show, the fairy dust settled, things went back to normal. The monologue neither lost him friends nor earned them. It turned out that Jack was right, all those people knew him. With the bright lights of the show growing dim with time, Jack was no longer the brave "overcomer of adversity" with courage approaching superhero proportions, he was no longer an object of their admiration. He had transformed once again into the mild-man- nered boy who continued to do life as best he could, working hard to earn the grades that would eventually raise his GPA, bagging groceries at Safeway, and not expecting friends to call or text. Even so, I knew Jack felt good about what he had done. As he said, 'This is a story that needs to be told.'

And so he did, on his own terms.

A MOTHER'S EPILOGUE

BECAUSE SAM ENROLLED in the high school STEM (Science Technology Engineering and Mathematics) program, Jack followed suit and went into the high school STEM program. When Jack's grades eventually got him accepted at the University of Wyoming, he allowed inertia to sweep him into the College of Engineering. The only problem was, Jack did not think like an engineer, nor did he have that natural love of math that is common among engineering types. Jack was not practiced in the art of identifying his own preferences. He stoically trudged through whatever hand he was dealt, stayed in the lane where he was placed, not expecting too much in return. Was this just an aspect of Jack's personality or was it more fallout from my "you can do this" or, as it played out for Jack, "you are doing this," approach to parenting? Regardless, it was now time for Jack to choose what HE wanted for himself.

As of this writing Jack is finishing his senior year in Environmental Science. He has discovered a passion for sustainability, and he cares deeply about the fate of our planet in this brave new world of wildfires, drought, and weather extremes. This past summer he held a research internship focused on creating climate resistant hybrid crops that may someday feed the world.

Jack still loves to read. He remains drawn to tragically underestimated characters who defy their station and rise up to alter their destiny. He has left behind his elementary school obsession with Dav Pilkey's "de-pantsed" Mr. Krupp, and has fallen in love with Stephen King novels for their flawed heroes who, because of their difficult circumstances, develop extraordinary powers.

He lives in an on-campus apartment with three other boys. I have learned that some things don't change when they leave the nest. Just as we continue to feel the searing pain of our kids' hurts, we also continue to kick up our heels in that happy dance with their every success. In fact, the degree to which we feel pain and pride for our children may intensify with time and space. I knew Jack had been regularly playing Dungeons and Dragons with some kids on campus. But when he FaceTimed me and told me that they had given him a surprise birthday party, I wanted to throw open the kitchen window and shout to the world, "My kid has friends!" He could not stop smiling as he told me that they had decorated his apartment to mimic the birthday party characters on their favorite TV show *The Office* had given their love-to-hate boss, Michael Scott.

Back home, this summer he signed up for and ran a couple of 5K races. Running is now a pursuit he has taken into adulthood. I now smile, quietly satisfied that all the honors that eluded Jack in high school: finishing among the top seven, taking home trophies, and even getting called onto the stage by the coaches, turned out, in the long run, to be not nearly as valuable as the lesson Jack took away from crosscountry—how to persevere against the odds.

Wonder of wonders, the boy who would not be left behind *did* go on to do everything his twin sister did. Now he is seeking new opportunities and tackling different challenges. Last fall he studied forestry and sustainability abroad in Finland. Jack, the "labeled" kid who began his school career in the multiply handicapped preschool class, who professionals projected would not learn to write, open a locker, or get the words out, studied in a foreign country, traveled Europe, lived with students from all over the world, and is following his interest in environmental sustainability.

Even so, moms will be moms, and old habits die hard. When Jack comes home to visit, do laundry, or just to get a home-cooked meal, I still call him down when it is time to crush the garlic—just to get in a couple more reps. It can't hurt, right? (Forgive me, son.)

While Jack has cleared many hurdles, he still experiences the pernicious judgments that are reserved for those in this world who have the audacity to be different. Last summer, he applied for a United States Dairy Association (USDA) Fellowship at Colorado State University. First, he landed on the waiting list, which with persistence and a bit of luck eventually turned into a spot on the fellowship team.

Through a completely different set of associations, I found myself out for the evening with a Ph.D, who, although not affiliated with Jack's fellowship program, was a colleague with someone on the program staff. The two of us were enjoying a concert with our daughters when she launched into the following commentary: "As soon as you look at him you know that there is something wrong with him." She continued. "Jack misrepresented himself in the fellowship application, he did not reveal his limitations." While supremely offended by the first statement, I ignored it because, frankly, "what do you even say to that?" But I did take on the second.

Partly because our daughters were standing close by and partly because we had become friendly over time, I gave her the benefit of the doubt. I abandoned my naturally defensive posture and chose instead a "teaching" stance, although no doubt she detected the hurt churning in the veiled sarcasm that lurked just below the surface of my measured response.

"Actually, Gretchen," I began, "that is not on Jack, I was the one who counseled him to not list a disability." I went on to explain that "the application expressly read: 'Do you have any limitations that will *not* allow you to carry out the duties listed?' Now, if the duties listed included 'applicant must salsa dance with flourish' or 'applicant must speak to large groups with the melodic tenor of a radio announcer,' I would have advised him to list each of his limitations. However, since the duties included: 'applicant will plant and test soil samples, gather data, run computer applications and analyze data,' I could find no limitation. Can you?"

Although it was difficult, I listened as she further expounded on her concerns. I learned that one summer day as Jack was busy testing and logging dirt samples (apparently, the stuff environmental science undergraduate fellowships are made of), Gretchen stopped by the lab. She approached him to say hi, and Jack, who had only met her once before in our home, apparently had not recognized her. This must have struck her as odd, because as I raised a quizzical brow, she offered this instance as further evidence that proved Jack had 'misrepresented himself' in terms of his fitness for the fellowship. I was not there that day, but it is possible that Jack did not place her because he did not expect to see her at the lab, or perhaps he was so intent on his work that he was caught off guard. It could also be that he was just not able to regroup in the moment and pretend that he knew someone just because they knew him. (You know that thing we all do when someone enthusiastically descends upon us in the supermarket and we immediately scour our brains for a connection. How do we know this person? Is she from school? church? the neighborhood? the bleachers at a kid's sporting event? Only, we don't give away that we don't know them, we change course in a nanosecond and just go with it. 'She obviously knows me so I will fake it.' Now, equally enthusiastically we reply, 'Hey! how are you? I haven't seen you in so long!'). Jack was not practiced in this art of social subterfuge.

This awkward encounter boiled down to a commentary about privileged and less privileged classes of people as defined by appearance and social poise. I could not help but think that any of my other three young adult children would have been immediately forgiven for not being able to identify a person they had met once in a different context. Or if not completely forgiven for their memory lapse, the person would have chalked it up to typical college student behavior. Perhaps they had "spaced out" or were exhausted from having partied too much the night before. Whatever the conclusion, they certainly would not have been tagged as having "something wrong with them" or "misrepresenting themselves."

But such is life in a world where judging and labeling come as naturally as taking in a breath and exhaling. My brave son will likely continue to encounter misguided folk who underestimate him, and it will be his job to continue proving them utterly wrong. But for now, Jack has graduation, job hunting, and graduate school on the horizon. As foretold in his monologue, his future is big and bright and only God knows the plans in store for him.

As for me, I am an eternal optimist, but also a scathing skeptic. Sometimes I don't believe it myself. Is the Jack who drops in on weekends really the boy who could not pick up his head, blow out his birthday candles, or lift himself out of the pool? Was he the boy who was painfully slow at everything, and simply could not get the words out? Was he the boy who was placed in multiply handicapped preschool and then years of special education? Did an occupational therapist really tell us he would never write and then sentence him to wearing oven mitts because he could not keep his fingers out of his mouth? Is this college senior before us the same kid who was at serious risk of high school failure?

We humans are a resilient lot. I am the type that remembers the positive and then discards, or at least buries, the negative…and to some extent I expect this is true of everyone. When things change for the better or the suffering subsides, we often question the veracity of the pain we felt. Evidence pregnancy and childbirth: when the ordeal is behind us and we are home cuddling our perfect new creation, we minimize the nausea, aching feet, fatigue, and pain, all of which mercifully allow us (if we choose) to get back in the game and try for number two.

Similarly, improvement, particularly when it is agonizingly gradual, has a way of sneaking up on us and tricking us into believing that things really weren't as they were. As life has transformed for Jack over the years, I have had moments where I have mused "Was it ever that bad?" When I am with Jack today, I sometimes shake my head and squint to bring the past into focus. Then I remember the genetics doc pronouncing the diagnosis and I know it was all real. "Sotos syndrome" could have defined my child, but I chose to raise him as if he had no limitations.

That one decision and the countless little ones that followed have made all the difference.

INVITE DEBORAH TO YOUR BOOK CLUB OR PARENT GROUP!

AS A SPECIAL OFFER to *Capable* readers, Dr. Deborah Winking has offered to visit your book club or parent group in person or via Zoom.

Contact Deborah directly to schedule an appearance with your group. Go to https://www.highexpectationsparenting.com/ and click "Book a Visit."

THE 10 HABITS OF HIGH EXPECTATIONS PARENTS

Raising "capable" kids regardless of their challenges

1. **Believe** that effort creates aptitude.
2. **Set a vision of capable** for your child and adjust it as necessary.
3. **Identify your fears and tame them** to allow your child to pursue his best life.
4. **Challenge your child** in ways that regularly take him (and you) outside your comfort zone.
5. **Use words that send your child the message** that you think he is capable.
6. **Act in ways that send your child the message** that you think he is capable.
7. **Set the expectation** that others treat your child as capable.
8. **Offer your child choices and hold him accountable** for the consequences of his choices.
9. **Celebrate your child's successes** and use them to build a narrative of success.
10. **Treat yourself with compassion;** make mistakes and learn from them.

CONTINUE YOUR OWN PARENTING JOURNEY WITH THE CAPABLE COMPANION GUIDE

To learn more, visit my website
https://www.highexpectationsparenting.com/
for more information on the practical companion guide
to *Capable*. Soon to be released on Amazon.

NOTES

1   National Center for Educational Statistics https://nces.ed.gov/programs/coe/indicator_cgg.asp)

2   NPR Story Corps 2015) https://www.npr.org/2015/07/10/421239869/babies-on-display-when-a-hospital-couldnt-save-them-a-sideshow-did

3   https://www.dailymail.co.uk/health/article-1306283

4   (Daniel Kish the real Batman https://ideas.ted.com/a-walk-with-daniel-kish-the-real-life-batman/)

5   Tough, P. (2012). How children succeed: Grit, curiosity, and the hidden power of character. Boston: Houghton Mifflin Harcourt

6   Dweck, C. S. (2006). **Mindset**: The new psychology of success. New York: Random House. Chicago

7   Duckworth, A. (2016). *Grit: The power of passion and perseverance.* Scribner/Simon & Schuster

8   *Saphier, J.(2016) High Expectations Teaching. Corwin.*

9   https://www.researchgate.net/publication/234732102_From_
    Aptitude_to_Effort_A_New_Foundation_for_Our_Schools

10 Dweck, ibid.

11 Ibid.

12 Learning Without Tears TM https://www.lwtears.com/hwt/
    handwriting-integrated-print-digital-solution?gclid=Cj0KC-
    QiAvP6ABhCjARIsAH37rbT7c9o0TLYyweBPJucz1Ss2ezK-
    P0x-nYyB1QehImMB_sslS7Ck3IM4aAkwNEALw_wcB

13 Multi-tiered systems of support or MTSS interventions, which
    were mandated in public schools in 2015, now provide some
    students without a special education label with additional
    academic supports if data shows that they are performing a
    year or more below grade level, but it still holds true that special
    education services are not available to non-labeled students.

14 https://www.cbc.ca/radio/quirks/feb-9-2019-psy-
    chology-of-solitary-confinement-mind-over-genes-
    genocide-and-climate-change-and-more-1.5008739/
    when-is-your-brain-stronger-than-your-genes-how-the-
    mind-can-fool-the-body-1.5008750

Made in the USA
Columbia, SC
27 May 2021